LOUISE BLANCHARD BETHUNE

LOUISE BLANCHARD BETHUNE

every woman her own architect

Kelly Hayes McAlonie

EXCELSIOR
EDITIONS

Excelsior Editions is an imprint of State University of New York Press

For information, contact State University of New York Press, Albany, NY
www.sunypress.edu

Library of Congress Cataloging-in-Publication Data

Name: Hayes McAlonie, Kelly, author.
Title: Louise Blanchard Bethune / Kelly Hayes McAlonie.
Description: Albany : State University of New York Press, [2023] | Series:
    Excelsior Editions | Includes bibliographical references and index.
Identifiers: LCCN 2022035321 | ISBN 9781438492872 (hardcover : alk. paper) |
    ISBN 9781438492896 (ebook) | ISBN 9781438492889 (pbk. : alk. paper)
Subjects: LCSH: Bethune, Louise, 1856–1913. | Architects—United States—
    Biography. | Women architects—United States—Biography.
Classification: LCC NA737.B485 H385 2023 | DDC 720.92 [B]—dc23/eng/20220824
LC record available at https://lccn.loc.gov/2022035321

10 9 8 7 6 5 4 3 2 1

For Brian
with whom all things are possible

Contents

Illustrations

Acknowledgments

This book represents a twenty-year journey for me. Along the way, many people helped me in my research, analysis of the details that I uncovered, and reviewing my manuscript while it was in development. First, I am grateful to Adriana Barbasch for endowing me with her twenty-five years of research on Bethune. I will be eternally grateful to you for entrusting me with your significant body of research. Thanks to Kathy Less, Adriana's longtime colleague, for providing analysis and context. Nancy Herlan Brady found the second known photo of Louise and the first photo of Bethune, Bethune & Fuchs. In addition to the other images of Nancy's ancestor, Will Fuchs, this photo provides a beautiful glimpse into the lives of the Fuchs family and their friendship with the Bethune family. Zina Bethune provided wonderful anecdotal stories about Louise that she learned from her grandparents. Zina's husband, Sean Feeley, generously donated Zina's family records and other ephemera to the University at Buffalo. This is the Zina Bethune collection on Louise Bethune. I am deeply grateful to Sean for this invaluable gift.

The UB Libraries staff have been incredible colleagues and supporters. Austin Booth, Karen Senglaup, and Beth Adelman suggested my project as a candidate for the TOME project, for which I am incredibly grateful. Amy Vilz was my great collaborator in collecting the materials for the Zina Bethune collection on Louise Bethune. Amy, I miss you very much. I hope that your new adventure in the next life is as wonderful as you projected. Chris Hollister is the best cheerleader in academic publishing. I am indebted to his assistance in navigating the publishing world. Rose Orcutt was a tremendous help in tracking down architectural periodicals and in other areas of my research. UB colleagues Doug Levere and Jeff Smith have been terrific in providing Doug's photographs of Bethune's existing buildings for the book. These beautiful photographs bring her buildings to life and contextualize them in their contemporary surroundings. The UB Gender Institute has long supported me and this project. Thank you to the Executive Committee and especially Kari Winter, Carrie Braemen, and Becky Burke for facilitating the various symposia that featured Bethune's legacy, and for the awards I was lucky to receive from the institute. My colleagues and staff at University Facilities and Campus Planning provided invaluable support while writing this book.

My partners at State University of New York Press have been very supportive of me and my project. Tim Stookesberry has guided me through the process. My editor, Richard Carlin, gave me the critical feedback, advice, and confidence to tell my version of Louise's story. Thank you, Richard—without your guidance, I would not have completed this project and personal goal.

The entire staff at the Buffalo History Museum have been dear friends, and we have worked together to tell Bethune's story to the people of Western New York and beyond. Melissa Brown invited me to co-curate the first exhibit, *Buffalo's Bethune*, which was held during the National Trust Conference in Buffalo in 2011. Cynthia Van Ness has always been generous with her time, knowledge, and research. In 2007, when she showed me the 1892 article on the Buffalo Women's Wheel and Athletic Club that included Bethune, it opened a new avenue of exploration for me. It demonstrated that there was more to Louise Bethune's story than simply the buildings that she designed.

My dear friends in Buffalo have provided critical support to me. Despina Stratigakos has been a devoted friend and colleague for many years. Her astute perspective on the impact of societal norms on turn-of-the-century professional women has been pivotal in how I have approached my manuscript and interpreted the research. Roxanne Button provides me with endless support and perspective on the considerations for women owners of small architectural firms—and Canadian tea when my inventory runs low. Barbara Campagna is my go-to architectural historian who assisted me in unraveling the stylistic changes and making sense of the undercurrents behind them. Barbara's insight and critical editorial eye on my manuscript kept me direct and on point. Mike Chadwick and Paul McDonnell were also helpful in reading specific chapters and offering their perspective as practicing architects in Buffalo. Karen King has championed my work for years and is leading the local effort to tell women's hidden histories through the Trailblazing Women of Western New York Monuments project. Lillian

Williams, my UB colleague and friend (and fellow Trailblazing scholar!), provided valuable insight on the fight for women's suffrage in Buffalo.

Martin Wachadlo generated the first comprehensive list of Bethune, Bethune & Fuchs buildings. I used Martin's list as my starting point and added to it to create the list of buildings in the appendix. Martin was also a great sounding board for questions I had on some of Bethune's local contemporaries in architecture. Additionally, Martin's articles on Richard Waite were a great resource for me. Jon Morris was generous in sharing his research on the Hotel Lafayette that he conducted while leading the restoration of the building in 2010. Rocco Termini has always supported my research and graciously hung our exhibit on Bethune in the restored Hotel Lafayette. Jake Schneider shared his research on the Jacob Dold Warehouse from his restoration of that building. Dana Saylor provided additional information on the Bricka & Enos Building (the John Greiner Estate project). Chuck LaChiusa's excellent website, https://buffaloah.com, has been a valuable resource while conducting my research.

AIA archivist Nancy Hadley has been a trusted advisor and valuable resource since I began researching Bethune's career. The Grosvenor Library, Buffalo and Erie County Public Library, staff assisted me while I studied the records of the Bethune/Blanchard genealogy research, the Daughters of the American Revolution Buffalo Chapter, and the Buffalo Women's Wheel and Athletic Club, and the Buffalo Genealogical Society. Diane Andrasik, the archivist with the Dunkirk Historical Society, assisted me in researching Horatio Brooks and finding photos of the Brooks Mansion before and after Bethune's renovation. The Woodlawn Historical Society provided me access to their early images of the Woodlawn Resort.

Deborah Gardner's PhD dissertation on John Kellum, "The Architecture of Commercialism: John Kellum and the Development of New York, 1840–1875," is the only reliable source on Kellum that I could find. Her generosity in providing context to that research and discussing the man who trained Richard Waite was invaluable. Deborah, I hope you publish your dissertation sometime in the future. Molly Lester offered me her unique perspective on the life and career of Minerva Parker Nichols. Carol Estornell shared early Moore College of Art ephemera, which mentioned Minerva's time at the Franklin Institute that also provided a glimpse of life at an early women's design college. Carla Blank has been a close colleague since she began researching her book on Bethune. She was generous with sharing her conclusions on gaps in Bethune's life and projects, which was the most helpful.

I have long counted my AIA family among my dearest network, especially Georgi Bailey, Eric and Nancy Goshow, Susan Chin, Emily Grandstaff-Rice, Brynnemarie Lanciotti, Graciela Carrillo, and Abby Suckle. My longtime friends from Buffalo Spree allowed me to write about Bethune in the first place. Thank you, Elizabeth Licata and Donna Hoke, for sticking with me all those years. Sandy Starks and Nancy Cardillo presented opportunities to honor Bethune's legacy at Forest Lawn Cemetery, and Nancy's revisions to my first draft were such a help. Michael Galen brought Bethune to life for me through his illustrations for the *Buffalo's Bethune* exhibit in 2011, which informed my approach to this book.

And most important, I am nothing without my family, who have had to endure ten years of lows and highs with my health and this personal project. My parents, Joan and Ed Hayes, are the foundation on which I stand daily. You have been there for me in every moment of need and joy. Brian is my partner in all things: co-curator of *Buffalo's Bethune*, literary critic, and emotional support. You and Olive are the loves of my life.

I thank you all.

Abbreviations

AABN: *American Architect and Building News*

AIA: American Institute of Architects

AE: *Architectural Era*

BHM: Buffalo History Museum

BREN: *Buffalo Real Estate News*

DAR: Daughters of the American Revolution

ER: *Engineering Record*

IABN: *Inland Architect and Building News*

RE & BN: *Real Estate and Building News*

SE: *Sanitary Engineer and Building News*

WAA: Western Association of Architects

Introduction

It was June 1876 in Buffalo, New York. Richard Waite, the most prominent architect in the city, was very busy. The construction of the Pierce Palace Hotel was about to begin, and there were other significant projects on the boards in his office. Waite's exciting new projects promised to elevate his firm's reputation beyond the confines of Western New York.

Summer is warm and pleasant in Buffalo, a welcome respite from the long and snow-filled days of wintertime for the Queen City of the Great Lakes. During one of these warm and busy days, nineteen-year-old Louise Blanchard entered Waite's office in the German Insurance Building at Lafayette Square, looking for employment. This was most unusual because there were no woman architects practicing at the time in the United States, or anywhere else for that matter. Architects were expected to do more than just draw plans for a building; they had to oversee construction, negotiate rates, maintain budgets—to manage the entire process that goes into successfully completing a project. Women just didn't seem to have the required capabilities to be successful architects. For starters, they were thought to lack the physical stamina to work on construction sites. Why, even their clothing—which included tight corsets and long skirts with bustles—precluded this kind of work. The idea of a woman performing the many duties of an architect was hardly thinkable.

Blanchard told Waite that she had wanted to be an architect since childhood. She said her friends mocked her in grade school, but she persevered in her ambition to pursue her dream. She graduated from Buffalo High School in 1874 and continued in its two-year college preparatory program with the intention of attending Cornell University's newly opened architectural department. She took advanced courses, tutored other students, and traveled in preparation for her continued studies. She hoped Waite would hire her for the summer until her program began. And—despite the common prejudice against women working in the profession—Waite hired her in June 1876, enabling Louise to fulfill her dream and become an architect.

This book traces the life and career of a largely forgotten woman and places her within the context of her city and the times in which she lived. Louise Blanchard Bethune was the first professional woman architect in the United States. She was raised and practiced in Buffalo, New York, while the city was experiencing unprecedented growth and wealth. She was accepted in the professional associations by the most well-respected architects of the time; Daniel Burnham, Louis Sullivan, and especially John Root were her colleagues and champions. Louise was not only admitted into the "boys' club" of professional associations—the American Institute of Architects (AIA)—but she also became one of its leaders during a crucial period in architecture's maturation from a craft and gentleman's pastime to a serious profession. How did this happen? And why is she unknown outside of small circles of architectural historians and Buffalo enthusiasts?

One reason for Louise's obscurity is that her professional and personal papers have been lost. While Louise founded her own architectural firm, its office records and most of its construction documents no longer exist. Many of the homes and other buildings that she designed have been destroyed over the decades. If Louise kept diaries, they, too, have been lost. Another reason is the collective amnesia of the profession's male members—purposeful or otherwise—regarding early women members. For years, there was only one known photograph of her, and little other information was available about her family or history. A few articles were written about Louise after she passed away in 1913, however, they were accompanied by others litigating a case that Louise had already successfully debunked in 1881: whether women had the intellectual and physical abilities to perform the work of an architect. Women experienced opposition to entry in certain local chapters of the American Institute of Architects until after World War I. Only a handful of women were admitted to the AIA until the 1920s, but it was not until the 1970s that the AIA began to address its longstanding indifference to its women members.

Another reason, I think, is because Louise was such an early trailblazer. Most of the nineteenth-century women architects left the profession when they married, or they focused on strictly residential architecture. Louise was the opposite; she married her colleague and business partner, Robert

Bethune, they had one child, and together they ran a very successful, albeit small, practice until Louise was forced to retire due to ill health in 1911. She designed schools and commercial structures as well as homes, handling the full gamut of architectural projects available at the time.

Louise Bethune was complicated: She was simultaneously very much of her era, and very far ahead of her time. As a professional in a male-dominated industry during the Gilded Age, she had to chart her own course. After winning an apprenticeship with Waite, she chose to forgo college training and then founded her own firm, confronting potential prejudice from male colleagues and builders and winning architectural commissions from—mostly male—clients. Yet, Louise's story is very familiar to contemporary women. She went into business with her spouse, and theirs was very much a partnership of equals. She balanced the conflicting demands of managing a firm, caring for her family, and pursuing personal interests with her friends. She believed that women should be treated equally in business and fought for pay equity, and she managed to fit a regular exercise regime into her busy day.

Louise faced more opposition within the profession than she admitted. Publicly, she stated that her male colleagues, clients, and contractors had been nothing but respectful of her and her opinions. However, we know that some AIA members were hesitant about admitting her to their ranks and only did so at the lowest level, and her firm fell out of favor with the City of Buffalo when it became apparent that Louise was a partner and not just an employee.

While she had close women friends, Louise was not the beneficiary of a women's network in support of her practice. While women who followed Louise received commissions from women of means, Louise did not find support among Buffalo's newly wealthy women—despite her fame. She was unable or unwilling to court favor from potential upper-class female clients as other women architects did and would do in the future.

Louise may appear to us today as a rather conventional, if not conservative, woman. We must remember that she was the head of a commercial business at a time when many of her clients were local businessmen and homeowners who would rarely have considered hiring a female architect. She couldn't align herself with the more progressive women who publicly called for voting rights and women's equality. Nonetheless, Louise would not be a victim; she wrote her own narrative. Beneath her veneer of Victorian manners and dress, she was a rebel and activist with a steely backbone and iron will. I am aware that as a white, Protestant woman born to educated parents Bethune benefited from the opportunities to advance from which people of color and immigrants were excluded. Nonetheless, she did face the common prejudices against women, not to mention the difficulty a woman faced to be successful in the architectural profession.

One of the most interesting aspects of Louise's story is that she was a bicycling enthusiast. She was the first woman in Buffalo to own a bicycle and was a founder of the Buffalo Women's Wheel and Athletic Club, the second all-female cycling organization in the country. Just as in the architectural profession, few women had previously adopted cycling as a sport and means of transportation because of the limitations of contemporary bicycle design, their bulky clothing, and the general feeling that only men had the physical strength to ride long distances. This was all eliminated by a group of pioneering women—many of whom were also part of the nascent women's rights movement—who defied common prejudices, adopted less-restrictive garb, and formed self-supporting clubs to encourage others to take up the sport.

This discovery led me to question the long-held belief promoted by her previous biographers that Louise was not a feminist. In researching the rich history of "wheeling" and its impact on the women's suffrage movement, and in my other research on her, I have found many indications that Louise was a staunch believer in women's equality and actively advocated for her beliefs. While earlier historians and biographers felt that Louise was not concerned with promoting women's rights, it became clear to me, after considering the social atmosphere of the time and viewing her life and activities in the context of other women of the era, that Louise was very engaged in women's equality on her own terms.

An 1892 profile that appeared in a Buffalo newspaper, titled "A Clever Woman's Work," perfectly captures Louise's stature as a forward-thinking woman. In it you see a woman who is in complete control of her life and career. The author marvels at the fact that Louise undertook all the many duties of a professional architect, including heavy onsite work and overseeing project costs. Despite its quaint language, this description of Louise could apply to a woman architect today:

> Mrs. Louise Bethune of this city is a very successful architect. And that does not mean that she is simply able to design and do office work, although she is proficient in this difficult line. But Mrs. Bethune does all that a capable, practical architect is expected to do. She handles all the dwelling houses that come to

the office of the firm of which she is a member. Designs, makes estimates and directs the work. More than half of her time is spent in personally superintending the building.

She goes from place to place on her bicycle, which she finds to be a great convenience. Mrs. Bethune is full of ideas, clever and well read. She devotes herself almost entirely to her work, rarely going out "on pleasure bent," and finds her lot a very happy and satisfactory one.[1]

Louise performed all these duties while wearing a corset and full skirt with bustle. Her mere presence on the streets of Buffalo actively challenged preconceived ideas of what a woman in a dress could do.

Louise lived during a time of profound changes in the architectural business as well as broader social forces that would greatly impact society. She worked in an industry that was maturing into a profession from a craft and technologically advancing in its use of building materials and new systems. Throughout her life, the women's movement increased in intensity, with advocates seeking reform on many fronts. She also lived in a city that was quickly growing in population and wealth just like the country at large. The society in which she navigated was moving from a rural economy to an urban, industrial one, with social upheaval and ethnic and class discrimination along the way. How this remarkable Gilded Age woman charted her own course by navigating these currents is the story I will tell.

Louise Blanchard Bethune, like many women at that time, changed her name when she married and soon after her husband became her business partner. Therefore, their personal and professional lives were inextricably interconnected. For consistency I have applied the following naming conventions: in each chapter I initially introduce them as "Louise Bethune" and "Robert Bethune." Thereafter, I reference them by their first name. Anytime I refer to "Bethune" for variety I am referencing Louise.

I first learned about Louise in 2002, when I attended the unveiling of a grave marker dedicated to her organized by Buffalo-based architect Adriana Barbasch. In 1986, the AIA had asked Adriana to research Bethune for a brochure on women in architecture. Adriana continued her research, contributing to several books on early women architects until 2004, when she retired. As one of two women on the AIA Buffalo/WNY Board, I was deeply struck by Louise's trailblazing spirit and accomplishments. My interest in her story might have ended then, except that when Adrianna retired, she offered to share her research with me.

Since receiving this cache of materials, I have lectured often and written articles on Louise, getting to know her from my twenty-first-century vantage point. In 2006, I successfully nominated Bethune to the Western New York Women's Hall of Fame. During that process, I met Louise and Robert's great-granddaughter and sole heir, Zina Bethune. Zina was an accomplished actor, ballet dancer, multimedia artist, and philanthropist. Zina and I stayed in touch, exchanging information on her ancestors as they were found until, in 2012, Zina was tragically killed in a car accident. To ensure the legacies of both women, Zina's husband, Sean Feeley, generously donated the historic family records, photo albums, and other ephemera to the University at Buffalo Special Collections.

The Zina Bethune Archive on Louise Bethune is a rich resource, containing unique images of Bethune and the people she held dear. A second source of information came from Nancy Herlan Brady, a descendent of business partner William Fuchs. Nancy shared a small collection of annotated photos of Fuchs from the 1890s. In this collection was a photograph of Bethune, Bethune & Fuchs, which became the second photo of Louise Bethune that was known to exist. This collection also included photos of their architectural office and candid family photos that included the Bethune family. These demonstrated the close relationship of the three partners. Additional sources came from many newspaper articles about her I have found. The Buffalo and Erie County Grosvenor Library holds records from the Women's Wheel and Athletic Club and the Buffalo Genealogical Society, two clubs in which Bethune was a member, have yielded information on her relationships with her friends, how she juggled a busy career, and pursued personal interests. The Grosvenor Library also holds the research that Louise compiled on the Bethune and Blanchard families. Her correspondence, mostly from the last decade of her life, provides good information on her declining health and her relationship with her immediate and extended family.

When I began my research on Louise, I was a junior architect learning my strengths and interests in the profession. In the years since, as I have grown as a professional, my life and career have eerily paralleled Louise's. Like Louise, I wanted to be an architect as a child and my passion has always been in educational design. I was fortunate to be able to dedicate my career to this type of work, which is a luxury Louise did not enjoy. Like her, I feel strongly about the importance of service to our professional association. I served on the AIA at the local, state, and national levels, becoming the second woman president of the Buffalo/WNY Chapter, which Louise founded. I later served as president of AIA New York State and served on the AIA National Strategic Council, mirroring Louise's participation with the national AIA. Following in her footsteps again, I was the first successful woman applicant after her living in Buffalo to become a fellow with the AIA. Where Louise suffered illness as a young child and at the end of her life, I suffered a life-threatening illness in the middle, when I contracted Guillain-Barré syndrome. Like Louise, I fought for my right to work, and I was even restricted in the clothing I could wear for a time, while I regained my strength and dexterity over a four-year period.

Our parallel lives in Buffalo and careers in architecture have provided me with strong points of reference while I have been writing this book. As I drive through the city, passing her buildings and visiting her gravesite, I can visualize the city Louise helped build, because many of the landmarks from her lifetime still stand. As I attend AIA meetings, I participate in discussions regarding the future of the profession and the academy that are similar in tone, if not the exact topics, in which she participated. As I attend project meetings, poring over floor plans, discussing budgets, schedule, and client needs, I am reminded of Louise's experiences holding similar conversations. I believe these parallels gave me a unique insight into her life and career and it certainly enhanced my passion in researching and telling her story.

Chapter 1

Becoming Louise

Early Life, Family, Education, and Apprenticeship

She had acquired habits of study and self-reliance which led her through
school life to disregard the usual class criterions.

—Willard and Livermore, *A Woman of the Century*

Figure 1.1. Louise Bethune in her teenage years. Zina Bethune Archive on Louise
Bethune, circa 1860–1962. Courtesy of the University Archives, University at
Buffalo.

A Family of Patriots

Louise Blanchard Bethune was born on July 21, 1856, in Waterloo, New York. She was the firstborn child of Dalson Wallace Blanchard and Emma Melona (Williams) Blanchard. She became a genealogical enthusiast in the last decade of her life, and our knowledge of her ancestry is a result of her research. According to her own account, Bethune's paternal ancestors were Huguenot refugees, and her maternal ancestors came from Wales to Massachusetts in 1640.[1]

Her mother's line included several distinguished early American patriots. Her maternal great-grandfather was Captain Ebenezer (Eben) Williams (1749–1847), who was born in Lebanon, Connecticut, and served during the Revolutionary War. The entire family were supportive of the American cause; Ebenezer's father Jonathon was an early activist, and his uncle, William Williams, was Lebanon's town clerk, a representative in Connecticut's General Assembly, and a signer of the Declaration of Independence.[2] Ebenezer rose through the ranks from enlisting as a minuteman to eventually becoming a captain.[3] According to family lore, during the war he received invitations to dine from both General Washington and the Marquis de Lafayette.[4]

Following the war, Williams moved to Richmond, Massachusetts, and, shortly after, met his future wife, Sarah (Sally) Stedman, who was born in Wethersfield, Connecticut. When Sarah was a young girl, a new minister, Reverend Perry, arrived in town, bringing his young bride with him. Mrs. Perry grew fond of little Sarah who was a regular visitor to their home, and she eventually lived with them as their eldest child. When the Perrys moved to Richmond, Sarah accompanied them,[5] and it was there that she first met her future husband, as one of her grandchildren later related: "When they reached Richmond, [Ebenezer] was the first gentleman they saw. He helped them out of their carriage. Grandma said she was a little afraid of him at first—he was so dignified and handsome. This must have been after the close of the war. They were married 28-April-1787, at the home of the Perrys."[6]

Ebenezer and Sarah remained in Richmond until 1808, moved to New York's Onondaga County, and then to Schoharie County in 1815, where they had a farm. While it does not appear that Ebenezer received a land grant for his service to the US Army, he received a pension, which he later successfully petitioned to be increased based on his long service.[7] The Williams's eldest child, Jonathon Whitney Williams, was Louise's grandfather. He was born in 1788 in Lenox, Massachusetts. In May of 1812, he married Elizabeth Fenner of Manlius, New York, while he also served as a captain in the War of 1812. Bethune's mother, Emma, was the tenth of twelve children, born in 1831.

On her father's side, Bethune was also descended from a veteran of the Revolutionary War, her paternal great-grandfather, Abiel Blanchard.[8] Bethune's paternal grandparents, Thomas and Sarah (Cunningham) Blanchard, moved from Vermont and Massachusetts, respectively, to Manlius, where they were married, owned a farm, and raised eight children.[9] Their son, Dalson, graduated from the Albany Normal School in 1848 as a teacher. He was possibly the first of his family to receive a postsecondary education, which was not uncommon at the time. Emma Williams and Dalson Blanchard were married in Manlius in 1852.

Located eleven miles east of Syracuse, the town was established in 1794 as the seventh of the twenty-five townships in the Military Tract of Central New York. The Military Tract was a vast amount of Haudenosaunee land—nearly two million acres—that was seized by the federal government and reallocated to soldiers and officers of the Revolutionary War as compensation for their service.[10] Many of the town's first white inhabitants were from New England, and in its first years of development it grew in population to become the most prominent community in the county.[11] By the time the Erie Canal was built in 1825, Manlius was already a bustling mercantile center.

The couple moved to Waterloo, New York, where Dalson taught science, and where Louise was born.[12] It may be a romantic notion to directly tie Louise's future architectural career with her Western New York upbringing and the women's suffrage movement that began there in Seneca Falls in 1848. However, the entire region was a center of innovation and expansion at this time. With that progress came progressive thought and action; it was no accident that the region was a hotbed for the abolitionist and women's rights movements. The catalyst for the region's wealth, innovation, and progressive movements was the development of the Erie Canal.

New Innovations Lead to New Ways of Thinking

In the decades following the Revolutionary War, the country emerged from the shadow of Great Britain as the world's leader in innovation and wealth.

Figures 1.2. and 1.3. Dalson and Emma Blanchard in the 1880s. Zina Bethune Archive on Louise Bethune, circa 1860–1962. Courtesy of the University Archives, University at Buffalo.

Several factors contributed to this ascent, including an extended national transportation network system and the growth of mechanized production methods in industry and the distribution of goods. US per capita output and consumption doubled, wealth increased, and the population grew exponentially thanks to the arrival of new immigrants.[13] The Erie Canal, which opened in 1825, provided the first means of transporting goods from the east coast to the country's interior without the need for portage. The 363-mile canal ran from Albany, at the Hudson River, to Buffalo, on the shores of Lake Erie, connecting the Atlantic Ocean at New York City to the Great Lakes and the Midwestern states. The immediate success of the Erie Canal made New York the economic and commercial powerhouse of the country. The national economy grew by 4.5 percent annually for the next quarter century.[14] The small towns of Buffalo, Rochester, Syracuse, Rome, and Utica became bustling commercial centers thanks to the commerce on the canal. Buffalo became the largest inland port in the United States and the population of Syracuse grew from 250 in 1820 to 22,000 in 1850.[15] A ribbon of ten new towns with names ending in "port" were founded between Syracuse and Buffalo. As the country expanded westward, the canal's importance grew, and cities such as Cleveland and Chicago became bustling mercantile and industrial centers along the transportation route on the Great Lakes. The Erie Canal, in essence, connected Chicago to New York, with Buffalo in the middle. The newly minted "Empire State" would become a hotbed for innovation and progressive thinking. Both entrepreneurial activity and technological innovation expanded exponentially. As economic historian Kenneth Sokoloff noted, "The completion of the Erie Canal in 1825 seems to have sparked big changes in the composition of output and a sharp rise in patenting along its route."

The Erie Canal was essentially the information superhighway of the 1800s. With this free flow of information came a surge of social movements such as abolitionism, women's rights, and utopianism to communities along its route. As noted by historian Judith Wellman, Seneca Falls and Waterloo in the 1840s were largely inhabited by people from outside the region, including New England, Eastern New York, and Southeastern Pennsylvania, as well as coming directly from other countries such as England and Ireland, seeking better lives; Quakers and African Americans came too.[16] The result was a mélange of cultures, languages, and points of view, which made it a place ripe for reform.

The antebellum period in the United States—generally considered to be between the War of 1812 and the US Civil War—marked a significant turning point in the young country's history. It was an era when its citizens began the first of many reckonings with the class and caste systems that formed the foundation of the "land of the free." The uneasy alliance among its disparate cultures and economies was beginning to unravel. Cries for equality for women and African slaves resounded. And from nowhere were these cries louder sung than Western New York. Buffalo and Niagara Falls were the last "stations" of Harriet Tubman's Underground Railroad. Ms. Tubman herself lived in Auburn, New York, in the heart of the Finger Lakes region and forty-five miles west of Syracuse. The abolitionist, statesman, and former slave Frederick Douglass lived in Rochester, New York, from 1847 to 1872, where he would publish his influential paper, the *North Star*, to advocate for abolition and women's suffrage. And, of course, women suffrage leaders Elizabeth Cady Stanton and Susan B. Anthony resided in Seneca Falls and nearby Rochester, respectively.

Stanton and Anthony were true products of the dramatic growth in both the state's commercial and intellectual spheres. As they wrote in their epic *History of Woman Suffrage*:

> New York with its metropolis, fine harbors, great lakes and rivers; its canals and railroads uniting the extremist limits, and controlling the commerce of the world; with its wise statesman and wily politicians, long holding the same relation to the nation at large that Paris is said to hold to France, has been proudly called by her sons and daughters the Empire State. But the most interesting fact in her history, to woman, is that she was the first State to emancipate wives from slavery of the old common law of England, and to secure to them equal property rights.[17]

The 1848 Seneca Falls Woman's Rights Convention was the spark that ignited the women's equal rights movement in the United States. It came about partly because of circumstance and partly because of the talent and will of the people involved. Essentially, the right people were at the right place at the right time. When Elizabeth Cady Stanton moved to Seneca Falls with her husband and young family from Boston in 1847, they were already active in the antislavery movement. The Stantons were friends with Rochester-based Frederick Douglass and Lucretia Mott, who had Quaker family in the area and visited often. The idea for the convention on women's rights had been germinating for several years, beginning when Stanton first met Mott at the World's Anti-Slavery Convention in London in 1840.[18]

The subtext of the convention was New York's long-debated Married Women's Property Act, which was passed on April 7, 1848. In New York State in the mid-1840s, the right for married women to own property was one of the most hotly contested legal issues. Upon entering marriage, women became "civically dead," with no legal right to own property, money, or custodial rights of their children. Still viewing marriage through the lens of Christianity, the law saw the husband as the literal and symbolic head of the family and the wife as the heart. The husband earned the income and was expected to represent his wife at the ballot box and in the management of the family's assets. The wife's sphere of influence was centered in the home, in the care and management of the family. This value system is often described as the "Cult of Domesticity" or the "Cult of True Womanhood."[19] The Married Women's Property Act of 1848 granted women the right to own property and the profits made from this property following marriage and became the basis for similar laws in subsequent states in the 1850s.[20]

While the Convention at Seneca Falls is considered the beginning of the women's suffrage movement in the United States, the road to women's equality was more than simply suffrage. Early members of the movement—notably Stanton—came to believe that, through suffrage, women would earn true equality, which included equal pay for equal service. Pay equity was a reoccurring theme for Bethune in her career and she came to believe that this was the pathway for women to achieve equality. Indeed, it was because of New York's Married Women's Property Act that Bethune could legally own her firm and the real estate that she would acquire as a practicing architect and firm owner.

Young Louise

The Blanchard family settled in the small village of Forestville at the outbreak of the Civil War, where Dalson had his next teaching position. Located forty miles southwest of Buffalo and part of Hanover Township in Chautauqua County, Forestville's primary industry was lumber. The town had opened its saw and grist mills in 1809 and 1810, respectively. In 1851, the Erie Railroad was routed through the town, which inspired its industrial growth.[21] By the 1860s, the town's population was 574.[22] The town had opened its first school in 1816, and by the 1860s, this had grown into a school district with the county's first union free school opening in 1863, where Dalson probably taught.

According to her later account, Bethune was a sickly child and was homeschooled until the age of eleven.[23] Her mother, also an educator, would have taken the lead in her education. It was this experience, she wrote, that provided her with the self-reliance required to direct her academic studies and her later career.[24] She had always enjoyed drawing houses as a childhood pastime,[25] predicting her future career.

On October 4, 1864, the Blanchards welcomed twins into the family: Edwin Williams and Clara White. Sadly, Edwin died on October 15, 1865, at the age of one year, and Clara followed on January 9, 1869, at age four and a half; both were buried in Forestville. The cause of the twins' deaths is unknown, but infantile death was not uncommon in this era. The fact that Louise was "sickly" as a child and her siblings died before reaching the age of five might point to an inherited illness in the family. Or these deaths could have been tragically coincidental. Either way, it is difficult to imagine that these events were not devastating to Louise and her parents.

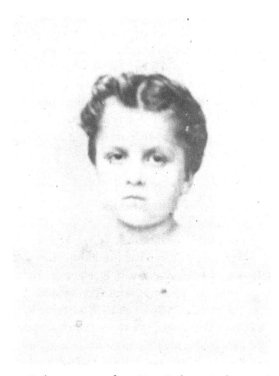

Figure 1.4 Louise Bethune as an infant. Zina Bethune Archive on Louise Bethune, circa 1860–1962. Courtesy of the University Archives, University at Buffalo.

In 1863, Dalson was drafted into the Union Army, however, it is uncertain whether he served;[26] if he did, this must have been another traumatic event in Louise's young life. During the last five of her nine years, she had gone from being an only child, to the eldest of three, and then losing her younger siblings; in addition, the family had relocated three times. Given all these events, it is understandable how she learned to be self-reliant in her youth. Indeed, several newly found photographs taken during this period show her unmistakable look of determination, which is also readily apparent in later photographs taken when she was an adult. Louise was her own person from childhood and her life experiences reinforced this need for self-reliance.

Bethune may not have come from a wealthy family, but she was born to a family of educators who provided her with individual academic instruction and a high degree of education. She gained an appreciation of lifelong learning at a young age.[27] From her father, Dalson, Louise inherited her academic approach, interests, work ethic, and high standards of conduct.[28] Bethune said that her father was known for his mental agility and accuracy.[29] Later in life Bethune noted that both she and her father were hard workers who didn't make or have time to discuss family matters or their common interests.

But it was from her mother, Emma, that Louise inherited her entrepreneurial spirit. Returning to work following the death of her son and surviving twin Clara, Emma first worked for her husband at Buffalo Public School No. 3 as an assistant, and then taught in Buffalo Public School No. 15 until approximately 1886.[30] In addition, Emma was a property owner, as we shall see.

School Years

Bethune's family settled in Buffalo in 1867, where Dalson first taught and then became a principal at Public School No. 3. Louise was eleven years old when they arrived and began attending public school. The city was in the midst of rapid industrial and economic growth that would continue throughout the late nineteenth and early twentieth centuries. Originating as a small trading village in 1789, the opening of the Erie Canal in 1825 set the stage for Buffalo to mature from being a town on the frontier to becoming a vibrant city with the promise of prosperity in its future. When the canal opened, Buffalo's population was 2,095; by 1865, its population

Figure 1.5. The Blanchard twins, Edwin and Clara, during the Chautauqua years. Zina Bethune Archive on Louise Bethune, circa 1860–1962. Courtesy of the University Archives, University at Buffalo.

Figure 1.6. Louise Bethune as a child in the 1860s. Zina Bethune Archive on Louise Bethune, circa 1860–1962. Courtesy of the University Archives, University at Buffalo.

had expanded to 94,210.[31] Louise was inspired by the atmosphere of growth and innovation that was occurring all around her.

When the Blanchard family moved to Buffalo, city leaders were about to embark upon a beautification program. In 1868, Olmsted, Vaux & Company was awarded the commission to design the city's park system. Fresh from his success building New York's Central Park, Frederick Law Olmsted designed three parks in Buffalo (the Front, the Park, and the Parade) and a parkway system that would unite the entire city. Neighborhoods adjacent to the parks and parkways began to be developed and, ultimately, they became the choice areas in the city. Richmond Avenue, a section of one of the critical parkways connecting the Front to the Park, was developed from a dirt path known as Rogers Street. It became a fashionable address for Buffalo's newly minted entrepreneurs, and adjacent streets flourished as a home for middle-class families. The Blanchard family would eventually live at 255 Porter Avenue, just two blocks from Front Park and on the link of the Front-Park Parkway. Their choice of neighborhood underscores their aspirations for upward mobility in a city that was prospering and in a growth mindset.

Following the move to Buffalo and the passing of her daughter Clara, Emma Blanchard returned to teaching. Bethune attended Buffalo Central School; it was during this time that Louise became interested in architecture. Several profiles written during her lifetime state that "in her girlhood she showed great talent in planning houses and so decided to take up architecture as a life work."[32] Bethune would later document how her interest in architecture first began, most notably, in her profile in the reference work *A Woman of the Century*. A better version of the story appeared in an article from 1913, published just one month before she died: "One day in conversation with several friends a caustic remark led her to investigate several studies in architecture. She became so interested that she took the study of architecture as a profession. Thus an investigation begun in a spirit of playful self-defense soon became an absorbing interest."[33]

Although we don't know what this "caustic remark" was, it is likely that her friends doubted the ability of a woman to succeed in the male-dominated field of architecture. As we shall see, Louise always welcomed a challenge to prove her worth and to defend women's rights to a full life, including a professional career.

At Buffalo Central High School, Louise became known to her friends as Lulu.[34] The school's curriculum was designed to offer an array of scholastic choices for girls and boys to prepare them for their chosen path in life. There were three academic tracks from which to choose. Students were encouraged to give serious thought to selecting their track to ensure their success, and were encouraged to add courses to their baseline as they became comfortable with the material and pace of the school. Courses ranged from bookkeeping to advanced physics, to chemistry and geology in the sciences, introductory German, French, and Latin, and literature studies within these languages. For those with ambitions of pursuing a postsecondary education, the school also offered a one-year college preparatory program.

Bethune graduated with honors from the school in 1874.[35] Following her graduation, she taught or tutored students and continued the college preparatory program, which she completed in 1875. By now, she had decided to pursue an architectural career and was preparing to enroll in the newly opened architectural school at Cornell University.[36] In addition to her college preparatory course, she also continued her preparation through travel.[37] It is uncertain exactly how far she went, but it was probably not beyond the US and Canada.

Louise changed her plans to attend Cornell University when prominent local architect Richard Waite offered her a job. It is not known how or why this offer was extended; however, Waite must have been impressed by Louise's determination and have seen a glimpse of her strength of character, interest in learning, and willingness to work hard to achieve these goals. Her life was spent in preparation for this moment, and she seized it.

Educating the Woman Architect

The hours were from eight to six, and the pay was small, but her employer's library was at her service.

—Willard and Livermore, *A Woman of the Century*

The ambitious, eighteen-year-old Louise Blanchard walked into the office of Richard A. Waite, the most prominent architect in Buffalo, in 1876 and secured an internship. What was it about her that prompted Waite to provide her this opportunity? Her father was a principal in the Buffalo Public Schools, so it is possible she might have secured her position through that connection. Or Waite may have recognized a little of himself in her.

It was traditional for an architect to receive training through an internship rather than attending college; Louise may have come to this conclusion

Figure 1.7. Bethune, when she was known by her schoolmates as Lulu. Zina Bethune Archive on Louise Bethune, circa 1860–1962. Courtesy of the University Archives, University at Buffalo.

herself because she decided not to enroll at Cornell but to work for Waite. That this option was even available to her is remarkable, because it required the commitment by an established architect to be her mentor, which was rare for a woman. In fact, most of her successors attended architecture school because they could not find employment without a degree or diploma.[38] As Bethune herself commented in 1891: "The total number of women graduates from the various schools of the country can hardly exceed a dozen, and most of these seem to have renounced ambition with the attainment of a degree, but there are among them a few brilliant and energetic women for whom the future holds great possibilities."[39]

In the late 1800s, there were three training paths to becoming an architect: attend a design school for women, enroll in a coeducational architecture school, or obtain an apprenticeship with a practicing architect. However, much of the mainstream architectural world was unaware of or unopen to women's involvement in the field. In 1883, the editors of *The Art Interchange* advised a young woman who was interested in pursuing architecture as a career that they knew of no successful woman architects, because the duties of the profession required business acumen, artistic talent, and the technical skills to work directly with builders. They were apparently unaware that, by this date, Louise Bethune had already opened her architectural practice following a five-year apprenticeship. Other women had also begun the path toward a career in architecture.

There were advocates for women to access education in design and architecture as early as the 1850s. In a lecture given by Horace Mann in New York in 1852, the educational reformer and politician advanced the many career opportunities for which women would be suitable. He identified art and design as particularly suitable fields for women, noting their finer level of taste than men.[40] Mann was referring to the design school movement that began with the opening of the Franklin Institute School in Philadelphia in 1848. The Franklin and others that followed—the New England School of Design in Boston and the New York School of Design for Women—provided women with access to education in the fine and industrial arts, and eventually some women received architectural training. Bethune addressed these design schools in her 1891 lecture, noting that they did not have facilities to provide the requisite technical training for an architectural education.[41] The curriculum at the design schools often did not provide adequate technical skills for a woman to advance into the profession afterward.[42] However, they created a vital entry to a design program, and, as Bethune noted, this education could be supplemented with additional training.[43]

Several late nineteenth-century women architects matriculated through these programs. Minerva Parker Nichols, of Philadelphia, attended the Franklin Institute Drawing School, graduating in 1885 before apprenticing with the architect Edwin W. Thorne from 1886 to 1888.[44] Minerva and Louise would cross paths several times during their careers. They corresponded in the 1880s, comparing notes on the number of women who were entering the profession. And their stories would intersect during the Women's Building competition for the Columbian Exposition, as two of the only practicing women architects in the country at that time, although neither submitted a viable entry to the competition (see chapter 7). Two other prominent female architects to graduate from one of these programs were Mary Nevan Gannon and her business partner, Alice J. Hands. They attended the inaugural class of the New York School of Applied Design for Women in 1892, graduating in 1894.[45] Gannon and Hands would run a successful firm in New York from 1894 to approximately 1899, winning several design competitions, and, like Bethune, were advocates for equal pay for women for equal service.[46]

By the 1870s, a woman interested in pursuing architecture could also attend one of the architecture schools that were beginning to open. American architectural education was a combination of the École des Beaux Arts atelier or studio system set within the existing university educational structure and the teaching of building technologies. The first American school of architecture to open was at the Massachusetts Institute of Technology (MIT) in 1869, followed by the University of Illinois in 1870 and Cornell University in 1871. Additionally, land grant institutions that had opened with the 1862 Morrill Act following the Civil War offered coeducational opportunities for women. These institutions provided programs in agriculture and mechanical arts on federal land throughout the country. The AIA briefly considered opening a school of architecture themselves, but decided that architecture schools offered by established universities were a better option for the profession.[47] These coeducational land-grant colleges were particularly good options, because many private institutions did not admit women until the twentieth century. As Ada Louise Huxtable noted, "By 1910 more than 50 women had been trained as architects in the U.S.A., although half of the existing architecture schools still denied admission to women."[48]

In the United States from the Civil War to 1900, thirty-nine academically trained women graduated from architectural schools.[49] The first woman to graduate from architecture school was Mary L. Page from the University of Illinois, receiving a certificate in architecture in 1878 and a BS in 1879.[50] She established a drafting, blueprint, and abstract service company called Whitman & Page with classmate Robert Farwell Whitman, and later taught in Washington State.[51]

Bethune was adamant that women be provided with the same educational opportunities as men in architecture. She noted, "Women cannot pursue architectural studies to advantage in a private apartment. Co-education is a privilege."[52] She regularly corresponded with directors of various schools of architecture to inquire on the status of their women students and advocate for coeducational training.[53]

As we've noted, Bethune originally intended to attend Cornell to further her architectural education.[54] A land-grant institution, Cornell began accepting women into its program almost immediately, with Margaret (Madge, as Bethune called her) Hicks being the first woman student admitted to the school. Hicks graduated in 1880. Had Bethune chosen to attend Cornell in 1876 as intended, she and Hicks may have been classmates and graduated the same year. Hicks was the first woman architect to publish work in a professional architectural journal; *American Architect and Building*

News published her student project, a "workman's cottage," on April 13, 1878. In 1883, Christian Universalist minister and suffrage activist Phebe Hannaford commended Hicks for her advocacy for social reform in her commencement essay "Tenement House."[55] According to Bethune, Hicks worked for an architect named Sillsbee in Syracuse upon graduation.[56] Sadly, Hicks died in 1883 before she could practice independently.[57]

The third option for women, and the most conventional option for an aspiring male architect, was to obtain an apprenticeship with a practicing architect. Julia Howe, the women's rights advocate, suggested that women agitate to be articled to an architect in 1873.[58] This was easier said than done, because it required an architect willing to offer a salaried position to an untrained woman. The male-dominated apprentice system was generally closed to women, despite the fact that, as Bethune noted, "there is a woman in nearly every architect's office in this city, but these are employed as bookkeepers, copyists and type writers, not as draftswomen."[59] While Bethune felt that any woman with the aptitude and desire could follow her in becoming an apprentice at an established firm, there are few instances of women who did, without receiving some design training in advance of securing a position in a firm.

It is difficult to quantify the number of women who tried unsuccessfully to pursue apprenticeship, but Bethune was the first to succeed. As of 1891, she knew of only a few others who had pursued this track.[60] Katharine Cotheal Budd, the first woman member of the AIA's New York chapter, may have been one of them. Budd received private instruction from William R. Ware, an architectural professor at Columbia University. Her apprenticeship was composed of work for several noteworthy architects in New York and Paris in the 1880s.[61]

Apprenticeship

It is no exaggeration to say that during the first three years of my office studying I did not sit fifteen minutes consecutively out of the day.

—Louise Bethune, "Women as Architects," 1884

In 1876, there were thirteen architects listed in the Buffalo City Directory; Richard A. Waite was considered one of the city's rising stars and influential tastemakers. Bethune worked in Waite's office from 1876 until October

Figure 1.8. Margaret Hicks. Courtesy of Division of Rare and Manuscript Collections, Cornell University Library.

Figure 1.9. Illustration by Margaret Hicks for a workman's cottage, which was published in *American Architect and Building News*, April 13, 1878.

of 1881. During her apprenticeship, she also worked part-time for the architect F. W. Caulkins.[62] Her days were spent drafting in the office and conducting site visits, all under Waite's direct supervision. Waite prided himself on the fact that he did not accept work in which he could not be personally involved. He closely supervised the work of everyone in the office, including his apprentices.

In her writings, Bethune was very concerned that women receive a thorough architectural training, including in construction and site supervisions. She lamented women who shirked "the brick-and-mortar-rubber-boot-and-ladder-climbing period of investigative education," so it is safe to assume this was an important aspect of her own architectural training.[63] She described her studies in the sciences and arts as "endless," which prepared the apprentice for a career of lifelong study, an attitude that she learned from her mentor. According to Bethune, Waite had a very complete library, which was rare in those days,[64] and that she studied in it often. (Bethune also possessed an extensive library, which she referenced in her will, that was started during her apprenticeship.[65]) Finally, she continued the travel that she had begun while preparing for Cornell to increase her architectural vocabulary and studied the work of practicing architects.[66] While working in the office, Louise met her future husband, Robert Bethune, who was another of Waite's apprentices.

Kellum and Waite

Waite's willingness to hire a woman with no previous architectural training may have been inspired by a similar opportunity that he enjoyed early in his career. He was offered an internship with John Kellum, the most prominent architect in New York City in the 1860s.[67] Indeed, Waite had defied the odds and overcame poverty and lack of formal education to become an architectural force in several Great Lakes cities.

Born in Surrey, England, in 1848, his family immigrated to Buffalo in 1857 and met with early prosperity. However, both of his parents died in quick succession, forcing Waite to forgo his aspirations to become an engineer and pursue work as a brass finisher at the age of seventeen.[68] His brother, who had distinguished himself in the Civil War, secured a position for Richard in the office of New York–based engineer John Ericsson. Ericsson is known today for his design of the ironclad ship, the USS *Monitor*, which helped change the course of naval warfare.[69] After two years, Ericsson saw that Waite's true passion was architecture and recommended him to Kellum. Waite worked for Kellum from approximately 1865 to 1868 and supplemented his training with sculpture classes at the Cooper Institute.[70]

By the mid-1860s, Kellum had a well-established practice, with some of the most successful businessmen in New York as his clients. He was known for his cast-iron commercial buildings, a building style that became prominent in lower Manhattan at the time. Kellum's list of clients included Tiffany & Co., the New York Stock Exchange, Mutual Life, the *New York Herald*, Steinway and Sons, the New York County (Tweed) Courthouse, and department store magnate Alexander T. Stewart. The breadth of the work—from residences to commercial, institutional, and industrial buildings—provided Waite with the skills needed to successfully operate his architectural practice in Buffalo a few years later.

RICHARD A. WAITE.

Figure 1.10. Bethune's mentor, Richard Waite. Photo of Waite from *Men of Buffalo*.

Despite or because of his successful business, Kellum was ostracized by New York's architectural establishment. John Kellum was a self-made man. He was born in 1809 in Hempstead, Long Island, where his father was a shoemaker of modest means. Following a very rudimentary public education, Kellum secured a position as a journeyman carpenter with a prominent master builder in Brooklyn in 1841. After four years of work and self-directed study, he began employment with the well-established architect Gamaliel King. In 1850, King made Kellum a partner.[71] The firm flourished with many of its commissions being cast-iron façade commercial structures and ecclesiastical buildings. In 1859, they amicably dissolved their partnership, and Kellum established his own practice, building on their earlier successes. Kellum unsuccessfully applied for admission to the AIA three times. Members criticized him for not having a thorough knowledge of the classical orders and overreliance on his assistants for design and draftsmanship. They also accused Kellum of overtly pandering to his wealthy clients, who might consider themselves amateur architects.[72] To members who were dedicated to transforming architecture into a profession with equal status to medicine and law, Kellum's humble background, outstanding success, and clear intention of running his firm as a business stood in sharp contrast to their more lofty ideals.

While Kellum is an obscure figure in architectural history now, his work was deeply influential in New York, even without the credibility of AIA membership. One example is the Tiffany & Co. store on Fifteenth and Union, which opened in 1869 and was in development during Waite's tenure with Kellum. Described by the *New York Times* as the "palace of jewels" when it opened, the five-story Italianate building had a cast-iron façade, for which Kellum was known. Its plate glass windows ran the full height of the first story, a remarkable feature for the day, which was intended to fully display the merchandise.[73] The arched windows on the upper floors became more curvilinear at each floor. The building demonstrated the vast amount of glass a cast-iron building could incorporate economically.

A noteworthy project that Waite worked on while he apprenticed to Kellum was the Working Women's Hotel. New York in the mid-1860s was deep in transition, with people moving to the city for work after the Civil War, particularly single, working-class women. Widowhood, a lack of marriage prospects, or other economic necessities led to this influx into the city. These women worked in domestic service or the clothing industry and generated the goods that were consumed by their wealthier sisters. The precarious state of housing for these women soon became a concern to the public, and Waite would have been aware of this problem through its extensive coverage in the city's newspapers; he also would have seen these women traveling to and from work during his own commute.

Kellum was commissioned by Alexander Stewart, the wealthy department store magnate, to design the Working Women's Hotel as a solution for this problem and a legacy project for Stewart. Stewart had opened the first department store in the US in 1846 and by the mid-1850s was one of the wealthiest businessmen in New York. In 1859, Stewart hired Kellum to design his new department store building, which was the first cast-iron department store in the country when it opened in 1862.[74] Stewart was so pleased with the results that he commissioned Kellum to design his palatial home on fashionable Fifth Avenue, the first and largest of many Gilded Age mansions of the era's new class of millionaires. Stewart became Kellum's most important client, and they became friends, which was typical of the close connections that Kellum maintained with many of his clients.

The design for the Working Women's Hotel began around 1867, and construction started in 1869.[75] However, both Kellum and Stewart died before it could be completed in 1877, so that neither architect nor client was available to guide it to completion or preserve the original intention of the project. The project failed the same year that it opened. By this time, Waite was running a very successful architecture firm in Buffalo and Bethune was already working for him. But his involvement with this earlier project may have made him more sensitive to the needs of women to succeed in the architectural professions—and open to offering an internship to Bethune.

In Buffalo, Waite enjoyed a reputation for his design and technical abilities within the architectural community and among his clients. He opened his practice in 1870, and by the mid-1870s he had won several substantial projects and design competitions, even winning work during the Crash of 1873 and subsequent recession.[76] In 1875, Waite was awarded the commission for the German Insurance Building in Lafayette Square, which was reminiscent of Kellum's work in New York. This ambitious project was the largest office building in Buffalo at the time and it introduced the fashionable Second Empire style, so prevalent in New York, to the growing and aspirational city. When the building opened, Waite established his office there in Room No. 13.[77] This is the building where Bethune worked during her apprenticeship. Waite remained in this office until he closed his practice and left Buffalo in early 1904.[78]

During Bethune's tenure with Waite, she worked on a portfolio of buildings of varying scales, materials, and typologies. This type of work—a

Figure 1.11. German Insurance Building on Lafayette Square, Richard A. Waite architect, 1875. Courtesy of the author.

combination of regionally based residential, commercial, and institutional projects—provided the basis of the work she and her husband would complete in their own practice. When she joined the firm, Waite was supervising the construction of the Pierce Palace and Invalids Hotel, which was both a facility for recuperation and healing and one of the first luxury hotels in Buffalo, and the commercial project, W. H. Glenny & Sons Building at 257 Main Street, which is still extant today. Two projects that Bethune probably worked on are the Canada Life Insurance Building, in Hamilton, Ontario, and the Genesee Hotel, which opened in 1881 and 1882, respectively. The Canada Life Insurance Building was designed in the Richardson Romanesque style, popularized by, and named for, the American architect H. H. Richardson, a style to which Waite gravitated as his career progressed. The building housed the national headquarters for the company. The five-story Connecticut brownstone structure dominated the corner on which it sat and was articulated with an immense turret, Roman arch windows, and copper roof. Demonstrating the impact of the building at the time in the region, it received praise from Oscar Wilde, who called it "one of the most beautiful buildings he had seen in this country" during his 1882 North American lecture tour.[79]

The Genesee Hotel was the third such structure on a site that dated back to when Buffalo was a frontier town. Waite's six-story Renaissance Revival structure was a response to the concerns of city leaders regarding the lack of refined accommodations for visitors in the 1870s. It was a six-story restrained Renaissance Revival structure. The muscular, cube-like brick building allowed for subtle flourishes at the level separating the second and third floors. Doorway entries on the first floor were banded together by a stone ribbon, articulated by archways capped with entablatures, also made of stone. These entablatures were repeated on the parapet. Ionic columns and an architrave supported the two-bay entry porch. Above it rested a stone balustrade that elegantly delineated the second-story balcony. The windows were articulated with simple stone lintels and sills. The hotel was a welcome addition to the cityscape and a signal to its citizens that Buffalo was on the rise. Mayor (and soon-to-be governor and president) Grover Cleveland attended its opening ceremony.[80]

Waite was a skilled and dedicated designer, consistently winning work based on the artistic merits of his submissions. Waite's colleagues respected him for his design work, technical skills, and professional integrity. An article from early 1882, while the hotel was still under construction, demonstrates the high regard in which Waite's architectural colleagues held him. It reported a rumor that was circulating of a structural failure on the stone balcony at the hotel's front entrance that had to be repaired. Waite vehemently denied that the failure was the result of a design error. Three other Buffalo architects were asked to comment for the article, including C. W. Caulkins, who discredited the charge. One of them "declared Mr. Waite too good an architect to have such a thing happen to a building he had planned."[81]

In the 1880s Waite's prominence in the Great Lakes cities would continue. In addition to building some of Buffalo's more important buildings in the decade to come, he would make even more significant contributions to Canadian cities, with the design of the Ontario Legislative Building in Toronto and the Canada Life Assurance Building and Grand Trunk Railway Company, Ltd., Station, both in Montreal.

Despite this success, Waite was a poor businessman, so his firm suffered significant financial setbacks when he temporarily moved to Ontario to complete a number of these projects. His brother and business partner, William, who was left to run the Buffalo office, was a bad manager. In addition, Waite's wife Sarah passed away in 1901, which deeply impacted him. By 1904, Richard Waite had moved to New York City to start anew

Figure 1.12. Pierce Place and Invalids Hotel, Richard A. Waite architect, 1876. Destroyed by fire 1881. Collection of the Buffalo History Museum, general photograph collection, Buildings—Residences—Hotels.

Figure 1.13. Canada Life Assurance Building, Hamilton, Ontario, Canada, Richard A. Waite architect, 1881. Courtesy of the author.

or to look for work. Census reports after 1904 list his occupation as "draughtsman."

Kellum, Waite, and Bethune were all outsiders who were determined to succeed and maximized their apprenticeship opportunities to become successful architects with their own firms. They were self-reliant and they were self-taught. They also saw architecture as a lifelong study. They had a passion for the science of buildings and act of building things. Kellum began his career in construction and Waite studied to become an engineer before he discovered architecture. Bethune spoke frequently about the importance of knowing the construction process and strongly encouraged women who followed her into the profession to learn these basics. She oversaw the construction of one-third of her firm's projects during its peak period.[82] Neither Waite nor Kellum took on work they could not personally supervise; Bethune was the same way.

All three architects enjoyed close relationships with their clients, who repeatedly sought them for projects. Kellum and Stewart's close working relationship resulted in a true friendship and some of Kellum's most significant work. As a sought-after architect in the 1870s, Waite enjoyed warm relationships with many of his clients, who were the leading businessmen of the time. Asked to serve on the jury for the Ontario Legislative Building, he was instead offered the commission. He also worked pro bono on at least one project: the Women's Industrial and Education Building in 1892. (The practice of working pro bono was one that Louise Bethune would never consider—she held the strongly felt principle that women should be paid for their efforts—but her husband Robert did.) Bethune also enjoyed personal friendships with Buffalo's leading citizens, including industrialist Spencer Kellogg, James Crooker from the Buffalo Public Schools, and entrepreneur Joseph A. Oaks; all would be repeat clients. Photos of their children and references to them were found in Bethune's personal letters.

All three architects relied on these values to see them through difficult periods in their careers. Kellum's peers would never accept or respect him. Both Waite and Bethune led their firms through crippling economic downturns, for Waite the 1873–1879 Depression, and for Bethune the Depression of 1893. Both would suffer setbacks late in their lives. For Waite, his business failed and he died poor. Bethune's health rapidly failed in the last three years of her life, leaving her far diminished. However, despite these setbacks, they enjoyed the respect and admiration of their clients and were praised by the press for their leading roles in their profession.

Chapter 2

Family and Firm

Figure 2.1. Louise Blanchard Bethune, circa 1881, possibly on her wedding day. Zina Bethune Archive on Louise Bethune, circa 1860–1962. Courtesy of the University Archives, University at Buffalo.

While Louise Bethune was an incredibly self-reliant woman, she had important support from her family—beginning with her parents—in formulating her values and establishing her life's work as an architect. Remarkably for a woman of the day, she founded her own firm shortly before her marriage, and initially her husband worked for her. Bethune's remarkable career trajectory also was the result of training and support from her mentor, Richard A. Waite. Her support system included her future husband and eventual business partner, Robert Bethune, and their protégé William Fuchs. Indeed, Bethune's professional and personal lives were very much intertwined, reflecting her strong belief that her work and home life were of equal importance—something that was unusual for a woman at that time, another striking example of her progressive thinking about a woman's role in society and at home.

Robert was Bethune's partner both in life and business. They met in Richard Waite's office as apprentices, married the same year Bethune opened her office, and remained in business together until she was forced to retire two years before she died. The Bethunes hired William (Will) Fuchs just before their only child, Charles, was born. He remained in their employ for the remainder of his career, eventually becoming their partner. Taken in its entirety, Bethune had a very tightly knit circle and support system.

Louise's mother, Emma, was also a role model as an entrepreneur involved with real estate. In 1879, she purchased three properties in the 300 block of Porter Avenue, including 325 Porter Ave., the Blanchard residence. After years of renting, the family finally owned a home and property. In November 1881, Emma transferred property on Porter Avenue near Fargo Street valued at $1,025 to Louise, presumably either to help finance Louise's new firm or because of her upcoming marriage in December.[1] Either way, just thirty years after the passage of the Women's Property Bill, Emma leveraged newly acquired wealth to fund her daughter's career and life aspirations.

Before their marriage, Robert boarded with the Blanchard family at their home at 255 Porter Ave. near Front Park beginning in 1880, according to the census.[2] Presumably, Louise and Robert were engaged at that time. After their marriage, the entire entourage moved to 325 Porter Ave., just one block away, where they remained until Dalson and Emma moved to 64 West Huron St. in 1891, ten years after Robert and Louise were married.[3] On August 16, 1891, Dalson Blanchard died suddenly of heart disease while on vacation at the family retreat in Mattapoisett, Massachusetts, near Plymouth.[4] According to reports at the time, Blanchard had been ill for some time but had improved with the sea air in Mattapoisett.[5]

Following Dalson's death, Emma and Louise continued to be development partners. In 1885, they jointly applied for a building permit to erect a frame structure in the rear of a lot on Porter Avenue at Fargo, possibly the same property that they jointly shared.[6] Bethune would follow her mother in building ownership and development. In 1891, Louise purchased a block of five townhouses at the corner of Huron and Franklin. Known as the Bull Property, it was renovated by Bethune as a mixed-use development. She and Robert moved their offices and their residence there.[7] Conveniently, and probably not coincidentally, the townhouses were situated just across the street from Louise's parents' new residence on 64 West Huron St. Consequently, Louise lived no further than a block from her parents until well into adulthood.

Emma eventually moved to Mattapoisett full-time in 1895.[8] She lived in the family home there with her sister Louisa (Aunt Lou to Louise) until her death in 1919, six years after Louise herself passed. In fact, in Bethune's will she bequeathed her property in Mattapoisett and her rental property at 881 Tonawanda St. in Buffalo to Emma, with her son, Charles, as the secondary beneficiary.

Robert Armour Bethune

Robert (Bob) Armour Bethune was born on June 7, 1855, to Donald and Mary Telfer (Gay) Bethune in Bowmanville, Ontario, Canada. Through genealogical research conducted by Louise, we know his family descended from the Bethunes of Balfour, Fifeshire, Scotland. Robert was directly descended from Rev. John Bethune (1751–1815) of the Isle of Skye and Veronica (Wadden) of Geneva, Switzerland. The Reverend was educated at King's College in Aberdeen, Scotland, and immigrated to the United States shortly before the beginning of the Revolutionary War. He served as chaplain during the war for the Royal Militia and was taken as a prisoner in Philadelphia. He was exchanged for an American soldier and became the chaplain for the Highland Emigrant regiment. He later established St. Gabriel's of Montreal, the first Presbyterian congregation in Canada. In 1787, the Reverend moved to Glengarry, Ontario, where he owned three thousand acres of land and spent the remainder of his life.

The Reverend's eldest child, Angus (1783–1858), was a fur trader and chief factor (or mercantile trading agent) with a high administrative position in the Hudson Bay Company. Angus and his wife, Louisa (Mackenzie), had six children and lived in Fort William, Ontario. Angus's eldest child,

Figure 2.2. Robert Bethune. Zina Bethune Archive on Louise Bethune, circa 1860–1962. Courtesy of the University Archives, University at Buffalo.

Donald (1820–1886), was Robert's father and became a lawyer. Donald and his wife Mary Telfer (Gay; 1827–1879) had five children, only two of whom lived past infancy: Robert and his sister, Louisa. The Bethunes lived in several towns in Ontario—Cobourg, Hamilton, Bowmanville, and Windsor—before settling in Detroit.[9]

In 1873, at the age of eighteen, Robert began a three-year apprenticeship under noted architect Gordon W. Lloyd (1832–1904), the most prominent architect in Detroit at the time. Born in Cambridge, England, Lloyd apprenticed for his uncle, Ewan Christian, an architect who had studied at the Royal Academy and had a successful practice in London. Christian had a general practice but was particularly successful in ecclesiastic design. Lloyd, too, made a name for himself in this area, and was the architect for many Episcopal churches throughout Michigan, Ontario, and the Midwest. Lloyd immigrated to Windsor, Ontario, in 1858 and maintained a practice in Detroit until his death in 1904. At the time of his death, Lloyd was considered the "Dean of Michigan architects"[10] and Robert considered him his mentor, similar to

Louise's relationship with Waite.[11] Among the more noteworthy projects that were in development during Robert's tenure with Lloyd were the First Congressional Church of Ann Arbor, Michigan (1872–1876), and the Trinity Anglican Church, St. Thomas, Ontario (built 1876–1877).

From 1876 to 1877, Robert worked for architect Leverette A. Pratt (1849–1924) in Bay City, Michigan. Pratt was a self-trained architect who entered the profession as a carpenter and master builder.[12] In 1880, Pratt formed a partnership with German architect Walter Koeppe. Pratt & Koeppe rose to become one of the most prominent firms in Bay City. Among their buildings is the town's City Hall (1894), which is listed on the National Register of Historic Places.[13]

Robert joined Richard Waite's firm in Buffalo in 1877, where he met Louise who was already working there. Both Robert and Louise served as interns in the firm and later referred to themselves as students of Waite,

Figure 2.3 A young Robert Bethune. Zina Bethune Archive on Louise Bethune, circa 1860–1962. Courtesy of the University Archives, University at Buffalo.

although Robert came to Buffalo with more experience.[14] Robert worked for Waite from 1877 to 1879 and then left the firm to join Field & Hayes, the contractors responsible for the construction of the Cantilever Bridge in Niagara Falls, New York.

Robert returned to Waite in 1880 and remained with the firm until he left to join Louise in practice, upon their marriage.[15] Given his background of working in three architectural firms and one engineering and construction company, it is probable Robert was fluent in most aspects of running an architectural practice, in particular construction documentation and administration. Indeed, when they opened Bethune & Bethune Architects, he was the more experienced architect of the two. By the end of the 1880s, Louise and Robert would build one of the busiest and most prominent architectural firms in the city of Buffalo.

Louise and Robert

Robert and Louise were married on Saturday, December 10, 1881, at the First Unitarian Church at Franklin and Eagle Streets.[16] The weather on their wedding day was pleasant for Buffalo in early December, with light snow in the early afternoon and an average temperature of 25 degrees.[17] The papers were filled with advertisements and general stories about Christmas preparations for the holiday season. Photos that were probably taken at their wedding show a softer and happier side of Louise than how she typically appeared. Wearing a colorful day dress with a row of buttons down the front, a soft white lace collar, and relatively modest taffeta bustle for the day, Louise was practical as always at her wedding. The dress may have been burgundy or claret red, because these were very fashionable colors for wedding dresses in the early to mid-1880s.[18] The one flourish she allowed herself was in her hat, which was adorned with a spray of delicate flowers and a feather.

The couple enjoyed a close and warm relationship and complemented each other in temperament and skills, although they were very different types of people. Physically, both were average in height: Louise at approximately five feet two, and Robert at around five feet five. Louise had a full figure, curly blond hair, and blue eyes.[19] Robert had dark brown hair and was thin as a young man but became portly by his thirties and into middle and old age. Louise was also very athletic as an adult, which is noteworthy for a woman of the Gilded Age in general, but particularly considering her history of childhood illness. Her friends in the Buffalo Women's Wheel and Athletic Club described Louise as an early riser and fearless bicyclist, often leading twenty-five-mile-long biking expeditions. She rode her bicycle around town, to the office and construction sites, where she would inspect the work of the contractors. Robert, on the other hand, was photographed as a boy and young man engaged in fishing and hunting.[20] However, later in life he was much more sedentary, unlike his wife.

Louise was self-confident, ambitious, and assertive. A natural leader, she relished being the first: the first woman architect and the first woman to own a bicycle in Buffalo, to name just two examples. She also was the type of person who became passionately involved in a project, club, or association but, after exhausting her interest, moved on to a new one with the same focus and passion. Louise discontinued her membership in the American Institute of Architects in 1904, despite her active role with her firm until 1911. After 1904, she turned her attention to genealogy and was elected president of the Buffalo Genealogy Club in 1907, extensively docu-

Figure 2.4. Robert and Louise Bethune, possibly on their wedding day, December 10, 1881. Zina Bethune Archive on Louise Bethune, circa 1860–1962. Courtesy of the University Archives, University at Buffalo.

menting hers and Robert's family trees in her later years.[21] Louise was also intellectually curious. She compensated for her lack of formal architectural education by using her mentor's library to supplement her apprenticeship. As a result, she became an intellectual elitist who valued academic pursuits, but this also made her dismissive of those less well educated.

Robert (or Bob, as he was called) was not a self-starter, but he was a closer. Following Louise's involvement in the American Institute of Architects, Robert was a card-carrying AIA member until his death in 1915. Robert did enjoy activities outside of work. He served on the board of the Music Hall and participated in several large musical productions and balls in the 1880s and '90s.[22] At least one sketch survives that shows that he was skilled at freehand drawing and enjoyed sketching. He was also interested in politics; both he and his father-in-law Dalson were active members of the local Republican Party. Robert regularly attended Republican state conventions throughout his adult life and both men signed a petition issued by the Erie County Republicans chastising their state party for election fraud in 1882.[23]

The Bethunes had one child, Charles William Bethune, who was born on April 24, 1883. Charles probably enjoyed a close relationship with his grandparents because they lived with his parents, and he spent time at their summer cottage in Mattapoisett. No doubt, family visits to Mattapoisett increased when Emma moved there, following Dalson's passing. The Bethune family albums include many photos of the Mattapoisett house and surroundings, so this might have been used as a family retreat over the years.[24]

Charles had a scientific mind and pursued several interests that fed his naturally inquisitive nature, including joining a geology club that took regular field trips to Niagara Falls and other destinations in the area. He was also a keen photographer, as is demonstrated by his many photos showing geographic formations. In 1901, Charles graduated from high school and entered the University of Buffalo School of Medicine in the class of 1905. He completed a postgraduate course in urology at Harvard Medical School in 1908 and became chief of services at Sisters of Charity Hospital in Buffalo. Charles continued to live with his parents until their deaths, first at 215 Franklin Ave. and then at Louise's properties on Tonawanda Street.[25] In 1906, Louise designed and had built a two-family residence for her, Robert, and Charles at 904 Tonawanda St. in Buffalo; it appears that Charles operated his practice from their home until 1911.[26]

Both Louise and Robert enjoyed close friendships. Louise surrounded herself with supportive, strong women friends such as her fellow members of the Women's Wheel and Athletic Club. Yet, she was also comfortable and confident in the company of men, including her AIA colleagues and

Figure 2.5. Charles W. Bethune, as a child. Zina Bethune Archive on Louise Bethune, circa 1860–1962. Courtesy of the University Archives, University at Buffalo.

genealogy chums. Louise was also direct and opinionated, and cared less about the opinions of others than Robert, within the strict bounds of society. Meeting minutes from the Women's Wheel and Athletic Club demonstrate an outspoken, engaged, and openly opinionated Louise. Although, she was less inclined to speak out at the male-dominated AIA meetings, she was a recognized and elected leader among her architectural colleagues.

Louise also had a sense of humor; she once described Robert to a friend as "a stout, amiable, elderly man in the extreme south-east corner of the dining room," adding slyly, "and all the adjectives in a lesser degree apply to Mrs. Bethune."[27] In 1911, Louise joked that during a long illness, because she was so unsteady on her feet, "Bob was very angry with me . . . and said the neighbors would think I had been drinking."[28]

Louise was the more energetic, organized, and hardworking, while Robert was more empathetic and cared for the people around him. In a letter to a friend in 1910, Louise commended Robert for how he cared for a lonely, elderly neighbor. And in 1905, he was celebrated in the local press

Figure 2.6. Robert, Louise, and Charles Bethune in the late 1880s. Zina Bethune Archive on Louise Bethune, circa 1860–1962. Courtesy of the University Archives, University at Buffalo.

Figure 2.7. Charles W. Bethune, while attending medical school. Zina Bethune Archive on Louise Bethune, circa 1860–1962. Courtesy of the University Archives, University at Buffalo.

for his selfless act of assisting his fellow theatergoers while he was attending a performance in Manhattan. According to the newspaper article, Robert quickly acted to refute a rumor of a fire that was circulating in the theater hall, which could easily have resulted in a panic, and a probable loss of life.[29]

Robert's caring nature was especially evident in his relationship with Louise. Repeatedly, he sacrificed—or at least deferred—his own career advancement in support of his wife and business partner. In 1885, both Robert and Louise intended to apply for membership to the newly formed Western Association of Architects. However, just before the convention, Robert rescinded his application out of concern that members would not support Louise if they applied at the same time because they would assume that her architectural portfolio was his work.[30] In 1888, for the same reason, Robert again waited to apply for membership to the AIA until Louise was successful.[31] And Robert may have lost additional opportunities by partnering with his wife; in 1901, as we shall see, the press noted that the firm had lost several municipal contracts because a woman held such a key position in it.

The couple's warm relationship was reflected by contemporary architects, as in this profile of Robert that appeared in 1884: "[Mr. Bethune] has been in business for himself about two years and has gained a footing among the leading builders and contractors. . . . Mrs. Bethune, his wife, is also a fine architect, and there is none of her sex . . . who are her superiors. Both Mr. and Mrs. Bethune are well known in Buffalo society and have a large circle of warm friends."[32]

Note, however, that this writer focused on Robert while incidentally mentioning Louise—even though the two were equal partners.

Louise would need this caring support throughout their married life, and, in particular, during her protracted illness before she died. A woman of action and constantly in motion, Louise pushed herself physically throughout her adult life. In addition to running the firm and her club/association work, she managed several rental properties, performing the maintenance on the properties herself. In 1910, her relentless schedule caught up with her and she was struck with a series of illnesses that left her bedridden for much of 1912 and 1913. Robert and their son Charles, by now a medical doctor, rallied to care for her, along with a paid nurse.[33]

Bethune & Bethune Architects

When Louise Bethune opened her office in October 1881, she was the sole practitioner. Following their marriage in December of that year, the firm became Bethune & Bethune Architects. Although the name of the firm changed, Louise remained the sole financial owner of the firm until 1886, when Robert provided additional capital to the operation.[34] The new practice opened at a favorable time; the 1881 city directory listed fifteen other architectural firms in competition with them.[35] Buffalo was a robust and bustling town with plenty of opportunity for a progressive firm such as theirs, that is, with a woman at the helm. For the next forty years, Buffalo would prove to be at the nexus of commercial and industrial innovation. As an example of the city's growing influence, Buffalo's former mayor and favorite son, Grover Cleveland, was elected president of the United States in 1884. With these expanding markets came a growing population, both American and immigrant. All of this was taking place in Buffalo when the entire country was exploding with optimism and growth. Progressive social change, investments in infrastructure, and advancements in building technology and its connection to reducing disease and fire and protecting the public were all to come during the next two decades, and architects would play a vital role in these changes.

As architectural historian Mary Woods states, during the profession's infancy in the US, most architects were sole practitioners, relying on occasional assistance from apprentices and students.[36] However, architectural partnerships began to occur as early as the 1820 to '30s, predating the development of the atelier, as promoted by H. H. Richardson in the 1870s, as well as the myth of the genius architect, as espoused by Frank Lloyd Wright thirty years later. Architects would come to understand that running a successful and sustainable practice required business acumen. In addition to having the prerequisite design talent, a successful firm required constant client relations, financial oversight, and a responsible organizational and production structure. Architecture is both art and business. To meet both ends, the partnership was born.

Initially, architectural partners maintained their own professional identities and associations to meet the demand for particular skill sets. However, these partnerships were short-lived, with little financial commitment from either party. A new type of partnership, however, was born in the 1870s, capitalizing on the individual skills of the partners, who would be stronger as part of a larger entity than they would be on their own. Typically, partnerships were born from need or perceived deficiencies. There are several examples of successful partnerships from this era, the most obvious of which was Chicago's Adler and Sullivan. Dankmar Adler was twelve years Louis Sullivan's senior, and provided the administrative and managerial skills to sustain a successful practice; Sullivan provided the firm's distinctive critical design talent. The combination created the unique marriage of opportunity and ingenuity (design talent). Without Adler's administrative organization, Sullivan's designs may never have been realized.[37] The Boston architect Ralph Adams Cram (1863–1942) provided clear insight on this philosophical approach to partnerships. As noted by Boyle, Cram recalled recognizing the need for a partner when he founded his office: "As I considered myself as the designing factor in a putative architectural firm, I must have a practical partner."[38] Cram would be involved in two partnerships: Cram and Wentworth and Cram and Ferguson.

Bethune & Bethune, of course, was no ordinary partnership. The two were partners in life and in business. Their decision to form an architectural practice would have had less to do with a need to supplement each other's skills than the simple desire to work together or not compete against each other by working at different firms. In the first couple of years, the firm's work was reported to journals and newspapers as being "from the office of R. Bethune, architect." That was probably not indicative of Robert being the principal partner, but simply that he was the one who was doing the reporting. They may have also been concerned that Louise's status as the first woman architect who had recently had a child might also influence their press coverage. By 1885, both partners were listed in the journals. Based on interviews Louise gave and biographies written on both Bethunes during their lifetime, they each assumed design responsibility, production of the construction documents, and the construction administration for their individual projects. In an 1884 interview in the *Buffalo Daily Courier*, Louise stated that she assumed full responsibility for the plumbing design in all the firm's projects; however, since this was early in the firm's existence, this practice might not have continued. In an 1892 *Buffalo Enquirer* profile, Louise said she assumed responsibility for all the "dwelling house" projects that came to the firm.[39]

In multiple profiles, Louise stated that, of all their projects, she preferred designing educational facilities. However, Robert also worked on schools and is credited with the design of a few Buffalo Public Schools, in particular Public School No. 16. Robert was also listed as the lead designer for a small number of hotels: the St. Francis in London, Ontario, and the Agency Building in Buffalo, and was the lead designer for the unbuilt Blackrock Market. Both Bethunes take credit for the Seventy-Fourth Regiment Armory; Louise drew the plans and Robert was the lead designer. Robert listed its building committee members as references for admission to the Western Association of Architects (WAA).[40] Also, he visited the Seventh Regiment Armory in New York to conduct research during its design phase.[41] And while Louise was the lead designer for the Hotel Lafayette, Robert was also very much involved, especially during the initial contractual and planning phases.

In the early 1890s, after William Fuchs was made their partner, Louise stated that she "has for some years taken entire charge of the office work, and complete superintendence of one third of the outside work."[42] By "office work," Bethune could have meant many different things. First, she could have been describing the administrative and financial work of running the firm. Alternatively, she could have meant the broader role of overseeing the design and documentation of all the work that took place in the office. Given the lead role in projects that Robert took and the fact that Louise was the sole financial owner for so many years, it probably meant that Louise assumed the former responsibilities for the firm.

In one extraordinary editorial written in 1901 in the local press, a reporter asked rhetorically why Robert had fallen out of favor as a consultant who had regularly received municipal projects. The writer answered his own question by stating that when Robert took his wife as a business partner, many of the aldermen lost faith in him because they did not trust a woman in business. The newspaper stated, "Look for the woman, and there is a woman, dearly beloved by Robert Bethune, who appears to have interfered with favorable glances which were cast upon him by the Aldermen."[43]

This direct assertion that government officials would be unwilling to work with a business that was co-owned by a woman was written twenty years after the Bethunes' firm was established, in the first decade of the twentieth century, and well into the women's suffrage era. This prejudice suggests the reason why Robert was listed as the lead architect for most of the firm's public projects, and it possibly explains why Louise's name was omitted from some projects or submissions. But most importantly, it highlights the fine line that the firm walked with its clients in who represented its work and the very tangible risk that a male architect took in his career by bringing on board a female partner, who was not to be trusted by virtue of her gender at this time.[44]

Starting in the mid-1890s, Bethune, Bethune & Fuchs's public commissions dramatically reduced. After this time, their work was based on the commercial, industrial, and hospitality sectors, which were funded by private clients. This may have been partially due to the Depression of 1893; however, it is clear from this article that this shift of commissions was a direct result of bias and discrimination, rather than lack of public funding. The fact that such public criticism of elected city officials was made in a local newspaper is not only extraordinary but also served as a possible warning to men not to work with women in business, or risk seeing their work reduced to "pretty small business," in the words of this reporter.

Ironically, Louise commented multiple times throughout her career that she experienced no hostility or discrimination from her male colleagues, clients, or the construction crews, who accepted her expertise, work ethic, and authority. This is an incredible position for a woman architect of the twenty-first century to claim, much less one of the Gilded Age. It demonstrates the authority and confidence that Louise could project in a professional setting. Obviously, the firm was very successful with or without publicly funded commissions, and she was certainly highly regarded as a businesswoman. However, Louise had detractors as well, despite her business acumen and knowledge as an architect, and the progressive zeitgeist of the region. Her comments reveal her single-minded determination and refusal to acknowledge any actions or sentiments that would limit her aspirations. This may have contributed to the fact that, as far as we know, her firm did not employ women apprentices. It would be natural to assume that Louise would have employed one or more of the newly educated women architectural graduates in her firm. There is no evidence that this occurred, or that, on the other hand, women applied for work and were not accepted. We know that Louise advocated for coeducation in architectural programs and corresponded with some of these programs' directors. If the firm did not employ women architects, it may have been because Louise was more comfortable demonstrating the equality of women rather than mentoring the next generation, or that the firm could not risk the appearance of agitating for women's equality.

William Fuchs Joins Bethune & Bethune

Bethune & Bethune was a small firm. After Will Fuchs joined, the firm probably only employed apprentices or student help, as shown in contemporary photographs of the office staff. Given the firm's small size and the intimate relationship between the founding partners, it is highly likely there was no clear division of responsibility—aside from administrative—and that the partners had their own projects and collaborated with each other as well.

William (Will) L. Fuchs was born in July 1865 in Buffalo to August and Helen Fuchs. August was born in Hesse-Darmstadt, Germany, in 1822 and immigrated to Paris in 1840, where he worked as a saddler and harness maker. In 1844, he came to New York City, where he worked for four years, and then moved to Buffalo in 1849, where he opened a wine store with his brother, Julius. The brothers grew this small business, aptly named Fuchs Bros., into one of the most successful grocery and liquor stores in the city.[45] August met and married Helen while living in New York and they both moved to Buffalo where they started their family. They had twelve children, five of whom survived into adulthood, including Will.[46] August was considered a leader in the German community in Buffalo, a self-made man who was "born plucky," according to his friends and associates,[47] and he was very active in the Roman Catholic Church. He was twice appointed as a park commissioner in the 1870s and 1880s, while the city was working with Frederick Law Olmsted on the expansion of its existing park system.[48] August died in December 1888 following a stroke.

Will Fuchs began working for the Bethunes in 1882, initially as a "draughtsman," and then, from 1884 onward, as an "architect."[49] His

Figure 2.8. Will Fuchs and an apprentice at the office. Courtesy of Nancy Herlan Brady.

employment coincided with Louise's pregnancy and the birth of her first and only child, Charles, who was born in April 1883.[50] Will was just seventeen years of age when he started at the firm, and, therefore, very much an entry-level employee. Fuchs would learn the profession of architecture solely from Louise and Robert. In 1890, Will was named the firm's third partner, and in 1893 he assumed a financial partnership role in the firm when it moved to a new location at Franklin and Huron Streets.[51] In 1889, Fuchs married Dorothea Devening, and their first child, Daniel, was born in 1891, the year after he became a partner with the firm. He designed their Queen Anne home at Ashland and Hodge, which they filled with five children, three of whom survived.[52] Fuchs continued to grow professionally during this time and took on added responsibilities as well. Following the deaths of both founding partners, Fuchs was left to run the firm beginning in 1915.[53]

Figure 2.9. Will Fuchs and his son, Daniel, with Robert Bethune, June 19, 1892. The Fuchs children referred to the Bethunes as "Bob and Mrs. Bob." Courtesy of Nancy Herlan Brady.

In addition to family and work activities, Will was active in several organizations. He was the president of the Buffalo Architectural Sketch Club and regularly published his work in local and professional journals. As a member of a successful family in the German community in Buffalo, Fuchs played an essential role in obtaining projects from friends and colleagues and followed Bethune into the role of being a developer himself, with mixed results. Not surprising, the Bethunes and the Fuchs families were close. In a photo album dedicated to Will's son Daniel, one photograph shows a beaming Will with baby Daniel on Will's bicycle next to a standing Robert, wearing a waistcoat and holding a cigar. Will named the photograph, "As a Wheelman, June 19, 1892," for his son. The Fuchs children knew their father's partners as "Bob," and "Mrs. Bob." Will's office photos show him posing with an intern and alone, and demonstrate a casual office environment. And while Charles Bethune was older than the Fuchs children, one can imagine that the two families spent time together outside the office.

Chapter 3

Home Work

Women as Architects

Do I think there is any branch of the profession in which women are particularly fitted to succeed? Decidedly, yes, in domestic architecture and particularly in arranging the details of the kitchen, pantry and dining room.

—Louise Bethune

Figure 3.1. Louise Blanchard Bethune in her early twenties with lifelong friend (or cousin) Frankie Sherman. Zina Bethune Archive on Louise Bethune, circa 1860–1962. Courtesy of the University Archives, University at Buffalo.

In the nineteenth century women began to take their place in society as professionals, challenging the male-dominated norms of long-established and emerging professions alike. At the same time, women's role in the home was becoming more important, with women generally considered the primary decision makers in the management of the domestic sphere, including overseeing the home's decoration and design. Both these trends had a great impact on Louise Bethune's early career. She oversaw all the residential work in the office, and, of her firm's extant buildings, most are residential projects. In this chapter, I will discuss Louise's attitude toward women's role in architecture, compare her work to other professional women trailblazers in architecture and other fields, and review the residential projects of her firm.

The year 1881 was an auspicious one for the women of Buffalo, whether they knew it or not. On January 6, socialite and advocate Maria Love opened the first crèche—or daycare—for working mothers in the United States. Known as the Fitch Crèche and modeled after the French system, Fitch was the first to implement a Froebel kindergarten in the US, which was an early childhood education program based on structured activity-based learning with an emphasis on creativity. That October, Buffalo opened the Ninth Congress for the Advancement of Women, which was held at the Buffalo Central Library. From October 19th to the 22nd, the city hosted luminaries of the country's progressive women's rights movement. It ultimately inspired Harriet Townsend to establish the Buffalo Women's Education and Industrial Union to promote education and social reform for women, regardless of social status. For thirty years, this organization provided educational and support programs for women in need and advocated for women's justice issues in New York State.

Louise opened her architectural office—by design or coincidence—in October of 1881, during the same month as the Ninth Congress convened. After five years of apprenticeship for Richard Waite, she was ready to strike out on her own. In that single act, Louise Bethune became the first professional woman architect in the country. However, the 1882 City of Buffalo directory only listed her husband R. A. Bethune, not Louise. While Louise was breaking barriers for women within the profession by establishing the firm, Robert was the first public face of the enterprise. It would take two years for Louise's name to appear in the city directory as an architect.[1]

Women as Professionals

In 1891 Louise was invited to give a lecture to Townsend's Women's Education and Industrial Union titled "Women and Architecture." Louise highlighted the early acceptance of women as architects as compared to other male-dominated fields: "The professions of medicine and law were far advanced before the much needed and highly appreciated woman physician and lawyer appeared. Women have entered the architectural profession at a much earlier stage of its existence even before it has received legislative recognition."[2] Given the fact that the leading American architectural association, the AIA, had been established only thirty-four years earlier, and architectural licenses were not yet recognized in any state, Louise's observation was certainly true.

In the mid-1870s, when Louise was deciding upon her career path, only a few professions were considered appropriate for women, based on their perceived intellectual capabilities, emotional tendencies, and fundamental responsibility to home and family. As historian Nancy Woloch writes, the term "professional woman" was considered a contradiction in terms, because professionalism meant specialization that was thought to be beyond the capacity of the female brain.[3] The expectation that a woman should be—and should *want* to be—tending the home fires meant that careers demanding long years of training and work duties, such as medicine and law, would require a woman to choose between marriage and family and a solitary, unmarried life.[4] Despite these beliefs, the number of women professionals steadily increased during the Gilded Age. The proportion of women professionals was double that of women in the general workforce from 1870 to 1930; in 1890, while 17 percent of the workforce was female, 36 percent of all professionals were women.[5]

In her 1863 book, *The Employments of Women: A Cyclopaedia of Woman's Work*, Virginia Penny gives an overview of what were then considered acceptable occupations for a woman to pursue. She listed 515 occupations that were, or could be, available to women in an array of categories, beginning with 38 professional careers. Interestingly, architects were included in the book but listed under the "Artist" category as opposed to "Professional." Penny's professional list included authors, deaconesses, government clerks, lawyers, librarians, missionaries, physicians, reporters, and teachers.

Teaching and writing were the two most widely accepted occupations for women at that time. Both were considered a natural evolution from women's domestic sphere. Women had been teaching in the US since the 1600s. Penny commended teaching as the most responsible office in life other than that of being a parent and she rejoiced in its relatively recent elevation as a learned profession. She noted that women were particularly suited to teaching, however she fretted that female education was largely superficial. Penny applauded Catherine Beecher for her activism in addressing this problem, because "woman must be taught to think for herself, and to act for herself."[6] However, Penny noted that male teachers were favored over female and men were better paid; male principals received a salary of 1.5 to 2 times that of their female counterparts.[7] This may have improved between the 1860s and 1880s, because public school education became more established during those decades. However, in Buffalo's 1885 city directory, of the thirty-eight principals in the public school system, only eight were female, demonstrating the preference for men in supervisory roles.[8]

Writing was considered an extension of education, and it had the added bonus of work that could be completed at home. As historian Frances Cogan notes, there was an enormous market for advice and etiquette books, manuals, cookbooks, and homemaking texts in the mid-to-late 1800s. A woman with a good education could write "conduct of life" books or write fiction, selling stories to magazines or completing novels.[9] Careers such as librarian and even reporter would also have fallen under the "education" category, and would therefore be within the realm of women's work.

In the 1850s, federal, state, and local governments began hiring women with good handwriting to copy important legal documents, speeches, and laws. This practice was greatly expanded during the Civil War.[10] When the typewriter was popularized in the 1870s, women, with their smaller, more nimble fingers, were considered better typists than men, which led to even more women working in offices. However, when men and women performed similar administrative duties in an office, women were generally considered as assistants and secretaries, while men were viewed as training for future managerial roles.

Prior to the Civil War, nursing was not considered a profession, but an extension of the domestic skills women were expected to have. Penny doesn't even mention it as a potential career. Clara Barton popularized it as a profession based on the Florence Nightingale model during the Civil War, and the first American school of nursing was opened in New York City in 1873. When it was finally recognized as a profession, women were encouraged to consider nursing as an "appropriate sphere for their activity and devotion."[11]

Traditionally male-dominated careers that fell outside of the accepted domestic realm were much harder for women to enter, and the more established the profession, the more difficult the task. The professionalization of medicine was a masculine effort to exclude women from the care roles that they typically performed until the eighteenth century as midwives and healers (now nurses).[12] However, by the mid-1800s, the medical profession was a less-rigorous organization than some of the other professions, which provided an opportunity for women. The first female American physician was Elizabeth Blackwell, who graduated from Geneva Medical College (the future Syracuse University School of Medicine) in 1849.[13] While her male classmates voted nearly unanimously for her admission to the college in 1847 as a prank, it paved the way for other women to follow her.[14] Blackwell went on to open the New York Infirmary for Indigent Women and Children in 1857, with her sister Emily, who followed her into medicine, the first women's and children's hospital in the country. The model was replicated by Elizabeth Garrett, the first woman physician in the UK, when she opened her women's and children's hospital in London in 1872.[15] While it wasn't easy for women to attend medical school—Harvard University, for instance, didn't admit its first woman until 1945—the justification for women physicians to treat women and children was undeniable.

The legal profession was far more established, better organized, and more difficult for women to penetrate. The notion that women as beacons of virtue and morality would come in regular contact with criminals including rapists, thieves, and murders was difficult for contemporary men to accept. Also, the courtroom was institutionalized as a male domain.[16] Obtaining the requisite training to be considered for the bar required both dedicated study and apprenticeship, which, like architecture, necessitated finding a willing mentor in the profession. The fight for women in law was closely associated with the fight for women's equality and suffrage in general, although women became lawyers decades before the passage of the Nineteenth Amendment in 1920. Arabella Babb Mansfield was the first woman admitted to a state bar association, in Iowa, in 1869. She had graduated from Iowa Wesleyan College, apprenticed for her brother in a law firm, and then passed the Iowa bar examination.[17] By 1910, there were approximately 1,500 women lawyers in America.[18]

The other long-established and revered profession was the clergy, the epitome of the men's club. Even though church work was well within the realm of "true womanhood," a woman's role in the church was limited to assistant in most cases. Women were encouraged to serve as missionaries and work overseas or in poor immigrant ghettos in large cities locally. Most churches did not allow women to become ministers, with very few exceptions. The Quaker faith allowed women to preach, and Lucretia Mott, the well-known suffragist, was a Quaker minister. Antoinette Brown was the first woman ordained as a Congregationalist minister in 1851, Olympia Brown was the first woman Universalist minister in 1863, and Anna

Howard Shaw was ordained a minister in the Methodist Episcopal Church in 1880 and later earned a medical degree in 1886. All these women were also active suffragists. Finally, Mary Baker founded the First Church of Christ Scientist, initially as a vehicle for (well-off) women to address their nervous and physical ailments.[19] These women were certainly the exception to the rule that clergy remained (and still remains in most cases) exclusively a male institution.

While women were beginning to seek higher education and consider pursuing professional careers as a means of personal fulfillment in addition to earning a living, society continued to view their options within the narrow view of gender. There had to be a reason for the woman to perform her duty in the profession. Even Louise hints at this in her "Women and Architecture" lecture when she describes women doctors and lawyers as being "much needed" as the rationale for their entry into these professions. The concept that a woman could have a career based on any criteria beyond her gender, such as interest or natural talent, might result in her taking the place of a man, who needed the job to support his family. Society felt that a woman's place was in the home, and if she did work, it should be in service to a duty that was an extension of her domestic role or fulfilled a need that her gender enabled her to best provide. And we must never forget that immigrants, women of color, and members of the lower economic class were excluded from this standard, as they assisted their male brother and husbands in the labor market to enable white, Protestant, and middle- and upper-class families to pursue this ideal.

Women as Architects and Tastemakers

As with other professions, women's first entry into architecture was through an acceptable pursuit: they wrote about architecture as opposed to practicing it, and their subject matter was primarily the domestic realm. The first book on architectural history published in the United States was by Louisa C. Tuthill, *The History of Architecture, from the Earliest Times; Its Present Condition in Europe and the United States*, published in 1848. Its dedication read, "To the ladies of the United States of America, the acknowledged arbiters of taste, this work is respectfully inscribed." Tuthill (1798–1879) had been writing for women since 1828. She was a member of a writers' movement that espoused the virtue of womanhood and connected it to the environment of the home, in particular its design, décor, and upkeep. As Lamia Doumato writes in the essay "Louisa Tuthill's Unique Achievement,"[20] these publications were part of a reaction to the dramatic changes that took place in America from 1815 to 1865. The Industrial Revolution and advancements in transportation greatly impacted the lives of Americans. The middle class sought to conserve traditional values, with the home environment central to this effort. As architectural historian Gwendolyn Wright notes, the "good homemaker could instill virtue in her family through careful choice of architectural detail and furnishing."[21] These writers combined decorating advice with commentary on new products and furniture, all with the underlying emphasis on the moral influence of the environment of the home, reinforcing the connection between the values of architecture and society.[22]

Catharine Beecher (1800–1878) was another architectural critic who wrote for the general public and building practitioners on residential design. Her 1869 book, *The American Woman's Home*—cowritten with her sister and famous novelist Harriet Beecher Stowe—was a best seller. She was a strong advocate for self-improvement, believing that the home was the best place to build it.[23] Her book advocated efficiencies through thoughtful space planning and mechanical services such as plumbing, to increase sanitation in the home.[24] It focused on maintaining the traditional values of the home while incorporating the modern technological advancements of the day. Catharine also wrote articles in builders' magazines on the latest research in sanitation and heating. As populations and disease increased in congested urban environments, the need for technologically sophisticated houses arose and a call for professional oversight began.

Other women who wrote on architecture for the general public included Clara Erskine Clement (1834–1916), Caroline W. Horton (1838–1895), Martha Joanna Reade Lamb (1826–1893), and Mariana Griswold Van Rensselaer (1851–1934), who is widely considered the first professional woman architectural critic and journalist.[25] Van Rensselaer wrote about all types of architecture; however, like Tuthill and Beecher before her, she paid particular attention to residential architecture and therefore reinforced the notion of domesticity and the home as a woman's realm.[26] As her career advanced, she became an important mediator between professional architects and the general public and potential clients, leading to Van Rensselaer receiving an honorary AIA membership in 1890.[27] Louise noted the importance of these women architectural critics to the field when she stated, "From Mrs. Tuthill in 1848 to Mrs. Van Rensselaer in 1891, is a greater stride than progress usually makes in one half-century."[28]

While there was hardly an overwhelming call for women architects, the obvious connection was made as early as 1857 by the architect Calvert Vaux, who wrote, "There can be no doubt that the study of domestic architecture is well suited to a feminine taste."[29] As homemakers or daughters of homemakers, it was often noted that women were in a far better position to comment on the practical details of the design of a house. "It must be obvious that women have a far more ultimate knowledge of the requirements of a home than men usually have," said an unnamed woman architect in the *New York Tribune* in 1901.[30] A woman's understanding of the layout of a kitchen and the importance of ample closet space were reoccurring themes. As with other professions, when women began to practice architecture, the public viewed their gender in the context of their professional expertise and saw a natural fit in domestic architecture.

At the 1879 congress of the Association for the Advancement of Women (AAW) in Madison, Wisconsin, Martha N. McKay presented a paper titled "Women as Architects." Her argument was based on two primary points: women's inherent expertise in residential architecture (both the single-family dwelling and multifamily structures) and their natural interest in increasing health, safety, and welfare standards in the built environment. She outlined the invaluable role of women as experts in their natural "sphere" and described the innate knowledge women have for running a household and operating a kitchen. She then related that expertise to the more socially relevant topic of tenement housing and proper sanitary design in all building types, in particular, residential buildings. McKay stated: "To-day, not alone in the house of the poorer classes are these serious faults, but where wealth has furnished the means for unlimited gratification of taste and the desire for comfort, science has been ignored, or has failed, in the matter of heating, ventilation, and sewerage."[31] She noted that those who suffered the most were young children: "Last year, the death-rate of one of our largest cities, was nearly ten per cent of all the children in that city, and seventy per cent of all these deaths occurred in, or in connection with, tenement-houses."[32]

American cities were growing steadily in the aftermath of the Civil War, inspired by the expansion of the Industrial Revolution and the significant increase in emigration from Europe, but without the proper infrastructure to accommodate the need for more residential buildings. While McKay began her paper with a description of the proper design of kitchen cabinets, she quickly transitioned into advocating for architects to address one of the humanitarian crises of the time: the spread of disease. More than a simple argument for gender equity, McKay's paper was a thesis on the value of a humanist philosophy and scientific approach to the design of the built environment. Societal and demographic pressures were demanding more from our political representatives and our building experts: "Were women in power—either upon school-boards or as the architects of school-build-ings,—a slight increase in the cost of fuel would not weigh against the health and life of the children."[33]

According to the AAW, McKay's paper inspired a negative reaction from the press, which reflected the general impression that "the idea that women could climb over rafters and ridgepoles as men did, was thought too ludicrous to be entertained."[34] While numerous articles written in American periodicals supported women working in the decorative side of architecture and design, they questioned whether women could perform the technical, or male side, of the profession. One article written for the Royal Institute of British Architects (RIBA) from November 1890 that was republished in the *American Architect and Building News* went further. Titled "Female Com-petition," it addressed the concern of some men about women becoming architects. To ease these fears, the author claimed that in the future women should design the "softer" side of architectural projects while the "masculine arts of construction . . . [should be left to] educated men."[35] Louise and her successors were exposed to similar critiques in the years to come and responded through their actions, particularly by visiting construction sites and overseeing the installation of "rafters and ridgepoles."

Bethune's Role in Residential Design

Louise embodied the very architect Martha McKay described: In addition to designing residential buildings, she oversaw the plumbing and ventilation aspects of all the firm's projects. This challenged the notion that women could only be tastemakers, while the technical and construction aspects of the profession should be left to men.

In several interviews conducted during her lifetime, Louise stated that she was responsible for the design of all of Bethune & Bethune's residential projects. Of the firm's approximately 180 known projects, 79 were sin-gle-family dwellings or mixed-use buildings with a residential component, or more than one-third of its portfolio.[36] Many Buffalo firms took on res-idential projects, as would be expected in a growing city with many small firms. Even a prominent architect such as Richard Waite accepted residential work. However, a cursory review of the projects reported by other Buffalo architects in the early to mid-1880s demonstrates that Bethune & Bethune had more residential projects than their contemporaries, with the exception of the many significant mansions designed by Green & Wicks.

Through her career, Louise was interviewed several times about her residential work. In 1884, she noted how she brought a woman's special expertise to residential design: "Few men stop to consider that it matters which side of the sink the shelf is set, but women who have ever washed dishes know that it makes the greatest difference. Women are not likely to forget either that the kitchen closet should not be far away from the sink, and that there must be a wide space provided for the bedstead in the bedroom."[37]

However, by 1891, she had cooled somewhat to residential work. She discouraged the idea that women should specialize in the area:

> The dwelling is the most pottering and worst-paid work an architect ever does. He always dreads it, not, as someone may have told you, because he must usually deal with a woman, but because he must strive to gratify the conflicting desires of an entire household, who dig up every hatchet for his benefit and hold daily powwows in his anteroom, and because he knows he loses money nearly every time. Dwelling house architecture, as a special branch for women, should be, at the present rate of remuneration, quite out of the question.[38]

Louise was clearly speaking from experience. She likely spent endless hours working with clients on the interior design of their homes. Because architects are paid on a percentage rate of the overall cost of the project, Louise's professional fees clearly did not compensate for the time and energy involved in these rather modest projects.

Louise also challenged conventional wisdom that women architects were innately experts in residential or any particular type of architecture. As she stated at the Women's Education and Industrial Union gathering in 1891, women were not greeted with open arms by the architectural profession: "When women entered the [medical profession] and became physicians they filled a long-felt want. There is no need whatever of a woman architect. No one wants her, no one yearns for her, and there is no special line in architecture to which she is better adapted than a man."[39]

It may appear that Louise was suggesting that women should not pursue careers in architecture. By saying "there is no special line in architecture" for women to pursue, she was critiquing the common idea that female architects should be limited to working exclusively within the cult of domesticity and be trapped in a practice of residential architecture. She was making the argument that society does not want women to pursue architecture as a profession, but if they *must* be architects then they should focus on domestic design. This, obviously, was a notion that she rejected. In Louise's view, women should have the freedom to pursue their chosen profession based on interest and aptitude, not on gender-defined bias.

Despite her rejection of residential work as a line of expertise, Louise assumed responsibility for all those projects throughout her career.[40] Of course, in 1884 she was speaking as a partner of a new firm and used this interview as a marketing opportunity. Because they were just starting out, any work was good work, and Bethune & Bethune certainly did take on many residential projects in those early years. By 1891, Louise had been in business for herself for ten years and had experience working on various types of projects. She was also in a better position to understand her own strengths and interests. Yet, she was also a woman of business and well understood that while she might not have thought that her gender predisposed her to one type of architecture, the public may have thought differently. Indeed, since the 1840s, the role of women as tastemakers of the home had been reinforced in society through a multitude of vehicles. The first woman architect would be enlisted to design houses for her clients whether she wanted to or not.

Louise described the inherent bias she was subjected to in an 1884 interview: "It is a curious phase of human nature which I have often had occasion to observe that while many people are conservative and unwilling in the first instance to trust themselves to the judgment of a woman, if their plans are being drawn in an office where there is a woman architect they will unconsciously appeal to her judgment more and more in all those domestic details concerning which she may naturally be expected to make suggestions from her experience."[41]

Louise was subject to negative bias from clients when she worked for Waite and in the first years of her office, but she was able to leverage her gender to gain influence and respect through residential projects.

Residential Design and Female Architects

Like Louise, her contemporaries initially used residential design as their entry into the field. Some focused exclusively on it while others followed Louise's model of working on different building types. In 1900 the American literary magazine *Frank Leslie's Popular Monthly* published an article titled "Women as Architects," which listed thirteen contemporary practicing women architects. Louise received only a passing mention, possibly because the article reflected the attitudes of the day in highlighting women who worked on residential or other acceptable commissions, such as women's colleges or clubs.

Minerva Parker Nichols was described as the best-known woman architect of the day, although she had probably retired by 1900.[42] While Parker's significant New Century Club House was highlighted, the article's author claimed that she valued most her residential work, where "architectural talent has been reinforced by the maternal instinct."[43] Elise Mercur Wagner (1864–1947), the first woman architect in Pittsburgh, designed the Woman's Building at the 1895 Cotton States and International Exposition in Atlanta, Georgia. She practiced from 1895 to 1910 and designed an impressive collection of buildings, including churches, schools, and female seminary buildings. However, according to Leslie's article, "as with most of these ladies, it is the home features of the work in which, with true feminine instinct, she takes special pride."[44]

Others featured in the article showed a similar proclivity, at least according to its author. Emily Elizabeth Holman (1854–1914) apprenticed for an architect throughout the 1880s and then opened her practice under the title "E. E. Holman Architect" (hiding her gender) in 1894. She designed various types of buildings but met with success in designing homes and summer cottages throughout the US and Canada. In addition to her practice, Holman wrote six house and cottage plan books between 1894 and 1908.[45]

Josephine Wright Chapman (1867–1943) hailed from an affluent Boston family and pursued the architectural profession against her family's wishes, pawning jewelry and clothing to finance her work.[46] In 1894, she began an apprenticeship in the office of Boston architect Clarence Blackhall and dedicated herself to learning the craft. In 1897, she struck out on her own and designed significant public buildings in Boston, such as the Craigie Arms Dormitory for Harvard University and St. Mark's Episcopal Church in Fitchburg, Massachusetts. Chapman designed the New England Building for the 1901 Pan American Exposition in Buffalo. However, following this work, Chapman had an epiphany, which ran counter to Louise's philosophy: "A woman's work is to design houses. Hereafter I am going to design houses." She devoted herself to residential design and refused commissions for public buildings. She thought that English homes were the best model and traveled to England every year to study its historic houses. In 1907, following the economic downturn, Chapman moved to New York and continued to pursue her mission as a residential architect. Like Holman, she contributed to the field through the publication of influential articles on home design and decoration, such as "How to Make the Home Beautiful."[47]

Between 1894 and 1900, architects Mary Nevan Gannon (1867–1932) and Alice J. Hands (1874–1971) had a firm in New York, the first partnership of women architects in the United States.[48] Classmates at the New York School of Applied Design for Women from 1892 to 1895, Gannon and Hands started winning design commissions as students. They did not actively specialize in housing projects but were drawn to address New York's need for low-income housing during the late 1890s, and their legacy lies in their innovative tenement housing design work.[49] According to Sarah Allaback, the partners inspected housing conditions in New York's Tenth Ward as members of a Sanitary Investigation Committee.[50] Mary Gannon and several friends lived in a tenement for four years to better understand urban poverty.[51] In 1895, they were hired to design fifteen model tenements in New York and Jersey City, which were praised in multiple publications for the amount of light and quality of the space provided. Gannon noted, "We believe it possible to erect dwellings for the poor, which shall be healthful, beautiful, and homelike, and where light, ventilation, and every convenience shall be provided at no greater cost."[52] Gannon and Hands proved Martha McKay's 1879 thesis that women architects should focus their energies on solutions to improve the conditions for the working poor and, therefore, society at large.

Like Louise, Gannon and Hands supervised construction of their buildings and advocated for equal pay for their work. In an interview in 1896 they stated, "A point upon which we are determined, is that we will not cut rates."[53] They believed strongly that women should receive equal recognition for their work as that of their male peers. In her preface for the *History of Architecture from the Earliest Times*, Tuthill wrote, "The immense resources for building in the United States, will be profitably and tastefully appropriated, whenever the people themselves have sufficient knowledge of the Art, to employ and remunerate scientific architects."[54] Louise Bethune would have completely agreed that the quality of the built environment would be improved when architects are valued and paid fairly for their services.

Gannon and Hands also designed several projects specifically for women clients and users. Two examples were in New York: the Women's Hotel at Broadway and Seventh Street, and the New Era Building, which held women's offices and clubrooms.

Figures 3.2. and 3.3. Mary Gannon and Alice Hands formed the first women's architectural partnership in the United States. *Godey's Magazine*, 1896.

The Queen Anne Style: Origins and Adaptations

Bethune's residential work was largely single-family dwellings that ranged in price from $2,500 to $35,000. At the time, most of their houses cost between $3,000 and $7,000 and were either wood frame or brick construction and often designed in the Queen Anne style. This style originated in England and was popular in America's imagination from the late 1870s to the early 1900s, which more or less paralleled Louise's career as a firm owner. Bethune & Bethune's residential buildings were remarkably and consistently in this style and later the Colonial style, which was closely linked to Queen Anne.[55]

As architect and enthusiast John James Stevenson wrote in *House Architecture* in 1880, the style had little to do with Queen Anne, because it was based on a style of English vernacular architecture from roughly the late 1600s, before her reign began, and extended after her death.[56] Indeed, Stevenson referred to it as the "English Renaissance style, to which accident had given the name of Queen Anne."[57] In the late nineteenth century, the style represented part of a movement away from the mass production that the Industrial Revolution made possible and toward something more authentic that referenced an earlier and simpler way of life.

The Queen Anne style had both political and feminist overtones in England. As architectural historian Mark Girouard notes, it was developed by a group of young architects who were devotees of the Gothic Revival movement of the mid-1800s and its architect-evangelist, A. W. Pugin. By the 1870s these young architects were growing weary of the strict aesthetic rules of Gothic Revival, while they sympathized with Pugin's advocacy for developing a national style. They also were keenly aware that the Gothic style was best suited to ecclesiastical buildings and was not especially useful for residential design. They saw Queen Anne as a natural evolution of Gothic, given the accommodations required to adapt a medieval style to the nineteenth century, with modern technology, new building types, and materials other than stone, such as brick and wood. The "vernacular" brick architecture of London's seventeenth and eighteenth centuries provided a historical reference that was familiar and easily adapted to residential and school design and other building types.[58]

The Queen Anne style had its greatest impact on residential design, which is partly why the style became associated with women in general and the suffrage movement, in particular. Concurrent to the introduction of Queen Anne, domestic design in England was under reassessment in the wake of the Industrial Revolution and the rapid urbanization of society. As Annemarie Adams writes in *Architecture in the Family Way*, during this time, English middle-class women demanded better designs to accommodate their needs. Housewives and activists alike became critics of the ubiquitous multileveled and compartmentalized terraced houses of the 1700–1800s as early as 1860. They claimed these older designs suited the lifestyle of the man and not the woman. As women became more vocal and their influence grew in the design and arrangement of homes, they began to advocate for spaces for themselves and their children. After 1870, the nursery became a necessary and permanent fixture in the Victorian home, and the need for women to have their own space was seen as essential for the modern mother.[59]

English suffragists advocated for women to take control and manage spaces within their homes by exerting their personal taste on the domestic realm. Unlike in the US, leading suffragists exhibited home designs in department stores to advertise their cause, which created opportunities for women to pursue careers in home design and decoration. Indeed, the first women interior designers were the cousins Agnes and Rhoda Garrett, who were both active suffragists. Agnes had two sisters, Millicent, who was one of the leaders in the fight for the vote, and Elizabeth Garrett Anderson, who was the first woman physician in England.[60] The Garrett sisters were also close friends with J. J. Stevenson, whose two sisters were also active in the women's movement. These connections led to commissions for Stevenson and his Queen Anne colleagues for women's buildings (hospitals, colleges) in this style and led to the "architectural feminism" that can be credited to these younger architects.[61]

Queen Anne never assumed the feminist association in the US, but it became a catalyst for the political question about what constitutes a national style. As with the English, Americans looked for architecture that referenced an earlier era and simpler way of life. The Boston architect Robert S. Peabody was a leading figure in adapting Queen Anne to the US. He understood the opportunity to draw from the country's vernacular buildings to create an American style. In a speech given to the Boston Society of Architects in 1887, he stated: "To those who believe in revivals, 'Queen Anne' is a very fit importation into our offices. There is no revival so little of an affectation on our soil, as that of the beautiful work of the Colonial days. . . . It is our legitimate field for imitation, and we have much of it to study right in our neighborhood."[62]

Following the Philadelphia Centennial Exposition of 1876, a call for a truly American architecture emerged, which writers like Louisa Tuthill had been advocating for years. As a result, American architects readily embraced Queen Anne and it became ubiquitous in the late nineteenth century, employed by architects and builders alike.

Interest in Queen Anne was part of a larger interest in English art and design that was widespread in the US in the 1870s and '80s. English art, architecture, and lifestyle magazines were popular as was the English exhibit at the Philadelphia Centennial Exposition, which celebrated sixteenth-century Elizabethan houses and crafts including wallpaper, glass, and needlework.[63] Another example of this interest was the American reception to the aesthetic movement, which was a philosophy that originated in England around this time that called for the elevation of beauty and authenticity. The English Queen Anne architects were eager participants in this movement, along with designer William Morris, artist J. M. Whistler, and the poet Oscar Wilde.

Wilde toured the US and major cities in Canada in 1882, lecturing on the virtue of beauty in the arts and referring to the movement in the UK as the "English Renaissance." In general, Americans saw Wilde as a spectacle. Yet there were kindred spirits of the aesthetic movement in America, beginning with poets Walt Whitman and essayist Ralph Waldo Emerson, landscape architect Frederick Law Olmsted, and architect Henry Hobson Richardson. This was the precursor to the arts and crafts movement of a decade later. Richardson Romanesque would also fall under this aesthetic rubric, but for residential architecture, it would largely be confined to grander mansions, which were a more appropriate scale and budget for stone construction and craftsmanship.

The Queen Anne style became a vessel to explore the philosophical ideas of beauty and authenticity, as well as regionalism, climate, and geographic settings in US, as Peabody advocated. East Coast architects, for instance, relished the ornamentation of the style and freely made use of details from seventeenth- and eighteenth-century New England buildings they claim were "Colonial." These later adaptations became known as the Colonial Revival and Shingle styles respectively. On the other hand Midwest architects chose a more reserved and less ornamental expression.[64] With Buffalo geographically located in the middle of these two regions, elements of both were used. Both Queen Anne in England and Colonial Revival in the US romanticize the same period in architectural history, which was the transition from the medieval era to the Renaissance, as noted by architectural historian Vincent Scully.[65]

Bethune & Bethune's residential portfolio generally reflected the Midwest restrained approach to the Queen Anne style, where ornamentation was spare and the focus was on massing and proportion. As opposed to the ornamental clay tile of England, the American Queen Anne houses were built with functional wood shingles and brick. And the necessary new technology of central heating in the US eliminated the need for interior doors, which allowed for more relaxed and irregular floor plans, which coincided with the country's looser social structure. This allowed architects to focus on the organization of the floor plan, break the box of previous styles, and play with exterior materials and textures.[66]

While Louise regularly designed in this style, she disparaged how it was interpreted and overused by builders, stating that the "real 'Queen Anne house' of the speculative builder is a serious practical joke."[67] This reflected the general attitude of most architects of the time and their skepticism of work not designed by a trained professional. Queen Anne was often subject to poor imitation by untrained builders and therefore subject to derision by members of the architectural profession. Also, by the time Bethune made that comment in 1891, many architects had moved on from the Queen Anne style, including Louise. However, Louise and Robert remained very much interested in the values espoused in the aesthetics movement. In 1901, they eagerly became inaugural members of the Society for Beautifying Buffalo.[68]

Bethune's Clients and Projects: Businessmen, Outsiders, and Trailblazers

Of Bethune & Bethune's 180 known projects, 79 were single-family dwellings or mixed-use buildings with a residential component. Its residential clients ranged from middle- to upper-middle-class clients. Four were also clients who had hired them to design their commercial or industrial business facilities, and nine were women. However, the firm did not attract clientele among the city's growing group of millionaires. From 1880 to 1910 the city enjoyed steady growth and wealth, including an increasing number of very rich citizens. Bethune & Bethune benefited from this growth in many ways, but not through patronage by the city's elite. During this period, Buffalo's architectural character dramatically changed with significant new structures, including mansions that lined the newly paved streets down Delaware Avenue, nicknamed "Millionaire's Row," and along Olmsted's parkways. These were designed for Buffalo's wealthiest families. Some commissioned nationally renowned architects such as H. H. Richardson; McKim, Mead & White;

and even the young maverick Frank Lloyd Wright. Others chose prominent local architects such as Richard Waite, Milton Beebe, and especially Green & Wicks, one of the most prolific firms in Buffalo's history.

No firm had a greater impact on Buffalo's architectural landscape than Edward B. Green and William Wicks. Contemporaries of Bethune & Bethune, the partners were from Central New York State and educated at Cornell and MIT, respectively. They opened their practice in Buffalo after relocating from Auburn, New York, in 1881.[69] Their first commissions were large suburban dwellings for upper-middle-class clients, which led to larger and more significant residential commissions. In 1887, Green married Harriet Edson, whose brother-in-law was Josiah Letchworth of the ironworks manufacturing giant Pratt & Letchworth, the largest producer of carriage, horse-rigging, and saddlery hardware in the nation.[70] If Green did not have connections with the city's wealthy elite prior to his marriage, he most certainly did afterward.

Green & Wicks were skilled designers, very well connected socially, and equally skilled at winning work by maintaining personal connections with their clients. In 1888, the firm won a prestigious design competition for the new home for the First Presbyterian Church at Symphony Circle. Green was a member of the church congregation at the time, which undoubtedly helped them win the job, while at the same time the jury felt that Green & Wicks's submission was superior to the others.[71] Another significant client was the Buffalo Club, the social club for Buffalo's male elite, of which Green was a member. This led to a commission for the Twentieth Century Club, one of the first women's social clubs in the US whose members were spouses of the Buffalo Club. One might have expected the ladies of the Twentieth Century Club to procure the services of the first woman architect for this prestigious commission; however, Green's wife was a member of the club and commissioning the same architect the men had used was also a signal of the women's equality.[72] Finally, Green enjoyed the endorsement and patronage of John Albright, one of the wealthiest businessmen in Buffalo. Albright commissioned him to design two mansions and several cultural buildings culminating with Albright's legacy project, the Albright Art Gallery in Delaware Park (now known as the Albright-Knox-Gundlach Art Museum).[73] Indeed, as a testament to their close relationship, Edward and Harriet Green's burial plots are adjacent to the Albright family mausoleum.[74] While Green & Wicks's portfolio did include more modest single-family dwellings in the 1890s and 1900s, they stopped taking on these projects around 1914, presumably because of the small fees, adding further validity to Louise's concern about compensation for women architects who became pigeonholed as residential architects.[75]

Bethune & Bethune were considered very good practical architects. However, neither Louise nor Robert attempted to cultivate the city's elite, instead focusing on other personal interests and business prospects. However, two of their residential commissions stand out because they were significantly larger and provided greater design budgets than their other residential projects: Kellogg House and Brooks Mansion. Both clients were industrialists.

In 1885, Spencer Kellogg hired Bethune & Bethune to design his new Kellogg & McDougall factory on Ganson Street in the city's industrial area. Kellogg (1851–1922) was a member of one of the first American families to enter the linseed oil business, just thirty-one years after production began in the US. He was of the third generation of his family to continue the

Figure 3.4. Spencer Kellogg. Photo from *Men of Buffalo*.

work. The original company was based in Amsterdam, New York. Kellogg's father died at a very young age and Spencer accepted a buyout from his uncles when he came of age. He moved to Buffalo in 1879 and formed a new linseed oil company called Kellogg & McDougall, in partnership with his brother-in-law, Sidney McDougall.

In 1887, Bethune & Bethune also completed the Kellogg residence at 211 Summer Street. While both partners were probably involved in the two projects, Louise submitted the Kellogg House in her portfolio for her AIA application and Robert listed the Kellogg & McDougall factory in his. As such, Louise was probably the lead partner for the residence and Robert likely oversaw the work on the factory.[76] When Kellogg hired Bethune & Bethune, he and his wife Jane were living on Niagara Street and had had the first two of their seven children.[77] Located between Richmond and Delaware Avenues, Summer Street was one of the very fashionable addresses for the affluent. This would have been an ideal location for a businessperson who was building his wealth and establishing himself in the community. The project included the $16,000 brick dwelling and a $3,500 barn.[78]

Figure 3.5. Spencer Kellogg House today, 211 Summer St. Photo by Douglas Levere, University at Buffalo.

Kellogg's brick Queen Anne house was designed with many of the characteristics of the style, but with comparatively little ornamental detail. The three-story structure has a hipped roof with two intersecting gable roofs, a turret, and several dormers, circular and rectilinear. The multiple two-story bays protrude beyond the confines of the brick façade. Medina sandstone lintels and sills define the double-hung windows throughout the structure. Ornamentation is restricted to Medina sandstone corbels, finials, and gable roof trim; brick relief detailing at the roof and sculptural chimney; and terra cotta panels at the front elevation. Stained glass and leaded glass were utilized throughout the building. The Medina sandstone lintels and terra cotta details break up the monolithic forms in the building. Many of the Queen Anne houses in the area are wood frame and siding, which allow for more ornamentation to be incorporated in the exterior elevations.

In 1905, the Kelloggs sold 211 Summer St. and hired Green & Wicks to design a $500,000 Georgian mansion at 805 Delaware Ave., a most desirable address for a successful entrepreneur. Spencer Kellogg had made his fortune and he spared no expense in his new residence, sending his architect to Europe for ideas from French and Italian architecture and art.[79] Louise and Robert were basking in the success of the Hotel Lafayette, their most celebrated project, and the many opportunities this project provided, so they may not have pursued this commission if given the opportunity. Still, the Bethunes' relationship with the Kellogg family was true and extended beyond their contractual obligations. There is a photograph in one of Louise's albums of Kellogg's nine-year-old child, Doris, on her pony on the Kellogg property at 211 Summer St.[80] The house is still extant and has been in service as an apartment building for decades.

Of all of Bethune & Bethune's residential work, none was as ambitious, complicated, and yielded such incredible results as the renovation of the Brooks Mansion in Dunkirk, New York. For that project, Bethune & Bethune transformed a rural manor house into an impressive Queen Anne mansion that would be a landmark for the town for decades and the home of its first hospital. Horatio G. Brooks (1828–1887) was born and raised in New Hampshire and moved to Chautauqua County in 1850 to work for the New York and Lake Erie Railroad. In 1869, he founded the Brooks Locomotive Works, which manufactured railroad engines. The company became the largest employer in Dunkirk, which had a population of 7,248 when it was incorporated in 1880.[81]

Horatio Brooks, his wife Julia, and their three daughters lived at 529 Central Ave. in a rambling Italianate brick house that was built in the late 1860s–early 1870s. The original Brooks house was composed of a simple hipped structure that was capped with a cupola and two chimneys at the building's front and back. Ornate corbels supported the deep eaves and there were arched windows throughout. Two semi-hexagon, two-story bays protruded at the side elevation. There is only one surviving rendering of this building, from the 1881 *Chautauqua Atlas*. From this rendering, there is an L-shaped, two-story wing, also in the Italianate style that appears to have been added after the main house was built.[82]

In 1885, Brooks hired Bethune & Bethune to renovate his Central Avenue house. The cost of the renovation was $35,000, more than twice that of the $15,000 Kellogg House, which was a new construction project. The renovation consisted of the demolition of the L-shaped addition; a new addition that doubled the footprint of the house and included a magnificent tower; an adjacent three-story turret with an ornate chimney; and an entirely new third floor, composed of a tall hipped-roof with balustrade deck and multiple dormers. Following the renovation, the building was more than double its original size. The original front elevation of the Italianate house was preserved, as were the two bays on the adjacent façade. Stone balconies were added to the second-floor bay windows and a semi-circular stone terrace was added between the bays on the first floor.

As Scully notes, the Queen Anne style brought several innovations to residential design in the US, which were rooted in an evolution of Colonial vernacular architecture. These innovations were the use of local building techniques and materials and the opening of the floor plan both inside and out. This resulted in the expansion of the veranda, the grouping of exterior windows to increase views and natural light, and enlarging the front hall into a hall room.[83] No floor plan remains from the original or renovated Brooks residences; however, the original Italianate structure's main space was a ballroom. Photos of the interior of the building after the Bethune renovation feature large sitting and gathering rooms. One must assume that the Bethunes' renovation included adding a hall room, because the other innovations that Scully described were included.

The distinguishing features of the renovation were the four-story tower and four-bay porch at the entrance of the mansion, the adjacent semi-hexagonal turret, and expansive roof with its many flourishes, chimneys, and dormers of varying sizes. The front porch had a hipped roof, with a balustrade and balcony above, in keeping with the design of the main roof of the house. The porch had a classical profile with a gable and pediment that extended over the circular driveway to ensure protection during inclement weather. The other bays replicated the classical profile with pilasters and spindles in the cornice and balustrade.

From the
1881 Atlas of
Chautauqua County

Truly Yours
H. G. Brooks

Figure 3.6. Horatio G. Brooks. *Chautauqua Atlas*, 1881.

RESIDENCE OF H.G.BROOKS, DUNKIRK, CHAUTAUQUA CO. N.Y.

Figure 3.7. Original Brooks House before the Bethune & Bethune renovation. *Chautauqua Atlas*, 1881.

Figure 3.8. Brooks Mansion, 1890s. Courtesy of the Dunkirk Historical Society.

The first two floors of the tower, as well as the remainder of the addition, repeated the arched windows of the original Italianate house, however clustered together as per the Queen Anne style. The defining element of the turret was the chimney, which was situated at the front elevation. It was designed with fluting in the brickwork at the third floor that was replicated in the other chimneys of the structure. The previously existing chimneys were also modified to the Queen Anne design. In all, there were thirteen dormers, including those in the tower and the turret. According to later reports, much of the interior woodwork was mahogany.[84] The interiors were well detailed but not overly ostentatious.

Sadly, Horatio Brooks died suddenly in 1887 of a massive brain hemorrhage, not long after his substantial renovation was complete. Julia Brooks lived in the mansion until her death in 1896. In May 1898, the Brooks's daughters donated the property to the Young Men's Association, to be renovated into a community hospital and public library, in honor of their parents. The Brooks Memorial Hospital at 529 Central Ave. was opened on March 4, 1899.

Among the leaders of the Queen Anne movement were Peabody & Stearns Architects. Relatively unknown today, the firm was one of the most influential in the early 1880s. The Brooks Mansion was comparable to the Peabody & Stearns resort structures, for which they were most famous at the time. Most of those structures were rambling, whimsical, and ostentatious, as one might expect in resort homes for the wealthy. There are similarities between Bethune's Brooks Mansion and The Breakers, the Newport, Rhode Island, summer home that Peabody & Stearns designed for Cornelius Vanderbilt in 1877–1879. While The Breakers was a wood structure, the use of the front tower and pavilion-like front porch to define the entry is similar in both projects. Also, both houses rely heavily on dormer windows to break up massing of the rooflines (multiple gable roofs at The Breakers and mansard roofs at the Brooks Mansion). However, even with this large building, Louise maintained a very conservative box-like floor plan, which may have reflected the client's values, and certainly reflected those of the architect.

Beyond conservative businessmen, a defining characteristic of some of Bethune & Bethune's clients was that they were trailblazers in their own right—one might equally consider them outsiders. One example is the seven Sutherland sisters, who hired the Bethunes to design a house on their family property outside of Lockport, New York. The sisters comprised a singing group that appeared with Barnum and Bailey's Greatest Show on Earth from the early 1880s to 1900s. They were famous, in part because of the length of each of the women's hair, which fell below their knees. Their parents, Fletcher and Mary, developed a hair tonic and used the girls' notoriety to market the product very successfully. This resulted in a franchise of hair products, providing the source of income for the family long after the group's singing career ended. The sisters were contemporaries of Louise, with the eldest (Sarah) born in 1845 and the youngest (Mary) born in 1862.

Another client was J. K. Murray, a highly accomplished baritone opera star originally from Liverpool, UK. He immigrated to the US in 1869 and settled in Pittsburgh, Pennsylvania. He toured with several opera companies before creating his own venture—the Murray-Lane Opera Company—with his wife, opera singer Clara Lane, in 1893. In 1892, approximately when he married, he commissioned Bethune, Bethune & Fuchs to design a house in Pittsburgh. However, it is not clear if the project was built.

Entrepreneur Joseph A. Oaks had a number of capital ventures. Bethune, Bethune & Fuchs was his preferred architecture firm, and Louise considered him a family friend. In 1898, the firm designed the factory to

Figure 3.9. Seven Sutherland Sisters. http://www.angelfire.com/art/rapunzellonghair/
rapunzellonghairarchive/portrait4.htm, public domain.

house his company, Jav-O Coffee. Sadly, this company was profitable only
for a couple of years before going out of business. The firm also designed the
Oakses' family home at 281 Parkside Ave., in 1898. The imposing Queen
Anne structure boasted a ballroom that would be well used by the future
tenants, the Cornell University Medical School Scalp and Blade Club. Oaks
became one of Louise's most consequential clients, because he was one of
the original financial partners supporting the Lafayette Hotel and, in fact,
hired the firm for that project in 1899.

Other exceptional clients were the Davidson family members. Two
houses were commissioned for them, one for Mrs. Thomas Davidson at 354
Ashland Ave. in Buffalo, and the other for the wealthy shipbuilder Capt.
James Davidson. Captain Davidson was born in Buffalo in 1841 and built
his wealth in Bay City, Michigan, where he owned a house at 249 Linwood
Ave. The captain hired Louise to design his new home in that city at 1710
Center Ave., in 1892.

Several Bethune & Bethune projects were built on adjoining lots,
suggesting that there was a relationship between the clients, or that one

client recommended the firm to their neighbor. The Noye House was one of the first commissions for the firm and was completed in 1883. Richard Noye was a successful Buffalo businessman who had made his fortune in the family company, John T. Noye & Sons, one of the earliest mill furnishers in the country. Noye commissioned the house for his brother's wife, the recently widowed Mrs. E. H. Noye, who was the actual client. The Noye House was located on Richmond Avenue, a very fashionable street at the time, and part of the Olmsted parkway system. The three-story house is an understated Queen Anne, with red brick on the first floor, clapboard on the second, and a steeply pitched hipped roof with a cross gable and multiple dormers defining the third floor. The sculptural chimney is the focal point of the structure, rising from the middle of the hipped roof. The adjoining lot holds a second Bethune & Bethune house, built for M. W. Taylor. This half-timbered, three-story Queen Anne is approximately the same scale and equally spare in ornamental detail as the Noye house.

Figure 3.10. The Warren House, 1890. Douglas Levere, University at Buffalo.

Figure 3.11. Comstock House, 1890. Douglas Levere, University at Buffalo.

The Comstock and Warren Houses are situated on adjoining lots on Lexington Avenue, an upper-middle-class street in Buffalo. Both buildings were designed and built at the same time and completed in 1890. George W. Comstock was the owner of a successful fur and hat store on Main Street; Melvin F. Warren was an officer with Buffalo's Bank of Commerce. In July 1889, Comstock purchased the property from Warren for $1.[85] The exact relationship between the two men, which would precipitate such a transfer of the property, is unknown. Both buildings are designed in the Queen Anne style and, despite the differences in their details, are very similar in massing and they respond to each other in their layouts. Both houses cost approximately the same and were both wood frame in construction with cross gable roofs and chimneys on their side elevations. Because these homes were from the later days of the Queen Anne style, they were generally modest in their detailing and ornamentation. The focus was more on massing and less on intricate ornamentation and details.

Many of Bethune & Bethune's residences were in the same or adjacent neighborhoods and were built on or very near Olmsted's parkway system, also known as the Emerald Necklace. Such was the case with the Davidson, Thorn, and Reiman Houses. These houses, and others—such as the Riley House at 310 West Utica St., the Bell House at 427 Prospect

Ave., and Bethune's neighbor, Miss Nisell's house at 329 Porter Ave.—were within two blocks of Olmsted's masterpiece. Mrs. Davidson's house, at 354 Ashland Ave., and George Thorn's house, at 40 Bidwell Parkway, were both built in 1885. The Mary A. Reiman House, at 186 Ashland Ave., came later, in 1900.

Beginning in the 1890s, Louise hoped to focus more on commercial and public buildings, stating in 1893 that she "has been the architect of many pretty dwellings, but gives her attention now to public buildings."[86] Despite her intention, she never fully escaped that line of work until late in her career. Her last known residential commission was the Girvin House in 1902, a very modest two-story Colonial, for which there are surviving construction documents. Her last residential design was in 1907 for the house she and Robert would share with their son, Charles, at 904 Tonawanda St. Charles would operate his medical practice here from 1908 to 1910 for a year until he established his practice at 228 Niagara St.[87] Even Louise should be allowed to make exceptions for her family.

Figures 3.12. Thorn House, 1885. Douglas Levere, University at Buffalo.

Figures 3.13. Thorn House, 1885. Douglas Levere, University at Buffalo.

Figures 3.14 Thorn House, 1885. Douglas Levere, University at Buffalo.

Chapter 4

Welcome to the Club

Let us drink a toast to the lady member . . . Mrs. Bethune. . . . Long
may she live and may there be many more.

—American Institute of Architects

Figure 4.1. Louise Bethune around the time she was admitted into the WAA. Zina
Bethune Archive on Louise Bethune, circa 1860–1962. Courtesy of the University
Archives, University at Buffalo.

During the early to mid-1880s, Louise Bethune made history three times: when she opened her own office and then was elected into the two leading American professional architectural associations. In 1881, she became the first professional woman architect to open an office, which led to some notoriety regionally. However, her acceptance in the two architectural associations signified her status as an architect nationally. In 1885, she successfully applied to the newly formed Western Association of Architects, the first woman to do so. Her admission placed her on the national stage and profoundly impacted her male counterparts' view of women as architects and the very notion of professionalism. Then, two years later, she was admitted to the American Institute of Architects (AIA)—the first woman to be accepted in that national organization.

Defining an area of expertise was—and still is—an important strategy for architects to develop and maintain credibility and ensure the long-term health of the business. Another form of establishing credibility is obtaining licensure or certification. However, in the 1880s, no licensure law existed for architects in the US, and so admission into professional associations provided the only vital recognition that an architect was a professional with high ethical standards.[1]

Throughout much of the 1800s, members of the architectural profession fought for the credibility that other occupations, such as the law and medicine, enjoyed. For architecture, as an occupation that was founded upon the craft of construction and the arts, the aura of professionalism was hard-fought in the United States and in the Western world in general. Because there were no schools of architecture in the US until later in the nineteenth century and no licensure until the early twentieth century, architects needed to create their credibility through membership in a professional association.

The First Professional Association and the Founding of the AIA

The first society of architects was likely the Brethren of the Workshop of Vitruvius Society, which was founded in 1803 in New York. This was a short-lived society composed of men who worked in the art, craft, and construction side of the profession. Many members of this small group were builders and carpenters.[2] The first true American organization for professional architects was the American Institution of Architecture. Founded in New York in 1836, the association was concerned with improving architectural education and the public recognition of architects. It was one of many professional associations to be founded in the 1820s and 1830s. The two leaders of the eleven-person organization were Alexander Jackson Davis and Thomas U. Walter. While the organization strived for national influence, the members were active only in New York City and Philadelphia. They tried to open a school in New York, but this did not happen. According to architectural historian Mary Woods, the confluence of a competition between the members from Philadelphia and New York, the lack of engagement with the general public, the juxtaposition of exclusivity in its membership during an age of egalitarianism, and the financial panic of 1837 all led to the demise of the association.[3]

Twenty years later, architects tried again to organize. On February 23, 1857, architect Richard Upjohn convened a group of twelve New York colleagues, including Thomas Walter, to discuss the creation of a professional association. The original name proposed was the New York Society of Architects. Walter suggested the American Institute of Architects (AIA) in the hopes it would become national in its reach. The first few years of the AIA were productive ones, with membership steadily growing. Sadly, this momentum began to wane with the outbreak of the Civil War, but was revived again in the mid-1860s after the war ended. In the 1860s–1870s, the AIA primarily focused on architectural education, setting rules for design competitions, establishing standard professional fees, and growing its national membership by creating chapters in cities around the country. Like its predecessor, in 1867 the AIA explored the idea of establishing a school of architecture in New York City. However, this ambitious initiative was abandoned after three years of unsuccessful advocacy and the AIA pivoted toward endorsing architecture departments in established universities.[4]

The AIA's focus on establishing standard fees and rejecting design competitions that relied on submissions of unpaid work was part of their mission to elevate the profession in the mind of the general public. Its members advocated for standardized professional fees commensurate with the construction costs of a building. This was in contrast to the daily wage paid to artisans or mechanics and was an effort to differentiate their work as a professional architectural service. They adopted a rate of 5 percent of a project's cost in 1866. However, this could not be mandated to the membership and certainly not to the clients. According to Woods, most architects in the late 1890s were charging a far lower percentage for their services.[5] As such, the fee schedule was a suggested rate of charges.

The membership was united in its concern over participating in design competitions for public buildings, which often did not recompense the architects for their time or stipulate the amount to be paid for the winning submission. In 1870, the AIA adopted an institute code stipulating members would not participate in open design competitions unless entrants were paid. The winning architect would be compensated for work based on a scheduled percentage fee and would provide supervision of the construction. The AIA also stipulated the selection committee include an architect on the jury.[6] Louise referred to this rule when refusing to compete for the Women's Building design competition for the Columbian Exposition in 1891 (see chapter 8).

The AIA encouraged cities and regions to establish local chapters.[7] Nonetheless, there was concern that the AIA was elitist. While it was a national organization, the institute was still largely based in the Northeast. In 1882, twenty-five years after the founding of the AIA, membership had grown to 362, 65 percent of whom were from the Northeast chapters, and over 21 percent practicing in New York City.[8]

Figure 4.2. The American Institute of Architects, 1883 convention. Courtesy of the American Institute of Architects Archives, Washington, DC.

Given the imbalance of the membership favoring the Northeast, it was likely inevitable that architects in the growing western regions of the country would establish their own professional association. In 1884, the Western Association of Architects was established, and its first convention took place on November 12–15 of that year. By this time, the WAA had already enlisted 126 members, all from western cities including 72 members from Chicago, as well as St. Louis, Minneapolis, Kansas City, and Des Moines.[9]

The Western Association of Architects

The WAA was led by architects—some of whom were also members of the AIA—who thought the AIA was too focused on its northeast membership, denying leadership roles for its western members.[10] Indeed, from 1857 to 1891, the AIA had elected just three presidents, and all were from New York and Philadelphia.[11] The true force behind the WAA was Daniel Burnham (not an AIA member), who served in a leadership position throughout most of the existence of the association. In his address at that first convention, Burnham spoke of the evolution of the architect from master builder to contemporary professional. He stressed the unique challenges of the western American architects as torchbearer for the design excellence and quality of the monuments of the Old World, without mentors on hand to guide their practice. He saw them as pioneers in a pioneering land. Therefore, he actively encouraged the "restoration of the spirit of brotherhood" to overcome their isolation.[12]

Despite any competition between them, the WAA and AIA shared many areas of concern. They immediately established standing committees to work on resolutions on design competitions and professional fees. They also created a committee on the revision of state statutes regarding building laws.[13] Yet, there were several topics on which the AIA and the WAA differed. One was in their position on professional architectural licensing, a topic also under discussion in Europe. As Woods describes, Britain and France explored the possibility of a state-mandated certification. French architects advocated for government officials to review the technical skills of the architect, and not adjudicate their design skills. British architects opposed any form of regulation because they argued that no certification committee could fairly assess the design skills of the architect.[14] Decades earlier, Prussia had mandated certification of its municipal architects to safeguard welfare and public safety. The WAA sought a similar certification process that would endorse the architect as a professional working for the public good. The AIA strongly opposed licensure, because it would be based on the technical skills of the architect rather than artistry, which they viewed as the foundation of the profession.[15]

A second point on which the WAA and the AIA differed was governance. WAA members believed in a more democratic process in decision-making, while the AIA formed a board of directors to represent its membership as a more efficient and robust method of conducting business.[16]

The most contentious disagreement between the two organizations was their philosophy regarding membership, including the admission process and membership standing. As an architect noted when learning of the founding of the WAA, "I hope [the WAA] will be broader in spirit than the eastern [AIA] is reported to be."[17] The AIA was just far too selective and elitist to advance the profession amid the industrial era in the aftermath of the Civil War and as the US was blossoming into an international economic powerhouse. AIA members were concerned about maintaining the prominent reputation of the institute and had strict criteria for admission, which is why they saw no need for a licensing process.[18] The AIA had two levels of membership: the Associate and the Fellow. The thought was that junior members would join as Associates and would be elevated to Fellows as they developed in stature within the profession. The AIA contended that the dual membership levels would ultimately provide the association with the ability to increase its numbers by having multiple entry points for admission, based on experience and stature within the profession.[19]

When initially formed, the WAA had been quite liberal in its admission of members, including members who came from the building trades in addition to those with professional training/education.[20] However, they retracted this practice after complaints from the more professional membership.[21] By 1886 the WAA had created the Committee on Professional Membership to address its previous admission of builders. Nonetheless, the WAA strenuously opposed the AIA's two-tiered membership policy. They believed that members should be equal, period. As Adler stated, "We think that the personal standing of an architect does not depend upon whether he writes FAIA after his name or not, but that it depends entirely upon the volume of work he does and the quality of that work, and upon his general conduct."[22]

The WAA leadership immediately knew that a large organization would provide the association with the strength to impact the public perception of the profession. They also understood the power it would possess to lobby legislators who had the authority to develop procurement standards for awarding public work. However, this obvious open-door admissions policy attracted architects who would otherwise have no vehicle to effect change in their profession. One of these individuals was the first woman architect, Louise Bethune.

Enter the Lady Architect

> If the lady is practicing architecture, and is in good standing, there is no reason why she should not be one of us.
>
> —WAA 1885 Convention Proceedings, AIA Archives

In 1885, just one year after the WAA was established, Louise applied for membership.[23] The WAA was considered the more progressive association

MEMBERS OF THE WESTERN ASSOCIATION OF ARCHITECTS,
At St. Louis Convention, November 18, 1885.

Figure 4.3. The Western Association of Architects at the 1885 convention in St. Louis. It was at this convention that Louise Bethune was elected to the association. *The Inland Architect and News Record*, January 1886.

of the two, so she probably applied to the WAA prior to the AIA for this reason.[24] However, admission to the WAA was not automatic, as neither the WAA nor the AIA had a woman member.[25] In 1885, Louise and Robert Bethune traveled to Chicago and conferred with WAA leadership—including Daniel Burnham, Louis Sullivan, and John Root—regarding their applications.[26] During this meeting, the parties developed the strategy for Louise's unprecedented admission.

Initially, both Louise and Robert submitted their applications for membership to the WAA. However, Robert withdrew his nomination before his application was reviewed, presumably at the advice of the WAA leadership and in anticipation of a charge that the firm's work was his alone.[27] With her application, Louise submitted a portfolio of her work to demonstrate her abilities as an architect.[28] She had previously intended to attend the WAA convention but decided against the appropriateness of such a gesture, given the fact that she was not a member, and potential embarrassment of not being admitted while present. The yearly membership was reviewed at the WAA national convention in St. Louis in November. Burnham chose to separate Bethune's nomination from the other members, to ensure the association would be prepared to include the admission of women as members to their constitution. This was a carefully orchestrated action to yield a positive outcome to the board's intention of opening their membership to women. The meeting's proceedings capture the drama of the moment:

> The president called the meeting to order and said: There is a bit of unfinished business before we can proceed. All the members recommended by the directors for admission were voted in except one, and nothing was done on that subject.

> Mr. Burnham: That was with reference to a lady.

> The President: Now I will ask if the committee are prepared to recommend that party in all respects except the fact that she is a lady?

> Mr. Sullivan: Yes, sir.

> The President: What shall be done with this question?

Mr. Burnham, of the Board of Directors: May I say that what the board desires is to be instructed upon the principle of admitting women as members of the association. That is the thing. If the decision is given us to admit women, we will make the recommendation. We would like the decision, now, of the convention, as to whether it desires to admit women as members of the association. We want the By-Laws interpreted.

A member: I would like to know what the opinion of the Board of Directors is.

Mr. Burnham: We are all agreed; we are very much in favor of it.

Mr. Cochrane: Then I would recommend that the secretary cast the ballot for the lady.

A member: Is the lady practicing?

The President: Yes, sir.

Mr. Cochrane: Let the secretary cast the ballot as he did for the others.

The motion was seconded.

Mr. Sullivan: What we desired was a vote of instructions as to the admission of women as a general thing.

A member: It seems to me that if you carry the motion as made by Mr. Cochrane, that it will suggest a precedent for future consideration. If the lady is practicing architecture, and is in good standing, there is no reason why she should not be one of us.

The President: The motion is made and seconded that this lady applicant be admitted to membership. All in favor of this will say aye.

Motion was adopted.

The President: Mrs. Louisa [*sic*] Bethune is the applicant. Her husband was an applicant but withdrew. She has done work by herself and been very successful. She is unanimously elected a member.[29]

As it is apparent from these proceedings, while the board members were seeking direction from the membership, they were signaling their strong support for the candidate. Sullivan, Burnham, and Root were particularly supportive of Louise's candidacy. Even more importantly, they used the opportunity to address the broader issue of the admission of women to the WAA, as opposed to solely the individual case of Louise Bethune.

While she was an ideal candidate to champion the admission of women in the association—given her experience and body of work—Louise's submission was somewhat complicated because she was in partnership with her husband. A skeptic could easily argue that she was riding on the coattails of her husband's work. With Robert's retraction of his submission, Louise was able to submit her application based on her own merit. (Robert successfully applied for membership to the WAA in 1887.[30]) The report in the *Inland Architect*, the official journal of the WAA, portrayed the deliberations of the membership regarding Louise's application as a fait accompli. However, reports from the AIA records demonstrate there were concerns from some WAA members. A. J. Bloor, AIA secretary and guest to the convention, later reported to its board:

> The afternoon session of the first day was signalized immediately on its opening by the election of a lady, Mrs. Louisa [*sic*] Bethune, of Buffalo, NY, to the membership of the Association as a practicing architect, a unanimous affirmative ballot being cast by the Secretary on the motion of Mr. Cochrane, an old member of the Institute. In private, I was asked my views on the question of her admittance, and, as an individual, I expressed myself in favor of it. It appeared that her husband is an architect practitioner, which suggests facilities that might not otherwise exist in the matter of supervision of buildings in process of erection.[31]

It is evident that while the progressive wing of the profession strongly favored its expansion to include women, not all members were comfortable with this strategy. Once again, their concern was that women could not supervise construction. After this historic vote, the WAA established its official definition of an architect in the organization's constitution as the following: "a professional *person* [as opposed to "man," which was originally suggested] whose sole occupation is to supply all data preliminary to the material, construction and competition of a building and to exercise administrative control over contracts stipulating terms of obligation and fulfillment between proprietor and contractor."[32]

Louise was deeply touched by the careful stewardship that the WAA leadership took to forward her candidacy. She understood her submission could make her the object of ridicule in architectural circles and she appreciated the orchestrated approach by the board. Following the convention, Louise wrote to John Root:

> My sincere thanks are certainly due to you and thro' you to all members of your society for the cordiality of the welcome you have accorded me and also for the extreme delicacy and adroit work with which the nomination and election were arranged. . . . I am particularly sensible of the kindness the association has rendered me, and the honor it has done itself in preserving admission from any taint of ridicule or notoriety. If the society's new member is no great acquisition, its new measure is certainly credible and progressive.[33]

Louise's admission to the WAA made national news. The story of her historic achievement was published by newspapers throughout the country, from Nashville to New Orleans, and especially in the Midwest. Most stories were positive about her breaking this barrier, although some just neutrally reported the fact. The *Buffalo Courier* and the *Woman's Exponent* in Salt Lake City took exception that the *Woman's Journal* referred to Louise as "a practicing architect of Chicago. . . . It is hard that Chicago should have the credit of the woman architect of whom Buffalo has such reason to feel proud."[34]

As might have been expected, her acceptance by the WAA led to more general articles on the best and least appropriate areas for women architects to practice. Edward Godwin, a "distinguished English architect" as the newspapers described him, was quoted at length on the subject. He asserted that women would be most useful in "designs in architecture, including furniture and decorations, illustrations of old work, cabinet work, metal work, monuments, carpets and hangings, painting on cabinets, wall paper designs, tiles, private and public buildings."[35] Godwin was a progressive and leader in the English Queen Anne movement, so he was probably very supportive of women becoming architects. Whether intended or not, his emphasis on the decorative and ornamental tasks of the profession, as opposed to the functional and structural, only reinforced a preexisting bias. Godwin also noted that "many young women possessed all the requisite talents to become architectural workers . . . [however] an impulsive, gay, free-as-air, lightsome sort of girl is not the stuff for an architect."[36] Here again, we encounter his obvious sexist attitude, demonstrating a prevailing attitude about women professionals that early women architects needed to counter head-on.

Following her admission to the WAA and later the AIA, Louise enjoyed the status of being the first and leading female architect. As a trailblazer, she was called upon frequently to speak about women in architecture, women professionals, and women's education. In 1889 she was part of a panel of professional women speaking to the Graduate Association in Buffalo, which also included the writer Mary Lee Perkins; Dr. Mary Moody, the first woman to graduate from the University of Buffalo Medical College; and Dr. Mary Wetmore, also a graduate from UB. In Louise's comments, she agreed with Godwin's commentary on the hard work involved in becoming an architect, and that not every woman would be suited to or interested in its study. However, she was unequivocal on a woman's ability to oversee construction:

> Women are entirely competent to become architects, but I do not believe the profession will ever be crowded, as it requires too much application and hard work. Unless a woman has a love and decided aptitude for the preparatory work she will tire of it quickly. This idea that a woman cannot superintend the erection of buildings is all nonsense. Any woman with a moderate amount of physical endurance can do it. As for dealing with carpenters and builders, there is no trouble at all. I have always found them an accommodating, agreeable class of men in all business transactions.[37]

The Struggle to Join the AIA

In February 1888, Louise applied for the highest level of membership of the AIA, the Fellow.[38] By this time, she had been a member of the WAA for over two years. However, longtime AIA secretary Alfred Bloor advised her instead to apply for the Associate level. Bloor reflected the view of many members when he told her that the Associate level was "largely an educational & probationary term, which may very properly be regarded by its incumbents as simply a stepping stone to the higher grade of Fellowship."[39] The AIA required two or more sponsors from the organization. Bloor agreed to sponsor her, along with AIA member G. W. Rapp, and he waived the requirement for a third, possibly because of her WAA membership and standing within that organization and profession at large.[40] Louise submitted drawings for the following projects: Hoffman's Millinery House, Police Station No. 2,[41] the renovation of the Buffalo School No. 4, and residences for William Mitchell, Spencer Kellogg, Horace G. Brooks, A. J. Meyer, and George Waterman (see chapter 3).[42] In addition to the recommendation letters from her AIA sponsors, the package included a letter of support from Sydney Smith, the 1888 president of the WAA, and John Root, who recommended her to be a Fellow.

At the 1888 AIA Convention, the group admitted seven members at the Associate level, elevated four members from Associate to Fellow, and admitted thirteen new members at the Fellowship level.[43] In other words, more than half of the applicants were admitted at the higher level. Of these thirteen new Fellows, their years of experience ranged from eight to thirty years, with W. W. Carlin being an outlier, with only four years (although this was probably an error in the written meeting minutes because he was six years older than Louise). Louise applied with twelve years of experience.[44] However, after "some discussion," the board admitted Louise as an Associate member.[45] Given her years of experience and that she had the endorsement of the WAA leadership, Louise could have made a compelling case for Fellowship. We don't know why Bloor recommended to Bethune that she apply as an Associate, but he did so with the consent of the AIA Board, and they could have elevated her if they accepted Root's suggestion.[46]

The difference in Bethune's admission process between the WAA and the AIA underlines the very different philosophies between the two organizations about their membership and women's role in architecture in general. The WAA was composed of progressive members who strongly supported women entering the profession and prospering. They actively worked to change professional norms by collaborating with potential trailblazers like Louise to present her application in a manner that supported a successful outcome. The WAA admission process was more democratic in nature, which also favored Louise. New members were voted upon in the open forum of the annual convention by all members. Members were initially vetted by the executive committee and then brought to the membership, with the expectation that they would be accepted. The convention forum allowed for an open dialogue, but it also inhibited discrete sidebar conversations where dissenting voices might gain traction. Because Burnham, Root, and Sullivan orchestrated Louise's membership vote, a dissenting member would have had to openly challenge the judgment of the executive committee to oppose Louise's application.

The AIA was much more conservative. They were focused on elevating the profession to be on par with law, medicine, and engineering. They had been working to establish this status for several decades and were at the cusp of a breakthrough, with the obvious need for expertise in the built environment, which was underscored by the maturation of the Industrial Revolution, the need for new building types, and the passage of additional laws addressing building safety. The AIA admitted its members through its the Board of Directors, at its own discretion, and reported the admissions at the convention, as opposed to holding a membership vote at that forum.

Louise applied for membership to the AIA at a very auspicious time in the AIA. She was already the first woman admitted to a professional association, by more than two years. She was a proven leader, because—as we shall see—she had established the Buffalo Society of Architects. By this time her firm had built significant factories, residential projects, and schools. Louise's nomination for the AIA was stronger than her WAA application because she had more important projects in her portfolio. To be clear, there is no indication that the AIA was opposed to a woman becoming a member. However, it is striking that the first woman to apply was admitted at the entry level, given Louise's compelling application.

Another factor that probably influenced the AIA's decision to admit Louise as a member was, by 1887, there were serious conversations underway regarding the merger of the AIA and WAA. Daniel Burnham, by now a member of both organizations, originally suggested the idea at the 1887 AIA Convention.[47] While the two groups had their differences regarding leadership and conflicting cultures, both organizations agreed that one larger entity advocating for the profession would benefit all members. These negotiations advanced in October 1888 at the AIA National Convention in Buffalo, where Bethune, as a new member, served on the host committee.[48] And while behind closed doors there may have been reservations regarding her admission to the AIA, she was warmly greeted at the convention. Day 2 of the convention ended with the following exchange:

Mr. Stone: Before we separate let us drink a toast to the lady member of the Buffalo Chapter, Mrs. Bethune.

Mr. Moser: Long may she live and may there be many more.[49]

Just after the AIA Convention in Buffalo, where the negotiations between the AIA and WAA got very serious, there was a shakeup in the executive committee elections during the WAA's annual convention in Chicago in November 1888. While members were aware of the importance of this committee as they continued their talks of a potential merger with the AIA, they were also a diehard democratic organization, and members thought that every position should be contested on the point of principle. It demonstrates how passionately some WAA members were willing to stand on principle. At the last minute, Buffalo-based architect William W. Carlin was nominated to the slate for the position of president beside the previously uncontested Daniel Burnham. Carlin, much to his embarrassment, won the election. In another unexpected term, Louise Bethune was elected second vice president of the Board of Directors, beating the other six candidates[50] and becoming the first woman to be elected to the association's Executive Committee. While Louise was active in WAA committee work, she had not yet assumed a leadership role within the association. Her election demonstrates the confidence her colleagues had in her work and stands in sharp contrast to her admission process to the AIA. One may wonder if the WAA members' personal interaction with Louise in Buffalo the prior month contributed to her election.

The consolidation of the two organizations took place at the AIA Convention, which was held on November 20–21, 1889, in Cincinnati, Ohio. Some of the longstanding philosophical differences between their members had not been resolved. To assuage the WAA concern about membership levels, all current WAA and AIA members were raised to Fellows upon consolidation—so Louise's tenure as merely an Associate was very brief. To address the concern about geographic diversity among the new association's leadership, the newly elected Executive Committee included positions filled by former AIA and WAA members.[51] Richard Morris Hunt was elected president, Buffalonian William W. Carlin was elected vice president, and John Root was elected secretary. Tragically, Root died in 1891 at the age of forty-one and Carlin died in 1894 at the age of forty-four, both leaving a void of progressive voices on the new board. Several WAA members refused to join the newly consolidated AIA until much later, if at all. One of these was Robert Bethune, who remained very active in the local AIA Buffalo/WNY Chapter but did not join the national AIA until 1902.[52] And although Louise remained a member of both the local and national AIA organizations, she was never involved nationally with the group after the consolidation. Indeed, she did not attend the 1901 AIA Convention that was held in Buffalo, although Robert was there.[53]

As a consolidated, more democratic, and geographically diverse body, the new AIA was ready to address issues to advance the profession. They negotiated terms for working with federal agencies and policies regarding entering design competitions. Both issues would directly impact both Daniel Burnham and Louise Bethune during the planning of the Columbian Exposition in Chicago in 1893.

The Women Who Followed . . . Eventually

Once Louise won her hard-earned positions with both the WAA and AIA, it would seem that the issue would have been settled for future generations. However, reviewing Louise's successors provides additional context to the continuing sexism that women architects experienced and the opposition they encountered from their male counterparts within the AIA.

Sallie T. Smith was the second professional woman architect in the United States, but her career is not well documented.[54] Born in Columbus, Mississippi, she attended Verona College in that state and then studied architecture with her father, W. S. Smith. He made Sallie a junior member of his firm, which moved to Birmingham, Alabama, in 1886.[55] In March 1887, daughter and father were among a group of architects to form the Association of Alabama Architects, which was associated with the WAA. Sallie was elected to the Alabama association to solicit new members throughout the state. At its 1887 convention, Sallie and W. S. Smith were admitted to the WAA.[56] However, neither Sallie nor her father joined the AIA after its consolidation with the WAA, and her name is not found in subsequent AIA member lists.

While the WAA admitted its second woman member only two years after their first, it took the AIA thirteen years. The next woman to be admitted to the AIA was Lois Howe (1864–1964) in 1901. According to Boston architect and AIA member C. H. Blackall, "Miss Howe came in to the Institute . . . because most of the members who voted on her thought Lois was a man's name."[57] However, she did not become a member of her local AIA chapter, the Boston Society of Architects, until 1916[58] and was not made a Fellow until 1931, the first woman after Louise to be given this status.[59] Henrietta Dozier (1872–1947) was admitted shortly after Howe in 1905. A graduate of MIT in 1899, Henrietta worked in Atlanta from 1900 to 1913 and served as the secretary of AIA Atlanta from 1910 to 1912 and then opened a practice in Orlando.

Ida Annah Ryan's (1873–1950) story demonstrates the struggle of early women architects for equality among their male counterparts. Before applying for AIA membership in 1907, Ryan wrote to the organization asking whether she could be considered for membership even though she was not a member of her local chapter, the Boston Society of Architects, because it was "positively closed to women," citing Lois Howe's failed attempt to join it. The AIA's reply must have given her the confidence to apply. However, her application was rejected by the Board of Directors on a ballot vote, with her application garnering nine letters of opposition. Of the three that survive, two opposed her because of her gender and stated they did not know her. Seth Temple wrote, "I have never known a woman who pretended to practice Architecture who was worthy to be included in so distinguished body." And C. H. Blackall asked "the Directors to consider whether it is wise to admit women at all unless they have achieved some signal [*sic*] distinction in the profession." A third member, D. Austin, from Boston, objected to her admittance on the grounds that she was not a member of her home chapter. The fact that her application was rejected almost twenty years after Louise's admission is astounding. Ida was finally successful in 1921 in joining the AIA, when women were more welcome.[60]

In 1918, the AIA admitted two women: Marcia Mead (1879–1967) and Theodate Pope (1868–1946). Marcia was the first woman to graduate from Columbia University's architecture program. She had practiced with Anna Pendleton Schenck until Anna's death in 1915 and then continued as a sole practitioner, mentoring Esther Hill from 1923 to 1924, who was one of the first woman Canadian architects.[61] Theodate Pope was born into a wealthy Ohio family. While Princeton University did not accept women, she hired a Princeton professor for private lessons and designed the family estate in Connecticut under the tutelage of Charles McKim.[62] In the 1920s, after women got the right to vote with the passage of the Nineteenth Amendment, the AIA admitted more women, with ten new woman members in the 1920s alone, starting with Julia Morgan (1872–1957) in 1921.

Louise's story is remarkable when compared with her initial successors because her admission to two professional organizations was so early; she was not succeeded by another female member for thirteen years. Despite the best intentions of the early WAA leaders to encourage women to join the profession and the perseverance of her successors, there was a concerted effort to limit the architectural profession to men only by a significant portion of the AIA's membership. This broke down somewhat in the 1920s, but it was not until the 1970s, after the beginning of the second wave of feminism, that the AIA began to address the fact that its women members made up just 1 percent of its total roster. Louise was correct that women had entered the architectural profession far earlier in its development than other professions and initially there were promising signs that they would be welcomed as equals long before they would receive that status in other aspects of society. However, after that initial wave, the profession closed ranks, and women would struggle to achieve the equal status that Louise experienced until well into the twentieth century.

Unlike several female architects who followed her, Louise did not benefit from the patronage of women, which could have been available to her in such an affluent industrial city as Buffalo. Other women architects were hired by women patrons, such as Minerva Parker Nichols in Philadelphia. However, there is no evidence that Minerva applied for membership to the AIA; she may have questioned whether she would be admitted. She also may not have felt the need for its endorsement, given her status with her largely female clientele. Throughout her career, Louise never could rely on women patrons, instead relying on public work and industrial and commercial clients.

The Buffalo Society of Architects

Immediately upon her admission to the WAA in 1885, Bethune joined the membership committee with the charge of establishing a presence in New York State.[63] On March 10, 1886, she organized the first meeting of the Buffalo Society of Architects with a membership of twelve. The Buffalo Society of Architects steadily grew and was very active by the time it received its charter from the AIA and became AIA Buffalo/WNY, in March 1890.[64] Much of the work of the society was in concert with the advocacy of the national associations, in particular lobbying for paid design competitions with educated jurors and actively and financially supporting the passage of a professional licensing bill for architects in New York State.

The Buffalo association was active in other areas, too. In 1888 it successfully worked with the city on the passage of the Building Laws as a revision of the Charter of the City. The society also successfully protested to the federal government against the original design of Buffalo's new Post Office Building in 1893, and unsuccessfully opposed the Buffalo Public Schools regarding the terms of the design competition for a new high school in 1901. The Buffalo Society was also instrumental in forming the Western New York Association of Architects in October 1886, the only regional component of the AIA until the creation of AIA New York State in 1931.[65] This organization encompassed Buffalo, Rochester, Syracuse, Ithaca, and Binghamton, and extended to Albany. Carlin discussed the importance of regional components as president of the WAA in 1889, stating that it was "largely through these that we must look for improvement in matters of legislation."[66] The members of the association stated: "The objects of the association are to unite in fellowship the architects of Western New York, to combine their efforts to promote the artistic, scientific and practical efficiency of the profession, and to cultivate and encourage the study of kindred arts."[67]

While a vibrant and active national association was vital in promoting the profession to the general public and the federal government, the state and regional chapters would be on the front lines in advocating for professional licensing, increased architectural education opportunities, and other state legislative issues. As such, the Western New York Association of Architects was particularly focused on passing a professional licensing bill for architects. Indeed, in Carlin's address in 1889, he was optimistic that the New York state legislature would pass such a bill within the year. The bill called for the creation of a board of architects to oversee the regulation of architects. The board would consist of one professor from Columbia University, one professor from Cornell University, two architects from the Western New York Association, two architects from the New York Chapter of the AIA, and one architect from central New York State.[68] The association worked with the AIA New York Chapter to jointly lobby for the passage of the bill in the state legislature's 1892 session. At a meeting of the New York State on Committee Law on February 4, 1892, the following groups supported the bill: AIA, Architectural League, AIA New York Chapter, Western New York Chapter, AIA Buffalo/WNY (Robert Bethune represented the chapter), Buffalo Sketch Club, and the superintendent of construction of the Albany Capitol.[69]

The bill was passed by both houses, giving Governor Flower thirty days to sign, which he never did, apparently due to opposition from select architects in New York City who had access to the governor.[70] Also, it was reported that the governor considered the legislation an opportunity for organizing a trade union.[71] Ultimately Illinois became the first state to legislate an architectural professional licensing bill in 1897 through the advocacy of Adler and N. Clifford Ricker, director of the Architecture Department at the University of Illinois. The loss of this tremendous effort dampened the enthusiasm of the Western New York's membership, as was demonstrated in the relative inactivity of their annual reports. Licensure in New York State was passed finally in 1915.[72] The Western New York Association of Architects did, however, also work hard to build enduring bridges between professional architects and schools of architecture, conducting regular visits and meetings at the schools of architecture at Syracuse and Cornell universities. Professors from both schools were also very active in the organization.

However, the geographic region of the Western New York Association of Architects eventually became too large to maintain a vibrant engagement model. The Executive Committee recommended merging with the very active AIA Buffalo/WNY Chapter, which the members outside of Buffalo resoundingly rejected. Ultimately, the regional association became the Central New York Chapter of the AIA in 1897.[73] And while gender issues were never part of the regular discourse of this or any architectural association, Bethune, by her mere presence, forced the issue. In the opening address by the WAA president to the Western New York Association of Architects in 1888, the issue was raised—somewhat obliquely: "Gentlemen—I wish I could add ladies, but I hope the day is not very far distant when I can add that to it . . ."[74]

This comment reflects WAA's optimistic attitude about the future of women in architecture. However, despite Louise's early success, she was not followed by large numbers of women pursuing the profession in the region. Because the Bethune, Bethune & Fuchs office records do not survive, there is no record that she hired women as interns. The first woman architect to succeed Bethune in Buffalo as a firm owner was Bonnie Foit Albert, who established her office in 1977, ninety-six years after Louise established her firm.[75] In Upstate New York, following Louise, twelve women became members of the AIA before 1970. Helen Chittenden Gillespie of Syracuse was the first of these women, whose AIA membership began in 1943.[76]

Describing Louise as a "trailblazer" within the AIA could be said to be inaccurate, because women did not immediately follow her into the organization and the institutional memory regarding her historic admission was lost when they started to apply. Instead, she was a lone warrior, who benefited from good timing, progressive advocates within the profession,

Figure 4.4. WAA New York State members, 1888. Robert Bethune is standing first on the right and W. W. Carlin is standing seventh from left. *Architectural Era*, May 1888.

and, most importantly, unfailing strength and perseverance. She refused to be a victim and never outwardly criticized her AIA colleagues. However, she did note that women professionals were not treated equally to their male counterparts. And she chose to not be involved in the national AIA after the merger.[77] Her inactivity, as someone who had been so very active just two years earlier, demonstrates her attitude toward the association. Ultimately, Louise would deeply impact her women successors, but it would be those who entered the profession one hundred years after her, among the baby boom and the generations that followed, who rediscovered her story and celebrated it.

Chapter 5

The Architecture of Education

Mrs. Bethune has made a special study of schools and has been particularly successful in that direction, but refuses to confine herself exclusively to that branch, believing that women who are pioneers in any profession should be proficient in every department.

—Willard and Livermore, *A Woman of the Century*

Figure 5.1. Bethune, Bethune & Fuchs (far right) and an unidentified apprentice photo from the late 1880s. Courtesy of the Nancy Herlan Brady.

The period of the mid- to late 1880s was very productive for Bethune & Bethune. Their small practice was growing, as was their family with the birth of their son, Charles. In addition to residential and industrial projects, they were ready to expand their practice to include public architecture and began to design educational buildings, starting with plans for the new Buffalo Public Schools system.[1] The firm designed schools as urban districts were forming, and educational building standards were being developed. They would design seven of the original twenty-five new buildings and four building renovations or additions in the first master plan project for Buffalo. As a rapidly growing city on the edge of the frontier, Buffalo would struggle to provide adequate facilities to meet the population's needs. However, this rapid growth enabled the city's architects to respond by designing some of the early examples of the new model for educational architecture.

A study of the educational facilities in the mid- to late 1800s demonstrates the maturation of the United States and its understanding of the cost to build, and then maintain, its democracy. The question regarding who should rightfully participate in our democratic system dictated who should be educated, and the value placed on that democratic involvement, in turn, led to the realization that the public must finance it. The design of the schools built during this era also demonstrates the research that was conducted in North America and Europe on how to teach children most effectively, which coincided with the genuine concern for public safety and how buildings can protect from disease and illness. Bethune & Bethune were among a small group of architects who participated with their clients to find the best architectural solutions in educational design, one of the most pressing concerns of their day.

Educating for Democracy

According to educational historian Lawrence Cremin, the country's founders' aspirations for their future education system had four points, which reflected Enlightenment philosophy. First, democracy required an educational system that promoted piety, civility, and interest in learning. Second, American education would be a uniform system that would reflect American values and the country's culture. This modern education would be rooted in American language, literature, and culture to create an American character liberated from the one-thousand-year-old European system. Third, American education would be useful and designed to improve the human condition. Following Enlightenment-era principles, it would be based on the newly understood laws of nature through the sciences and laws of humankind through economics and politics. And fourth, the education system would be a model for others. As Cremin proclaimed, "The goal was nothing less than a new republican individual, of virtuous character, abiding patriotism, and prudent wisdom, fashioned by education into an independent yet loyal citizen."[2]

By the 1800s, the US saw exponential growth in population, through progressive immigration policy, and the establishment of new industry, brought about by the science and technological advancements of the Industrial Revolution. These two factors led to the country shifting from a rural society based upon an agrarian economy to an urban-based population employed in industry. This shift would dramatically impact the educational system within the US and the architecture that supported it. During this time, education in the country's cities would be transformed from the village schoolhouse model to an urban bureaucratic system.[3] Education now had to provide the context for the expectations of an industrial and professional life. Where rural life and the family-industry-based economy valued general literacy and mathematical competencies, the new industrial economy had very different expectations, where careers and employment were not inherited but earned, and a standard of professionalism needed to be established. New standards needed to be developed for school attendance, conduct, and attire, to provide the necessary skills for students to gain employment in the new industrial era.

School Architecture

The first American village schools were single-room buildings that were community run and accommodated children of various ages in one classroom. They were commonly known as grammar schools, which were based upon the British educational model.[4] The curriculum was largely focused on reading, writing, and arithmetic, although rural schools often relied on the curriculum content at hand.[5] More than simply places for education, schools often served as the center of the community's activities and served multiple functions, such as places of worship on Sundays and assembly halls in the evening. The communities themselves were rather small, their residents closely knit and maybe even related.

Early urban schools were built using the same model, with a single room to house all ages. As enrollments increased, so did the size of the schools. Eventually, these schools held large assembly halls, with rooms that sometimes accommodated more than one hundred children. One building might contain several of these assembly-style halls, and sometimes more than one teacher might be assigned to the room at the same time. Generally, the teacher was responsible for all the instruction there. The model allowed for a very high student-to-teacher ratio, which was economically advantageous for schools. Each district, usually encompassing a city neighborhood, might be served by a single schoolhouse, and a city might have many districts within its borders.

As the 1800s progressed, educational reformers began to advocate for schools with smaller class sizes. Architectural historian Dale Allen Gyure notes that the graded school concept originated in Boston in 1847 and had a far-reaching influence on school design.[6] Horace Mann, secretary of the Massachusetts Board of Education (1837–1848), and Henry Barnard, commissioner of public schools in Rhode Island (1845–1849) and superintendent of common schools in Connecticut (1850–1855), were particularly influential in establishing grading policies of school matriculation in the country. Both Mann and Barnard drew connections between the quality of education and school architecture. As Barnard wrote in *School Architecture*, there is a "close connection between a good school-house and a good school. . . . To make an edifice good for school purposes, it should be built for children at school, and their teacher."[7] Barnard also believed that school buildings could teach important lessons to students about organization, order, and beauty.[8] Quincy Grammar School-House in Boston was the first fully graded school in North America, which opened in 1847.[9] The four-story building was designed for seven hundred students, with four grades and three classes per grade. The symmetrical floor plan had a double-loaded corridor with two fifty-six-student classrooms on each side and a staircase at each end. The fourth floor contained a large assembly hall. This building established the standard of small class sizes and segregation of the student body based upon age and grade.

Neil Gislason observed that three factors led to educational architecture's modernization during the nineteenth century. First, an increase in government funding and political support for public education provided funding for new building. Education reformers often connected the design of the school to the quality of the instruction delivered. From this advocacy grew an understanding of the importance of public investment in institutional architecture, generally, and particularly in schools. The second factor was the impact the public health movement had on schools. The increased population in cities brought poverty and disease that, in turn, necessitated that civic leaders turn their attention to health and safety issues. Finally, the newly industrialized economy required expansion of the curriculum with courses in the natural sciences such as chemistry, physics, and technical courses, which required specialized teaching environments.

Several publications that were written between 1850 and 1885 described the importance of good design in educational architecture. In addition to Barnard's book, British architect Edward Robert Robson published the international survey, *School Architecture*, in 1874. The book provided a comprehensive study of educational architecture in the US, United Kingdom, Ireland, France, Austria, and Germany. He singled out Americans for their interest in improving education, noting, "No people make more determined efforts to obtain information on the subject of schools and schoolhouses from all available sources than those of the United States."[10] As American schools evolved in the 1800s, the German model provided their design precedent. Robson described the German education system and its schools as the best in the world. While the US was slowly implementing the graded system, Germany adopted "the separate or class system for every kind of school, high or low."[11] The German schools Robson profiled were remarkably sophisticated compared to those of other countries in the study. They had developed standards that are comparable to twentieth-century educational expectations. Class sizes were limited to fifty students. Schools were a maximum of three stories in height, with corridors that generally had multiple staircases or means of egress. As Gyure notes, lighting and ventilation were the most important considerations in schoolroom design in the nineteenth century. Buildings were planned around maximizing natural light, so windows were placed on the student's left side where possible.

Maximizing lighting, proper ventilation, and replicating the German educational architecture model deeply impacted American school design in the 1880s.[12] By then, some American urban districts were beginning to develop very sophisticated school buildings, as was demonstrated by the US Bureau of Education publication *City School Systems in the United States*, written by John Dudley Philbrick in 1885. Philbrick was a disciple of Barnard and had been a principal at the Connecticut State Normal School and president of the National Educational Association. His report provides a comprehensive survey of the regions that were incorporating innovative strategies in their school planning and design. He also identified general requirements for schoolhouse design: height, size, school furniture, ground plan, fireproofing, ventilation, orientation, gymnasium design, water closets, entries and corridors, stairs and stairways, and the assembly hall.[13]

James Crooker and the Growth of Buffalo Public Schools

The first public school to open in Buffalo was in 1807, but the building burned down in 1813, along with much of Buffalo, during the War of 1812. A tax was levied to build its replacement in 1818. It took until 1830 for additional schools to be opened, when five more were built. These were all very small buildings—mostly one-room schoolhouses—each a combination of wood frame and brick construction.

The Buffalo Public School District was not founded until 1837, five years after the City of Buffalo was incorporated. Unfortunately, it coincided with a national economic depression, which led to the failure of two short-term administrations. Finally, Oliver G. Steele, a successful businessman, was enlisted to serve in the unpaid position of school superintendent later that year. He oversaw the construction of six new schoolhouses and worked with the New York State Legislature to ensure the schools were tuition free, thereby making Buffalo's the first free public education system in the state that was funded solely through taxes.[14] Steele also organized the system into fifteen districts, each financially responsible for its own educational facilities. While some districts had schools built, others rented facilities.

As Buffalo grew in population, schools were slowly added to the inventory, the most significant being the opening of Central High School in 1852. That same year, the City of Buffalo annexed the nearby town of Black Rock, which expanded the geographic size of the city from four and a half to forty-two square miles. Free education was one of the overriding factors in the annexation, because Black Rock had three schools, which were all tuition supported.[15] This growth inspired the next phase of construction for the system, when ten new schools were built, many serving rural and lightly populated areas. These buildings were brick or wood construction, two or three stories high, and were designed to accommodate an assembly pedagogical model for large-group instruction.

The real transformation of the Buffalo schools occurred in 1882 when James Crooker was elected superintendent. He led the most ambitious capital plan for the system to date, which coincided with a dramatic population growth, due largely to a surge in immigration. Crooker noted: "Buffalo is no longer a village. It is a rapidly growing and prosperous city, and destined to be a great commonwealth, and it behooves its citizens to act with wisdom and liberty in providing for its public schools."[16]

Born in 1835, Crooker was from southern Erie County and moved to Buffalo in the early 1860s. An experienced educator and administrator, he served as principal of seven Buffalo public schools, with School No. 31 being his last.[17] He also had been active in the Democratic Party for years and served as chairman of the Second Ward of Buffalo starting in 1880. He was elected superintendent as part of a Democratic wave that also made Grover Cleveland mayor of Buffalo.

From the outset, Crooker distinguished himself as a reformer and focused particular attention on the creation of a capital plan to improve the condition of Buffalo's schools. In his first *Superintendent's Report* for 1882, Crooker cited the condition of the schools as unacceptable.[18] He was concerned about the small size of the buildings, the overcrowding of children in them, and their inferior and outdated designs—particularly the many rental facilities, which had very poor lighting and lacked ventilation or adequate sanitary measures. He stated, "I am fully persuaded that a large proportion of the mortality among the youth of Buffalo may be traced to the evil consequences of the over-crowding of the schools."[19] The press supported Crooker's concerns, with the *Buffalo Courier* applauding him for his advocacy.[20] The *Buffalo Sunday Morning News* was even more outspoken, placing the blame directly upon the Common Council, which funded and provided oversight of the school system. In an article dated June 14, 1883, the *News* enthusiastically endorsed Crooker's position, particularly emphasizing the poor lighting in the classrooms.[21]

In 1883, the schools had a collective capacity of 16,544 but 20,067 students were registered, resulting in overcrowded conditions throughout the system.[22] But it was difficult to gain political support to build better facilities, because individual districts were responsible for their own capital funding. Crooker fought to correct this problem and finally united the system as one district in 1884.

Another problem was that the citizens of Buffalo had not yet embraced the notion that the public should invest in schools—or at least the affluent did not embrace the idea. Crooker focused on School No. 10 in the Delaware District, the most affluent of the city, as emblematic of this lack of investment. The *Buffalo Courier* asked the obvious question: "How could the richest and most cultured district in the city, have tolerated the condition of its public school?" It provided an equally obvious answer: that the affluent were not sending their children to the public school but to one of the excellent nearby private schools.[23]

Thanks to his advocacy, on May 29, 1882, Crooker obtained the funding to build a new school for District No. 10.[24] Buffalo architect M. E. Beebe was awarded the $37,000 project. School No. 10 began the most ambitious capital program in the system's history. As with all the schools built under Crooker's administration, the focus was on providing small class sizes that were separated by grade. Of equal importance was providing natural light to combat poor eyesight in school children and proper heating and ventilation to address the spread of disease and mortality in young children.[25]

During his tenure, Crooker would oversee the construction of twenty-five new schools and twelve additions to existing schools. Also, the population soared from 20,067 students to 35,576.[26] Crooker served until 1891, during which time Buffalo invested in its schools in an ambitious capital program that modernized the city's school system. These new school buildings were designed by a handful of Buffalo architectural firms, which competed in a public procurement process for the commissions. Bethune & Bethune was one of the most successful firms in winning these contracts, completing ten projects, including seven new buildings and three additions, far exceeding the other architectural firms that also competed for this design work.

The first school commission Bethune & Bethune received was in District No. 16 (later renamed School No. 8). This was the second new school project built by the city during Crooker's tenure as superintendent. The Committee on Schools was charged with the selection of its architect in early 1883. Seven firms submitted designs for consideration, with H. & C. S. Ellis of Rochester, New York, the preferred designer, but their entry exceeded the project budget of $45,000, so it was rejected. Of the remaining six entries, R. A. (Robert) Bethune's was the first-place winner, followed by a close second place entry by C. K. Porter. The committee commended R. A. Bethune's design: "The arrangement of rooms are good; are commodious, well lighted and have a good system of ventilation. One especial feature of this gentleman's plan is the arrangement of its water closets, being outside of the main building and still connected with it, and so well arranged for ventilation that any disagreeable odors that may arise cannot interfere with the school room."[27]

School No. 8 is the firm's only school project that did not list both partners as its architects. Robert may have been solely credited because

Bethune & Bethune feared that a woman architect could not win such a large public commission. However, because Charles was born on April 23, 1883, Louise may not have been available to contribute to the design. Or both could have been true: that Louise was unavailable due to her pregnancy and the partners were concerned about discrimination.

Located at the corner of Utica and Masten Streets, School No. 8 was designed to accommodate a thousand students. The three-story, Queen Anne–style structure was built in brick with Ohio sandstone details. The corridor was flanked on both sides by classrooms and egress stairs at each end. The first floor accommodated the youngest children, the second the middle children, and the third floor the oldest, with each room grouping students by age cohorts. The building was designed to encourage small-group learning, with classrooms designed to hold approximately fifty chil-

Figure 5.2. Rendering of Buffalo School No. 8, Bethune & Bethune Architects, 1883. Crooker, *Superintendent's Report, 1883–1884*.

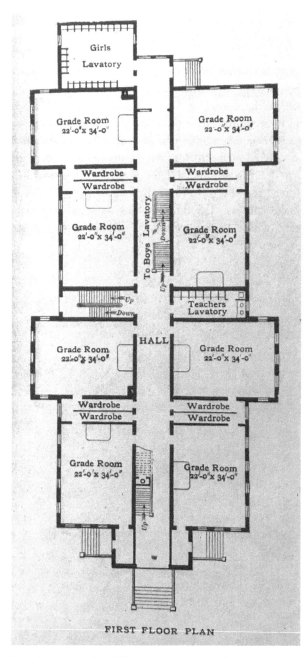

Figures 5.3. First-floor plan of Buffalo School No. 8, Bethune & Bethune Architects, 1883. Crooker, *Superintendent's Report, 1883–1884.*

dren, a similar size to the German model. The layout of each classroom was also based on the German standard, each with two exit doors, and the natural light from the exterior windows was intended to fall upon the student desks to the rear and left side. The window surface was designed to equal 25 percent of the floor area in each room.[28] Crooker noted that "those who have seen the plans . . . [believe it will be] the finest school building in the State, [and] probably take the lead over most of those in the country."[29]

In keeping with national standards, the architects focused attention on heating, plumbing, and ventilation. The *Buffalo Courier* article stated that Robert had studied various ventilation options and applauded his selection as a model for other schools. Each classroom was provided with both supply and return registers, situated to maximize heat and provide appropriate air circulation throughout the room. While a relatively simple plan, School No. 8 is a good example of architecture as a study in building science. The carefully conceived segregation of the age groups, the size and orientation of the classrooms, the consideration given to egress and general traffic of the students throughout the building—in addition to the study and attention paid to the mechanical and plumbing systems—demonstrate extensive research into an emerging building type. Crooker and the district teachers were also involved in the design process; he told the members of the Common Council that he expected all architects to consult with their clients as experts in education to avoid any unnecessary errors.[30] The success of this design established Bethune & Bethune for consideration for future schools and other public building commissions.

Crooker considered the new Buffalo schools built during this era as models in the art and science of educational design: "The department has been successful in having the most improved methods of school architecture carried into effect in the construction of the new buildings. . . . They are as perfect in sanitary conditions as the present knowledge and skill in the science and art of plumbing and other arrangements can make them."[31]

However, Crooker's claims that Buffalo established new national standards for educational building design should be placed in context. His annual reports were addressed to the members of the Common Council, who were politicians funding the most expensive expansion of educational architecture in the city's history. Nonetheless, the new schools certainly did demonstrate the city's investment in the public good and were examples of excellent educational design for their time. Crooker would work with all the architects selected to develop thoughtful designs and, in a very short nine years, turn Buffalo from being "twenty years behind the times," in his own words, to a single district with outstanding educational facilities.

When Crooker consolidated the Buffalo Public Schools into a single district in 1884, he created the flexibility to plan for new construction projects based upon neighborhood needs. A citywide district provided the tax base to implement his ambitious master plan. Crooker proved to be right, because the district continued to grow significantly in school attendance each year. Bethune & Bethune designed the first two buildings, Schools Nos. 38 and 39, under the new single-district model. The firm provided a description of the plans for these buildings to the city, giving us a rare glimpse of their design thinking. The floor plans featured hand lettering; we know that these were written by Louise through comparing the penmanship with other project drawings she authored, such as Police Station No. 2, which she submitted for her AIA membership application.

School No. 38 was designed to hold six hundred students in a small neighborhood on Buffalo's west side. The very small site was a 150-foot-by-156-foot corner lot, which resulted in an L-shaped floor plan. Bethune

Figure 5.4. Buffalo School No. 38, Bethune & Bethune Architects. Crooker, *Superintendent's Report, 1885–1886.*

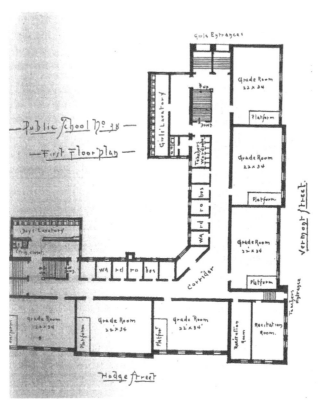

Figure 5.5. First-floor plan, Buffalo School No. 38, Bethune & Bethune Architects. Crooker, *Superintendent's Report, 1885–1886.*

& Bethune noted, "The charming, almost suburban, location of the site on two quiet streets, made it allowable to face each grade room directly on the street, while the corridors, wardrobes and lavatories occupy the rear portion of the building."[32] The diminutive Flemish Renaissance Revival building exuded a monumental character by placing the classrooms on the street sides of the corridors and featuring a symmetrical façade. The corner was marked with a square turret that held a two-tiered roof and eyebrow windows. The steep gable roofs of the two wings were punctuated with ornate gable end articulation, which was indicative of the style. The exterior was composed of brick and sandstone, and the roofs were of black Bangor slate. The smaller spaces, which held offices and utilitarian rooms, faced the interior of the site and allowed for considerable light in the corridors. The two-story building had six classrooms per floor, with the younger children on the first floor and the older children on the second floor. Each classroom was designed to hold fifty children and the teaching podium was situated so the exterior light would be on the student's left side, as per the German model. The basement held playrooms.

The architects gave special attention to the entrances of visitors and students. They placed the student entrances at each building end and hidden from street view, with the girls at one end and the boys at the other. Also, each of the two floors had a separate entry, to separate the children by age, in addition to gender. Visitors and teachers used the only door visible to the street, which was at the corner turret and near the principal's office. Although accessible from the main building, the lavatories were designed to function as separate from it, thereby isolating their ventilation. The architects also provided a description of the interior finishes. The floors were maple, the stairs and other trim were oak, and the furniture made of cherry wood. This provided a "wholesome and substantial appearance to the rooms and halls . . . enhanced by cheerful-colored woodwork and the softened light of the stained-glass window-heads."[33]

School No. 39 was, in Bethune & Bethune's opinion, "quite as perfect a building."[34] It was located on High Street on a large open lot with unobstructed light, giving the architects the freedom to expand; however, they chose to keep the building compact and symmetrical, with a layout closely resembling School No. 8. The cruciform arrangement allowed for entries at all four sides of the building. The two-story building was designed for eight hundred students and accommodated eight classrooms per floor. Thanks to the cruciform floor plan, many of the classrooms featured windows on two walls, and the classrooms were oriented in the German model to allow light to enter from the left of the students.

Many of the design features in School No. 38 were replicated in No. 39, so one may assume that the exterior and interior materials of the buildings were identical. However, their architectural styles differed. No. 38 directly addressed its street corner condition with the corner turret. The layout created the appearance of a much larger and more imposing building than it was. Children were protected here, as demonstrated in the monumental materials and the discreet entrances, which had them pass through schoolyard gates before they entered their private doorways. No. 39 was designed in the Queen Anne style and was set back on a large lot at the highest point in the city. The hipped roof over the cruciform building added to the monumentality of the building that was further exaggerated by the gable ends with brow windows, and the ornamental turret that was

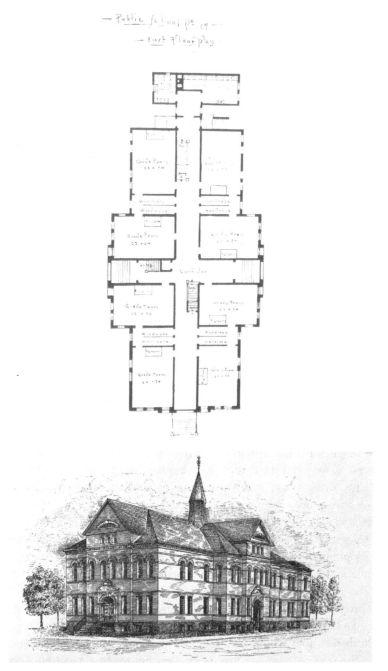

Figures 5.6 and 5.7. Buffalo School No. 39, Bethune & Bethune Architects. Crooker, *Superintendent's Report, 1885–1886.*

the building's focal point. The city budgeted No. 38 at $30,000, allowing $40,000 for No. 39 because of its larger size. It is to the credit of the architects that No. 38 achieved its monumental street presence despite this reduced amount.

The new buildings for the district were constructed of brick and, where possible, were two stories high as opposed to the three-story structures of wood construction previously erected.[35] Bethune & Bethune Schools No. 40 and No. 26 were two examples. These two-story brick buildings were designed in the Queen Anne style. No. 26 was designed to take advantage of its corner lot with a corner turret and public entrance, as did their earlier No. 38. No. 40 is unique in that the architects chose to emphasize the slightly elevated site with a front façade that soars with a steep gable roof and dramatic hexagonal turret. Arched windows and dormers accentuate the verticality.

Crooker always spoke of the need for state-of-the art ventilation and plumbing to ensure high sanitary conditions in the schools. In some annual reports, he dedicated pages to this topic to describe, in depth, the need to maintain these high standards and how he was ensuring they were met. Bethune & Bethune's School No. 48, on East Summer Street was designed with an innovative ventilation system. According to the *Buffalo Courier*, "Some radical changes have been introduced in the system of ventilation which was first introduced into the city schools by the same architects some years ago."[36] School No. 8 might have been the first school that featured innovations in ventilation, demonstrating the firm's contribution to the field at the regional, and even national, level. Opened in 1892, No. 48 was designed in the Beaux-Arts style, which was becoming fashionable in Buffalo. The monumental entrance portico predicted the firm's future work, while the roof dormers and cupola are reminiscent of their previous school projects.

The firm's attention to detail and particularly its concern that each school have proper ventilation is illustrated in an amusing exchange that Louise had with a local reporter for the *Buffalo Times* on September 4, 1886. The reporter was investigating an allegation of favoritism against the City of Buffalo public works commissioner regarding a contract for the ventilation equipment for two of Bethune & Bethune projects, School Nos. 18 and 31. The reporter paid an unannounced visit to the architects' office: "Mr. Bethune was absent but in his absence Mrs. Bethune, an accomplished lady with blonde hair and blue eyes who is herself a competent architect and her husband's able assistant, appeared to demand the reporter's business."

The reporter assumed that Louise was her husband's assistant, but he would soon learn that she had a deep understanding of all the issues regarding the buildings' ventilation systems. Asking Louise why they chose the specific type of ventilation equipment for these projects, she wryly asked why the question was being asked, and without waiting for a response, offered a long and in-depth answer describing how the equipment performed ("we have found that with less motive it spreads air more gently over large surface areas than any other"), in which building types it had been used, and in which significant buildings in the country it had been installed. Finally, she stated, "We have no preferences in the matter personally. . . . We have written to ask [the competitor] where it could be seen in operation but received no answer and are forced to conclude there are none of them in use in the city. We would always prefer to recommend home devices." The reporter left the firm's office completely satisfied in the "testimony of an expert utterly unaware she was justifying [the commissioner's decision] amply in the eyes of all sensible people and taxpayers."[37] The article nicely demonstrates Louise's expertise in the technical matters of building science, the ethics of the firm in their decision-making process, and her commanding personality.

In addition to these new buildings, Bethune & Bethune (& Fuchs) designed renovations for four Buffalo schools: Nos. 4, 20, and 33, and Central High School. The work for No. 4 was significant because Louise submitted it to the AIA in her admission portfolio, which suggests that she led this project.[38] School projects were mostly delayed during the mid-1890s, presumably due to the Depression of 1893. Bethune, Bethune & Fuchs was one of four shortlisted firms for the design competition for Masten Park High School in 1895. However, Beebe & Son was the successful architect in the selection process. After 1896, Bethune, Bethune & Fuchs designed just two projects for the Buffalo Public Schools, the new BPS No. 12 and an addition to Louise's alma mater, Central High School. While School No. 12 was built, the Central High School addition was canceled after the contract was bid due to lack of funding, which must have been a disappointment for her.[39]

In 1891, Crooker was appointed by Governor Roswell P. Flower to serve as the New York State superintendent of public instruction, a position he held until 1895.[40] However, his relationship with Bethune & Bethune continued, because the firm was hired to design his new home at Beeches Point, near Youngstown, New York.[41] He would live in this home until his death in 1919, a testimony to the strong professional relationship developed over years of important work between a reformer client and his passionate architects.

Lockport Union High School

Outside of Buffalo, Bethune & Bethune (and later Bethune, Bethune & Fuchs) designed several schools, most notably the Union High School in Lockport, New York, approximately twenty miles north of Buffalo. A major hub of the Erie Canal, Lockport was an affluent community in the late 1800s, which is apparent in the scale and design of the Union High School.

The Lockport school system was founded in 1821, and its first schoolhouse was opened in 1822. At this time, Lockport was little more than a wooded frontier village. Yet, the commencement of the construction of the Erie Canal led to a rapid increase in economic development along with dramatic growth in population. In 1835, the population in Lockport was six thousand, which doubled by 1850.[42] The town developed the first union school, or consolidated school district, in New York State. The Union School Act of 1847 consolidated a group of existing independent schools in the town under one single governing body and served as a model for other communities in the state and the nation.[43]

Bethune, Bethune & Fuchs designed a replacement for the original school that was built in 1848, immediately following the passage of the Union School Act. The Lockport Board of Education issued a bond of $30,000 to finance the site for the new school and circulated a request for proposals. Although Louise would later say that she opposed design competitions in keeping with the AIA's position, the firm participated regularly in them for school work.[44] Following design, the project was estimated, and supplementary legislation for a second bond was issued. Bethune & Bethune reported in *Inland Architect* in 1889 that the project budget was $57,000,[45] but the *Buffalo Morning Express and Illustrated Buffalo Express* stated on the occasion of the laying of its cornerstone on July 13, 1890, that the project cost was $100,000.[46] The board had probably started the project with a $57,000 budget but was prepared to raise significantly more money to build the Bethune & Bethune school.

The Lockport Union High School was by far the largest and most sophisticated of all of Bethune & Bethune educational projects. The Richardson Romanesque–style two-story structure was built in brick with "brown" stone, possibly Medina sandstone, details. The building's main entrance was augmented by a stone arch, which was replicated at the other six entries. There are several defining features of this building, but the most significant is the bell tower. Four stories tall, the tower had massive windows with stone lintels and was capped by a crenulated open room for the bell and a hipped roof. A small round turret above it further augmented the tower.

In the middle of the building, over the intersection of the main rectilinear building and the flanking wings, stood a square cupola.

The first floor of the building contained two eighty-person assembly rooms, seven recitation rooms, wardrobes, dressing rooms, the library, and administrative offices for the Lockport Board of Education. The second floor was dedicated to the senior class, and the rooms were designed to accommodate the two vocational programs offered in commercial and science education. The creation of the locks at Lockport was one of the engineering marvels of the nineteenth century, which may have contributed to the strong emphasis on science education. The basement held playrooms for boys and girls. The interior finishes were of natural wood.

No interior photos of the building from this early period have surfaced. However, a Sanborn map from the 1920s illustrates the interior plan, albeit in a rudimentary manner. The central oak staircase at the north of the building appears to have been a significant space. In 1915, the building received a major addition consisting of a third floor, a new front entry, and an auditorium and gymnasium on the south of the building. This final version of the Union School stood until 1956, when it was demolished and replaced with a third building.[47]

Figure 5.8. Lockport Union High School, Lockport, New York, Bethune & Bethune Architects, 1891. Courtesy of the author.

Chapter 6

Innovation, Industry,
and Entertaining the Public

1888–1900

Figure 6.1. Louise Bethune working at her drafting table, circa 1895. Zina Bethune Archive on Louise Bethune, circa 1860–1962. Courtesy of the University Archives, University at Buffalo.

By the late 1880s, Louise and Robert Bethune had grown their firm beyond residential work and had successfully delivered sophisticated projects in the educational and commercial sectors. They were now ready to advance to the next level in their design work and influence on the community. The 1890s was a dramatic decade for the couple. In 1891, the Bethunes made longtime protégé and employee William Fuchs the firm's third partner, as they continued to receive significant institutional work. Although the firm suffered during the Depression of 1893 and its aftermath, the period between 1888 and 1902 was marked with important, new commissions. By 1900, the firm was winning multiple significant commissions and expanding its portfolio in scale and building type that fostered innovation.

The Growth of the Architectural Profession and Development of an American Style

The architectural profession in America changed dramatically during this period. Between the end of the Civil War and the mid-1880s, American architecture was defined by energy and optimism in the economy and democracy. America opened its first architectural schools, beginning with MIT, in 1869. By 1881, there were six schools of architecture in the Northeast and Midwest. These schools were largely based on the curriculum of France's Ecole des Beaux-Arts, which focused on a rigorous study of classical architecture. However, some schools concentrated on English stylistic philosophies, while this period also saw an interest in creative eclecticism in architectural style, with French Second Empire and English High Gothic as the predominant styles. Archeological discoveries provided new material for creativity, and ever-new styles were added to the architect's portfolio. Creativity was cherished over authenticity. Second Empire, High Gothic, Eastern Stick, Eastlake, Queen Anne, Richardson Romanesque, and Victorian Romanesque are some of the most noteworthy styles that were in regular use during this time. Stylistic choices were associated with meaning and values.[1]

By the mid-1880s, leaders in the profession actively began searching for order from the chaos of the twenty previous years. Two of the leading architectural periodicals of the time, *Inland Architect and News Record* and *American Architect and Building News*, regularly published papers that rigorously discussed architectural styles, along with their historical context, to ensure the architect understood the environment in which these styles were born. John Root, of Burnham & Root, described this shift away from free interpretation of historic styles:

> During the rapidly shifting phenomena of our day the prob-
> lem presented to us is to determine which are ephemeral, and
> which will become fixed in the architectural foundations of our
> age . . . before every one of us has passed a kaleidoscopic pan-
> orama of styles, for whose original development three thousand
> years were required. To what extent may we call any of these
> rapidly dissolving architectural impressions our own? What in
> heavens name are the present tendencies of architectural design
> in the world? What are they in America?[2]

The argument for an American style was especially debated. Some architects, such as Louis Sullivan, sought this through their own response to the programmatic needs and technologies of the time. But it was more common for architects and their clients to revisit the better understood classical principles, the systemically taught stylistic principles of balance, harmony, and decorum of Renaissance and Classical architecture.[3]

The number of inventions and technological advancements during this period also contributed to the change in building design. The combi-nation of the invention of the elevator and the increase in production of steel provided architects the capability to build higher than ever imagined. The rapid growth of cities and rising land prices necessitated taller struc-tures on a narrow footprint. Inventions such as the typewriter in 1868 and the telephone in 1876 helped to define the work environment for which architects designed.[4]

New technologies led to new building typologies. In addition to the multifamily residence and schools, factories, office, and commercial build-ings were inventions of the nineteenth century, without an architectural precedent to follow. Finally, as America began to look toward the twentieth century, safety and security became paramount. No longer an emerging nation, the country became an economic powerhouse, and it sought to strengthen itself for safety at home, in the form of its police force, and borders in the form of its armed forces. Thus, police stations, penitentiaries, and armories were added to the urban fabric. Bethune & Bethune designed all these building types.

During this era, Bethune & Bethune designed their buildings in the Flemish, Italian, and French Renaissance Revival styles. There is little documentation on the reasons behind their stylistic choices, and many of their buildings have been lost. However, in reviewing the designs and building photos that are known, it is clear these choices were deliberate, and the factors contributing to the designs included the type of building, site constraints, the scale of the building, the urban context, and the budget. The building type and site appear to have been the dominant factors in the choice of style Bethune & Bethune selected. Many of their small retail buildings were designed in Renaissance Revival. The most significant of their Second Renaissance Revival buildings was the Buffalo Livestock Exchange. The never-realized Shea's Theater, which was located on a very constrained urban site, was designed in the Italian Renaissance Style, perhaps in reference to medieval Florence's congested urban landscape. The more flamboyant Flemish Renaissance style was chosen for market buildings, factories such as the Buffalo Weaving & Belting Co. Factory and the Seventy-Fourth Regiment Armory. These buildings were all located on street corners and, therefore, had more generous sites that provided panoramic views of the buildings, and more space for ornate details typical of the Flemish Renaissance style. All these projects are testimony to a firm that had the skills and fortitude to weather a significant economic depression, diversify their portfolio, and thrive in a regional market despite the prejudice against hiring a female-headed firm that they experienced within the public sector.[5]

The Depression of 1893

The last decade of the nineteenth century opened on a positive note, particularly in Buffalo. Starting in 1893, the city's favorite son, Grover Cleveland, was back in the White House beginning his second, nonconsecutive term as president. Buffalo's economy was booming and its population exploding. Architectural firms such as Bethune & Bethune were poised to enjoy a very productive decade. The firm was commissioned to design a new office building for prominent lawyer J. B. Greene at the corner of Main and North Division Streets. The brick building was expected to be fourteen stories high, which would have made it the tallest structure in Buffalo by six stories. Reports claimed that the building would have a street frontage of 50 feet and would be 180 feet in height "from the ground to the cornice." A bank was committed to occupy the entire first floor. While design drawings for the project have not survived, its ambition was described in the press: "The sketches show a magnificent front view, massive and singularly imposing."[6] Despite significant promise and excitement, the building was not constructed. Greene became ill in 1891 and passed away in 1893, which might have been the reason for the project's demise. This delay also coincided with the Depression of 1893, which brought about one of the most severe economic contractions in the country's history, so lack of financing may also have contributed to its failure.

The depression originated with a panic in the stock market that was not equaled until the Crash of 1929. The impact of the depression on the building industry was particularly severe. During the depression, the production of construction materials dropped by 60 percent and building capacity to 65 percent.[7] The depression was catastrophic for architects throughout the country. Just coming off the glory of the Columbian Exposition, where the public marveled at the architectural magnificence of the White City, architects finally had their opportunity to demonstrate the value of design excellence and their leadership role in the building industry in service to the public good. With the Panic of 1893, publicly funded projects evaporated, and large-scale commercial endeavors were placed on hold or canceled. J. W. McLaughlin, outgoing president of AIA Ohio, summarized the situation in 1894 when he referred to both the exposition and the depression in his address at the state convention: "We, as architects, can take pride in the exhibition our nation made to the world, showing what we could do in the way of superb effects. . . . It is hardly necessary to remind you of what you all are perfectly aware; that we have passed through a year of great financial depression, and our own profession has been one of the first to feel its effects."[8]

From 1893 through 1897, the *American Architect and Building News* (*AABN*) issued reports from cities throughout the US verifying the impact of the economic depression. It was particularly severe because of the pressures placed on labor costs. While the prices of building materials sank, labor costs rose as workers demanded higher wages, which was credited for the cancellation of many construction projects.[9] In 1897, *AABN* blamed the depression for the increase of suicides among architects in the 1890s, noting that "we cannot help feeling that it indicates that the vital resistance have been unnaturally lowered by the long strain and anxiety to which all professional men whose income is dependent on sporadic commissions have been subjected."[10]

Some firms did not survive the depression. In 1895, Chicago architect Dankmar Adler left the firm he shared with Louis Sullivan in search of work to support his family, thus ending one of the most important architectural partnerships in American history. Other architects survived on whatever projects came their way, like Bethune & Bethune. Between 1893 and 1896, the firm completed only one public project, which was the $10,000 new Buffalo Police Station No. 10. Otherwise, their portfolio during the depression was an eclectic collection of large and small projects, mostly from private sources. The Buffalo business community applauded itself for its "healthy conservatism," stating that this helped the city weather the storm of the depression.[11]

Architects had a different opinion on the dividends reaped from lack of investment in construction. In an article from November 10, 1896—just seven days after the election of William McKinley—members of the architectural community voiced their newly formed optimistic view. They and their colleagues in manufacturing commented on contracts that were signed as a result of the election. Finally, firms were busy again. Robert Bethune was one of the architects interviewed for the story; he noted, "We have closed a number of contracts since the election that would probably never have been closed . . . and we expect lively business right along. There is plenty of room for building in Buffalo if business is good. If business is at a practical standstill, as it has been for a time back, then Buffalo has more buildings than are needed."[12]

Until the Depression of 1893, public projects were an important aspect of the firm's business. After 1896, they designed only two projects for the Buffalo Public Schools, the new $42,000 School No. 12 and an addition to Bethune's alma mater, Central High School. While School No. 12 was built, the Central High School addition was canceled after the contract was bid, due to lack of funding (see chapter 5).[13] Otherwise, the firm's major work, in addition to the mainstay of its residential projects, consisted of industrial and commercial work. This shift was due in part to the depression. It also coincided with a bias against Louise from the municipal public sector that began to appear in the 1890s, as was reported in the *Buffalo Times* in 1901 (see chapter 2).[14] Louise was aware of this problem, noting (without providing examples) in her 1891 lecture "Women in Architecture" that women architects along with those in other professions were not treated equally to their male counterparts.[15] As Louise grew in stature regionally and throughout the country, city hall had to confront the fact that while Robert was the public face of the firm, with whom they dealt, Louise was not an assistant in the firm but an equal partner. Whether the dramatic loss in public commissions from the City of Buffalo was the result of the depression or prejudice, following the economic recovery and the opening of the twentieth century, the firm focused primarily on projects in the private sector.

Protecting Public Safety

Throughout the 1880s and early 1890s, Bethune & Bethune completed a series of public safety projects for the city and county, including designing six police stations and an addition to the penitentiary for women. While relatively humble in scope, the police stations were important to the advancement of the firm because Louise submitted one of these projects, Police Station No. 2, for her admission to the AIA. A small set of documents for this project, showing the basic floor plans, have been found that clearly show that she designed the building herself. Police Station No. 8 was built in 1886 and is an excellent example of the scale of the other stations designed by the firm, and, generally, of the stations in Buffalo. The two-story brick building had a budget of $16,000. The Renaissance Revival style provided an austere formality for a relatively small building that conveyed strength and security.

The most ambitious of these public safety buildings was the Erie County Women's Penitentiary, an addition to the existing women's holding facility. The budget for the project was $63,000. However, the bids came in at about $5,000 less, which is a testament to the architects' skill at working with their client and effectively within the constraints of the project. Located on Root Street, the three-story brick building was 53 feet by 150 feet. It housed fifty cells, baths, kitchen, scullery, two laundries, dining, ironing, and sewing rooms, and a hospital. The architect and client outlined their goals for this project in the local press, noting that the "alterations to the present building will make this one of the best prisons in the country. It will be fireproof in every detail."[16]

The Seventy-Fourth Regiment Armory Building was the first significant civic project for the couple outside of their work for the Buffalo Public Schools. This project is emblematic of these buildings that were constructed after the Civil War. According to Nancy L. Todd in *New York's Historic Armories*, there were approximately 120 arsenals and armories built in New York State from the mid-1800s to the early 1900s. The building type evolved from earlier arsenals (built between 1799 and the 1850s) that were utilitarian administration and munitions storage facilities for the militia. Following the Civil War, arsenals evolved into armory buildings, which were far larger, multifunctional, and more elaborate in architectural design, at a time when the National Guard flourished as the country's domestic peacekeeper.[17] Several armories were built in Buffalo alone during this time. The new armories were located in neighborhoods in the heart of the city for specific units of the state's militia. The locations were selected for easy access for the militia members and to build a community for them. Another purpose was to serve as a reminder of the military strength of the country during times of civic unrest. Todd states that the 1879 Seventh Armory on Park Avenue in New York City defined the new building type and served as a model for future buildings. It was certainly a model for Bethune & Bethune. The Seventy-Fourth Armory was centrally located at the corner of Elmwood Avenue and Virginia Street and was a Flemish Renaissance Revival–style brick building composed of two structures. The 61-foot-by-120-foot three-story administration building served as the main entrance on the street, and the 116-foot-by-120-foot drill hall was set directly behind it. The administration building accentuated several architectural features, such as the arched entry and a stepped gable at the third floor. The square turret at the corner of the building was topped by a pyramid roof, eyelid dormers, and an ornate wrought iron flag stand. The *Buffalo Morning Express and Illustrated Buffalo Express* reported in 1886 that Robert Bethune had visited the Seventh Armory to "get points to aid in the building of the [rifle] range," which was 285 feet long, making it the second largest in the country, and was based on its New York precedent.[18]

While the Seventy-Fourth Regiment Armory was demolished in 1945, leaving few interior photos and no floors plans, the existing Seventh can provide clues on the interior of Robert and Louise's building. The administration building of the Seventh was designed with a center main entrance that opened into a grand hall with an imposing staircase. On the first floor, off the central corridor were public and administrative rooms, with the veteran's room at one end and the board of director's conference room at the other. The façade of the Seventy-Fourth suggests a similar configuration, with a significant room in the corner turret.

Two types of buildings inspired the structures of all the drill sheds built during this time: the exposition great hall and the train station.[19] Both building types had implemented steel trusses, which provided the unobstructed spaces that marked the Grand Central Depot in New York (1871), the Crystal Palace in London for the Great Exhibition (1851), and the halls at the Centennial Exposition in Philadelphia (1876). The long span structural systems were exposed and were a defining feature of the building. Of course, large, open spaces with hard surfaces create acoustical problems that require a skilled architect to resolve.

Figure 6.2. Seventy-Fourth Regiment Armory, Bethune & Bethune Architects. Courtesy of the author.

When the Seventy-Fourth Armory Building opened, it was celebrated by the military and the larger community: "The [design] . . . was inspected under the most favorable circumstances, the occasion being a reception and dress parade tendered the county supervisors by the militia."[20]

In 1899, the Seventy-Fourth Regiment moved to a new facility on Connecticut Street, which is its home today. The Bethunes' building was then used as the Elmwood Music Hall until 1938, when it was demolished. The mere fact that the building became the premier music venue in Buffalo in the early 1900s is a testament to the acoustical proficiencies of the space and the Bethunes' technical skills. They used the Seventy-Fourth Armory as a model for the design of the W. J. Connors Social and Athletic Club, which was built in 1896.

Designing for Commerce and Entertainment

Starting in the 1890s, the firm took on increasingly more commercial and entertainment projects, ranging from relatively modest shops and offices to significant multistory buildings and markets, which were ubiquitous throughout Buffalo. As the Bethunes' prestige and network grew in the city, so did the opportunity to work on interesting entertainment venues, such as a baseball grandstand, a theater, and beach resort.

One significant project was very close to home, because they were also the client: a new office location for the firm at Franklin and Huron Streets in 1891. As further evidence of the dominant role Louise continued to play in the firm she founded, she purchased five renovated brick buildings for offices, saving the corner building for the firm's office and rented the remaining four to outside tenants.[21] They were only in this location for seven years, because Louise sold the property in December 1898 for $30,000.[22] One must assume that Louise reaped a substantial profit because the sale occurred after the end of the depression.

Buffalo had many markets at this time in various neighborhoods that served an array of purposes. Bethune & Bethune was involved in the design of several new or renovated markets. The Elk Street Market, established in 1845, was one of the largest venues in the city. It was originally designed in the Greek Revival style, complete with an octagonal cupola and main building flanked with a Doric colonnade. By the 1880s, the market was very worn indeed, and it had dramatically expanded to encompass two city blocks on both sides of Elk Street. Bethune & Bethune was retained to design a $12,000 renovation and addition in 1889. The project included modernizing the original building and adding a new shed to house some of the outdoor stalls, which dwarfed the activity of the original building.

The Elk Street Market renovation led to other similar projects, such as renovations to the Clinton Market and the new Black Rock Market. When the press announced the plans for a new, privately owned market in the Black Rock neighborhood, it was welcome news for citizens in North Buffalo, who had long petitioned for one.[23] Reports noted that their plan would result in "a commodious, substantial building, not quite as large as the present markets, but constructed on more modern lines."[24]

The firm designed the $100,000 building in the Flemish Renaissance Revival style. The three-story, L-shaped, brick building was three hundred feet by fifty feet on the West Street (main) elevation. It was planned to hold two rows of twenty stalls flanking a sixteen-foot-wide center aisle. In many respects, it was similar to the original Elk Street Market of 1845 as well as the ancient Greek Agora, where all the activity was confined to the interior and portico of the building. The thirty-foot portico roof rested on the colonnade for the outside stalls and pedestrians walking around the market. Unfortunately, the private investor withdrew from the project later in 1903. Because the City Council had declared a resolution in support of the market, it was then pressured to fund it publicly.[25] Sadly, this was not to be. The Black Rock Market was never built due to its cost and lack of political will.[26] Of all the firm's buildings that were never realized, this one is the most unfortunate. Flemish Renaissance Revival was relatively rare in this very eclectic era, and Bethune & Bethune kept it in their arsenal of stylistic choices. Today, none of its buildings in this style survive.

The Robert K. Smither store however is still standing. Smither was a druggist in business with George Thurston, with multiple drug stores throughout Buffalo. In addition to being a successful businessman, Smither was also very prominent in the community and Buffalo politics. For years he was active in the Erie County Pharmaceutical Association and the Queen City Society for the Prevention of Cruelty to Children. A leader in the local Republican Party (of which Robert and Louise's father were active members), Smither was a city alderman throughout the 1890s, and in the late 1880s he served on the Erie County Penitentiary Board. He was on this board when Bethune & Bethune designed the Women's Prison, which might explain why he commissioned them for the new branch of his store in 1899.

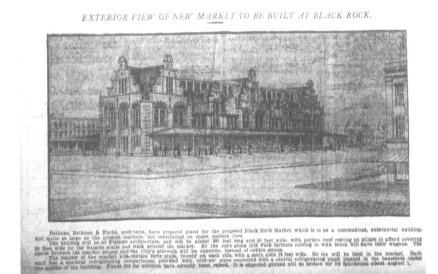

Figure 6.3. Rendering of Black Rock Market, Bethune, Bethune & Fuchs Architects. *Buffalo Evening News*, July 23, 1903.

Figure 6.4. R. K. Smither Building, Bethune & Bethune Architects, built in 1889.
Photo by Douglas Levere, University at Buffalo.

The Smither Building was typical of the mixed-use buildings in Buffalo
at the time, with commercial activities on the street level and residential
quarters above. It housed two storefronts on the first floor and apartments
on the second and third floors. The three-story, red brick structure was
designed in the Italianate style. The first story façade was a symmetrical cast
iron, brick, and glass storefront with pilasters at each corner. A clerestory
window facing the street corner featured the words "DRUGS * CANDY"
inset in stained glass, identifying the Smither & Thurston Pharmacy. The
front chimneys had decorative dental brickwork as well. Bethune & Bethune
completed an addition to the Smither Building in 1890, immediately upon
completion of the original structure.

Like the Smither Building, the Jehle Grocery is still standing. Built
in the Renaissance Revival style, the commission was probably a result of
a personal connection with the client. Fred Jehle was a very well-respected
merchant in the heart of what is now the Elmwood neighborhood. He
opened his grocery store in 1874, and by the late 1890s his daughter was
married and his two sons were in business with him. When it was time for
a new store, he commissioned Bethune & Bethune for the project. While

Figure 6.5. Jehle Grocery, Bethune, Bethune & Fuchs Architects, built in 1899. Photo by Douglas Levere, University at Buffalo.

there is no evidence as to why he chose their firm, Will Fuchs and his wife, Dorothea, lived just a half a block away from the Jehle's 311 Bryant St. store, at 193 Ashland Ave. One can easily imagine that Dorothea shopped there regularly. Fuchs's father, Augustus, and uncle Julius, known as the Fuchs Brothers, also ran a grocery, wine, and cigar wholesaling business, which is another possible connection. Also, both German families were active in the Roman Catholic Church. It is clear from the press that Jehle was an engaged client, noting that the new "attractive building [was] being erected according to his suggestion."[27]

The Disastrous Fuchs Brothers Building

One of the most dramatic and damaging incidents for the firm occurred with the collapse of the Fuchs brothers office building. Designed by junior partner Will Fuchs—also one of its developers—this failure hurt the firm's reputation while revealing the need for updated local building codes as more ambitious new buildings were constructed.

Originally, in January 1895, the Fuchs brothers were hired by Michael Shea, the proprietor of Shea's Music Hall, to build a theater on land that they owned on Washington Street. This was the first development scheme pursued by William and his brother Edwin. Because Will was one of its owners, he led the project as the architect in charge of construction for the Bethune firm. The $150,000 project was designed to be 90 feet wide, 160 feet deep, and 75 feet high, and would replace another large Shea's theater, which had been lost in a fire.[28] The design was developed to the point where the architects released an elevation of the front façade, which "follows the style of the Italian renaissance and is simple and unpretentious, yet tasteful and pretty."[29] One month earlier it was described as "the finest music hall in the country outside of New York."[30] While floor plans have not survived, newspaper accounts described the general layout and listed the location of the rooms, stating that the design was nearly complete. Great care was made to separate the bar and limit any drinking to the balcony area, and to use high-quality interior finishes to underscore the propriety and dignity the proprietor wished to convey. While there might be vaudeville acts that pass through, this music hall was to compete with older, more established theaters for other types of attractions as well.[31] However, by May, the project was abandoned due to a lack of financial support, possibly due to the depression. The terms of the agreement stipulated that the Fuchs Brothers would build the theater, and Michael Shea would commit to a ten-year lease of the venue. However, the developers had difficulty securing a loan for a music hall and were forced to serve notice to Shea and withdraw from the project.[32]

Instead, the Fuchs Brothers proceeded with the design of a mixed-use project. The new four-story brick building would cost $30,000 and would accommodate commercial activity on the first floor and apartments on the upper three floors.[33] This relatively modest mixed-use project ultimately exposed through great tragedy a serious flaw in municipal construction standards that would demonstrate the need for rigorous building codes. Construction injuries were common during this period, and the Fuchs Office Building was no exception. In fact, a serious injury was reported just two weeks after the building permit was issued. A laborer was accidentally buried to his chin during the excavation of the site.[34] But the worst was yet to come. On December 19, a rear wall of the nearly completed building fell outward and, ultimately, the entire wall was lost. Luckily, the accident occurred late in the afternoon, and none of the construction crew members were injured. The foreman attributed the incident to frost in the mortar, and plans were made to replace the wall.[35] Two days later, the roof collapsed, demolishing floors below in the process. The crew anticipated this failure, and construction had already been halted. City officials were called in to oversee the site.[36]

John Reimann, superintendent of buildings for the City of Buffalo, proclaimed the fault was in construction means and methods as dictated by the city, and no fault of the architects. The contractors were following the construction standards at the time, but these were outdated for the size and complexity of the building. His report on the accident stated: "The building laws now in use were the first and only ones framed, and for the modern system of building now in use are no longer adequate. This has long been the opinion of architects in this city, and a comparison with the building ordinances of other cities will convince one that this view is correct."[37]

In the aftermath of the collapse of the Fuchs Office Building, early in 1896 Superintendent Reimann suggested that Buffalo hire an architect for the purpose of designing and assuming the professional responsibilities of projects funded by the City of Buffalo. Members of the AIA's Buffalo/ Western New York chapter reviewed this proposal, ironically at the Bethune, Bethune & Fuchs office. They objected to the city's plan on the grounds that a city employee could not deliver a project of the quality nor as economically as architects in private practice could. They cited examples of other cities such as Boston and Chicago, which had experimented with an employee architect in the 1880s but had abandoned the model because it was costly. Instead, they advocated for the selection of consulting architects through a competitive process by an expert and impartial jury.[38]

The architects were certainly concerned about a potential loss of commissions if an in-house architect designed all public work funded by the city, but they were also concerned about the quality of design. These issues previously had arisen concerning the design and designer for the new US Post Office in Buffalo. The Tarsney Act had been passed by Congress in 1893, which required architectural competitions for significant federal buildings. The AIA had been assured the architect would be selected by a national competition. However, in March 1894, Henry G. Carlisle, the US secretary of the treasury, announced that the supervising architect Jeremiah O'Rourke, a federal employee, had prepared a design that had been approved prior to the signing of the Tarsney Act. Led by President Daniel Burnham, the AIA fought this decision at both local and national levels on the grounds of improving the quality of architectural design of public buildings. While the AIA was unsuccessful in its lobbying efforts regarding the design of the Post Office, it successfully opposed Reimann's plans; municipal projects continued to be completed by private architectural firms.[39]

The Fuchs Office Building disaster was an example of the many competing pressures for architects at the turn of the nineteenth century. With the profession still in the process of defining itself, the need to maintain quality in construction and design and the efforts architects took to gain credibility, especially with the government, were issues that they would struggle with for years to come.

New Opportunities

As Bethune & Bethune began to leverage its growing network and reputation, opportunities arose for the firm that might otherwise not have been available to it. And, in general, the projects with the most opportunity for design and innovation were in the commercial and entertainment sectors. One unique project was Woodlawn Beach Resort. Like so many that opened during this era, this destination provided a recreational opportunity for people of all classes, just as they were flocking to urban centers. It was part of an international vacation movement that led to resorts opening on coastlines throughout Europe and North America. Eventually, these resorts became so popular that they spread to interior lakefronts in New York, Michigan, and Ontario, Canada.

Cottage Company had purchased 150 acres of land on the south shore of Lake Erie, just outside of Hamburg, New York. The land had a mile and a quarter of lakeshore and a beach that was excellent for swimming. The developers intended to build a pier to accommodate a steamboat and a "first-class summer resort, with a fine hotel, dancing pavilions, and other summer attractions."[40] The following month, Bethune & Bethune announced that they had been selected as the architects.[41]

The resort was opened on August 2, 1892. It boasted a pier to accommodate the steamboat *Corona*, bathing facilities, restaurant, dancing pavilion, toboggan slide into the water, roller coaster and carousel, and ice cream pavilion. By the following year, the Woodlawn Beach Company had divided its land into properties for purchase and had placed them on the market.[42] By 1894, newspapers were reporting the tremendous success of the resort, with 1,600 people staying that summer. Some were camping, some were housed in temporary cottages, and others were patrons of the Woodlawn Heights Hotel,[43] the only property for which there is a historical photo, which opened in 1893.[44] The hotel was a simple Queen Anne, three-story, wood frame structure with a commanding hipped roof and two-story front veranda. Given the close time between the announcement of the resort and the opening of the hotel, one must assume that Bethune & Bethune designed all the original structures of the resort, including the hotel. The number of attendees grew each year, peaking at five thousand per summer season.[45] Woodlawn Beach Resort remained open for decades but never regained the allure of its early years in the 1890s.

Another seasonal building was the baseball grandstand for the Buffalo Bisons. In 1889, Buffalo's baseball team moved to a new location at Michigan Avenue and East Ferry Street. The site was originally called Olympic Park, and Bethune & Bethune received the commission to design the new grandstand and fence. Bids were awarded in February 1890, and the project was completed later that year.[46] The grandstand was a relatively modest structure, which could accommodate several thousand people. It was an L-shaped pavilion that encompassed the entire infield, extending approximately from first to third bases. An enclosed upper viewing dormer defined the intersection of the gable roofs at each side. In 1907, the park's name was changed to Buffalo Baseball Park. The Bethune & Bethune grandstand remained in use until 1923, when it was demolished and replaced with a concrete structure known as Offermann Stadium.[47]

The Buffalo Livestock Exchange Building brought tremendous attention to the firm and client. In 1890, it was the second largest exchange in the country. Construction plans for its new home were celebrated in the press: "As the drawing shows, it is to be a substantial, handsome building, creditable alike to the architects who designed it and the association that will own and occupy it."[48] Located on the east side of Buffalo, the exchange was comprised of the three-story Bethune & Bethune building and seventy-five acres of land to hold the yards for the livestock.

Construction for the building began in late July 1890; the building opened in 1892 at the corner of William and Depot Streets, directly across from the New York Stock Yards. The $60,000 building measured 120 feet by 90 feet. The Second Renaissance Revival structure was primarily brick. Arched and double-hung windows were lined with stone sills, and the cornice and onion-shaped cupola were clad in copper. The oak doors at the main entrance vestibule on Williams Street had an ornamental iron fence and grills. The building was used for managerial and public use. The basement contained a restaurant, kitchen, pantries, and barbershop. The first and second floors housed the Stock Exchange offices, and the third floor held a forty-seven-by- eighty-seven-foot public hall and ticket offices. The building's design—housing a relatively utilitarian function—continued to be celebrated into the twentieth century.

As the nineteenth century drew to a close, Bethune & Bethune began to receive a growing number of commissions for factories, while Buffalo's

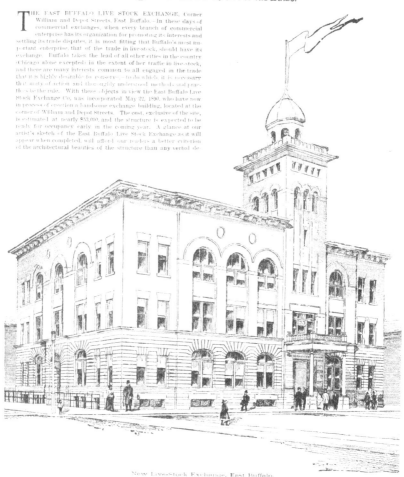

THE EAST BUFFALO LIVE STOCK EXCHANGE, Corner William and Depot Streets, East Buffalo.—In these days of commercial exchanges, when every branch of commercial enterprise has its organization for promoting its interests and settling its trade disputes, it is most fitting that Buffalo's most important enterprise, that of the trade in live-stock, should have its exchange. Buffalo takes the lead of all other cities in the country (Chicago alone excepted) in the extent of her traffic in live-stock, and there are many interests common to all engaged in the trade that it is highly desirable to conserve,—to do which it is necessary that unity of action and thoroughly understood methods and practices be the rule. With these objects in view the East Buffalo Live Stock Exchange Co. was incorporated May 22, 1890, who have now in process of erection a handsome exchange building, located at the corner of William and Depot Streets. The cost, exclusive of the site, is estimated at nearly $53,000, and the structure is expected to be ready for occupancy early in the coming year. A glance at our artist's sketch of the East Buffalo Live Stock Exchange as it will appear when completed, will afford our readers a better criterion of the architectural beauties of the structure than any verbal de-

New Live-Stock Exchange, East Buffalo.

scription. The officers of the exchange are as follows: president, John Hughes; vice-president, Norman W. Ransom; secretary, W. S. Kerr, treasurer, R. W. Watkins; trustees W. A. Reinhart, B. Williamson, Joseph Stevens, Ira Ivey, W. S. Kerr, Hiram Waltz, L. A. Leeck, Harry Hole, George W. Stacy, C. Kline. The principles upon which this organization has been founded, as well as the rules for its guidance, cannot but inspire universal confidence, and we predict for it a growth in business and influence, wealth and membership in a ratio proportionate to the ever-increasing development of the Queen City of the Empire State.

Figure 6.6. Buffalo Livestock Exchange, Bethune & Bethune, 1890. George M. Bailey, *Illustrated Buffalo: Queen City of the Lakes.*

industrial sectors continued to expand. The firm continued to receive these commissions through the next decade, and its designs would be consistent with the more modern structures built in the Midwest during this time, which led the way to the modern movement (see chapter 9). Here we review those factories that reflect the architectural styles of the Gilded Age when factory life was beginning to become a vital force in Buffalo.

The most significant of the firm's factories from this era is the Buffalo Weaving & Belting Company Factory at 234 Chandler St., which became a major industrial zone at the turn of the century. Located in North Buffalo, Chandler Street borders the historic Black Rock neighborhood and, more importantly in the late 1800s, the Beltline of the New York State Railroad. The Beltline was developed after the Civil War, as part of a general railroad network expansion within the Great Lakes. Along the Beltline was a series of nodes with industrial and pedestrian access points that facilitated the opening of several new industrial zones, including on Chandler Street, where the Weaving & Belting Company was an early and essential presence. The company began to build in 1892 and quickly expanded to have one of the largest factories in this district. Bethune & Bethune designed three fireproof factory buildings for it in 1903.

The construction documents for the Flemish Renaissance Revival–style one-story brick structure have survived. The building was typical of nine-

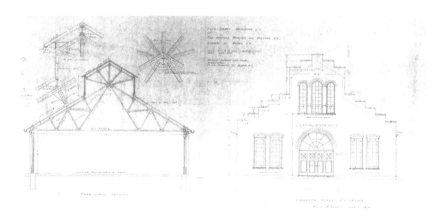

Figure 6.7. Buffalo Weaving & Belting Company Factory, front elevation, June 1903. Courtesy of the author.

teenth-century factory design in that it was composed of one very long and narrow structure, which was the most economical to build and allowed for the most natural light. The skylight that was incorporated in an open-truss roof structure allowed for maximum natural light and dictated the design of the front façade. The stepped brickwork along the roof gable perfectly camouflaged the skylight from street view. The upper triple-arched windows provided additional light into the truss and sat in the center of the gable. This south elevation provided the only ornamentation on the building. On the street level, the front entry was composed of four doors, over which sat a semicircular clerestory arch with fan-light tracery. Two arched windows flanked the front entrance. The other two buildings were designed with consistent vocabulary, albeit more simply. Sadly, the first building was destroyed by fire in 2002.

. The Cosack & Koerner Company Lithography Plant is another example of factory design in the late nineteenth century. Cosack was the largest printing company in the US, propelled by its successful commission for printing the exhibit material for the Centennial Exhibition in Philadelphia in 1876. In 1885, Bethune & Bethune was commissioned to design the home for the ever-expanding company to hold the art, printing, and administrative functions in one building. The fact that Louise and Robert received this important commission so early in their careers is a testament to the reputation they already enjoyed. The three-story brick building held the "largest press-room in the United States, measuring 70 by 200 feet and 40 feet high, without a single post; partition; belt, shaft or pulley. . . . The roof is supported by 14 trusses of immense strength, resting on brick and stone abutments."[49] A contemporary illustration demonstrates the importance of proper lighting in this factory building and illustrates how the structure was organized and used.[50] Interestingly, the building featured several technologic innovations for its time, such as incandescent light for the entire plant, with power generated by two boilers in the building's basement.

Ben Sabins, a tenant in the Elk Street Market, hired the firm to design a $7,000 warehouse at 586 Michigan Street in 1892. The firm also was hired to design a four-story store and factory for Sarah Howard a year after her husband, Howell Howard, passed away. The $18,000 building was located at 208–212 Terrace, replacing a two-story industrial building owned by Howard Iron Works. We can imagine the appeal of employing a female business pioneer to design a project for new entrepreneur Sarah Howard.

In August 1898 Bethune & Bethune filed plans with the City of Buffalo for a temporary brick terminal station for the Cataract Power and

Conduit Company on its property at 2290 Niagara Street. The permanent station would be built the following year.[51] The engineering accomplishment that enabled the generation of electricity at Niagara Falls was one of the great breakthroughs of the day, ushering in the modern technological age by providing the infrastructure required for future discoveries. Bethune, Bethune & Fuchs played a small part in the project to transmit electricity to Buffalo from Niagara Falls.

Figure 6.8. Cosack & Koerner Company Lithography, Bethune & Bethune 1885. Illustration from Elstner Publishing Company, *The Industries of Buffalo: A Resume of the Mercantile and Manufacturing Progress of the Queen City of the Lakes,* 1887.

Finally, in 1898, Bethune & Bethune designed a factory for Joseph A. Oaks, at Grote and N.W. Switch for the new Jav-O Cereal Coffee Company, of which he was a director. That company would go out of business in 1900, and the property sold.[52] The $5,000, two-story building was modest compared to the other projects for which Oaks hired the firm. That same year, they designed a $10,000 residence for his family on Parkside Avenue (see chapter 4), and Oaks was an early financial investor in the Lafayette Hotel (see chapter 9). He would play an instrumental role in Bethune & Bethune receiving this commission, which would be the most important in the firm's portfolio.

Chapter 7

Riding into the Future

The Wheelwoman and Feminist

Every woman her own architect.

—Louise Bethune

Figure 7.1. Photo of Louise Bethune with her bicycle on a country ride, circa 1890. Zina Bethune Archive on Louise Bethune, circa 1860–1962. Courtesy of the University Archives, University at Buffalo.

Susan B. Anthony famously said in an interview, "Let me tell you what I think of bicycling. I think it has done more to emancipate women than anything else in the world. It gives women a feeling of freedom and self-reliance."[1] One of the most fascinating aspects of Louise Bethune's life is that she was a founding member of the Buffalo Women's Wheel and Athletic Club, the second women's bicycling club in the United States. Louise's role in this new and controversial pastime demonstrates her maverick spirit and commitment to women's equality. This chapter will explore how the bicycling craze impacted the women's movement through fashion and challenging what a woman could physically do. Similarly, early women architects questioned society's belief in women's lack of physical capabilities. Both endeavors challenged what the world thought a woman in a dress could—and should—do.

A common assumption about Louise is that she was not a feminist. This is largely because of a comment made in her address to the Women's Union in 1891: "The objects of the business woman are quite distinct from those of the professional agitator. Her aims are conservative rather than aggressive; her strength lies in adaptability, not in reform, and her desire is to conciliate rather than to antagonize."[2]

But Louise demonstrated in many ways her belief in women's equality. She was part of a small but necessary cohort of women who served as a bridge between the True Woman and the New Woman, two ideals of womanhood. The True Woman cherished the traditional role of woman as mother and caretaker of the home, versus the New Woman, an independent professional woman who pursued outdoor activities and considered herself equal to men. Women bicyclists, or wheelers as they were called, came to symbolize the New Woman movement during the Gilded Age. As a founding member of Buffalo's women's bicycle club, Louise was at the forefront of the wheeling craze that defined an era.

When the safety bicycle was invented in 1887—with its two wheels of equal size, a lower and more stable seat, and chain-and-sprocket mechanism—it provided women the ability to navigate the urban landscape with an independence that was never before imagined. But it took trailblazers in every city to give wheeling respectability and to become an accepted activity for women to pursue which, in turn, provided them with the confidence to challenge various other aspects of their station as women. The Gilded Age's fashion norms restricted the activities of women, professionally and in recreation. The confining corset and long skirt with heavy and cumbersome bustle greatly hindered the movements of women and were impossible to wear while on a bike. The wheeling craze demanded less restrictive cloth-ing, which confronted conventional Victorian women's attire, as did the profession of architecture.

The Wheelers of Buffalo

The modern bicycle owes its origins to the velocipede, which was unveiled in the summer of 1817 by the German Karl von Drais. For years Drais had been working to develop a horseless carriage. After several failed attempts at four-wheeled, human-powered vehicles, his velocipede or "running machine" held the public imagination for a few years. The wooden contraption looked much like bikes of today, without the pedals or chain. Riders sat on the seat and propelled ahead using their feet. A pastime of the wealthy and leisurely, the velocipede grew in popularity in Europe and the US for a few years until its riders were considered a nuisance on the streets. Eventually, it sank into oblivion while inventors pursued the notion of a mechanical horse—on two, three, and four wheels.

By the early 1870s the high-mount bicycle, also known as the ordinary, proved to be much more roadworthy, due to its new padded rubber tire that absorbed shocks and suspended the rider sufficiently high enough off the dusty roads. These new machines grew in popularity across the globe, and especially in Buffalo. Given the height of the ordinary and the difficulty it took to master riding it, it was still seen very much as a young man's rec-reational activity, and advertisements of the day celebrated the masculinity of its users. The invention of the tricycle provided opportunities for women and older or less athletic men to engage in the new sport. But it was not until the design of the "safety" bicycle in 1886 that wheeling graduated from being a novelty for daredevils to the transformational pastime of the age. This new bicycle had rubber pneumatic tires, spring seat, pedals attached to chain and sprocket, and was safe and comfortable to ride. The bicycle quickly gained popularity among the middle and upper classes in cities across Europe and the US.

In Buffalo and other cities, young men took to their two wheels with vigor, and soon began to create clubs such as the Buffalo Bicycle Club, which was founded in 1879. As a progressive and prosperous city in the mid-1800s, Buffalo became a special place for the bicycle craze that hit the US. The excellent condition of its roads helped; by 1896 Buffalo had two hundred miles of streets paved with asphalt.

Some saw the bicycle as a viable replacement for the horse in everyday urban life. At a cost of $150, the safety's price was approximately equal to that of a horse. And the bicycle did not require a stable or food to maintain it as the horse did. There was also the danger of riding a horse or relying on horsepower to pull wagons and buggies. This hit home to the Bethune family when Robert Bethune was injured while riding in a horse and buggy with two male colleagues in 1891. The horse was startled and took off; one man jumped and the other was thrown, leaving Robert as the sole passenger remaining on the wagon until the rough terrain destroyed it. The press stated that he endured "a great shock to his nervous system in addition to the bruises."[3]

While the bicycle offered nothing but endless amusement and physical activity for male riders, the pastime was fraught with difficulties for women who took up the sport, even following the invention of the safety. There was much concern that riding a bicycle would lead to the loss of a woman's virtue, because they now had the freedom to ride without a chaperone or companion, which was a social convention for Victorian girls and young women. The bicycle was also considered dangerous to women's health. Some physicians warned that riding a bike could lead to infertility for women or sexually arouse them, and others cautioned that the strenuous activity was too much for them to bear. Finally, there was the matter of women's clothing. Contemporary dress featured a full-length skirt, bustle, and corset. This costume was not conducive to athletic activity and could be unsafe to wear on a bicycle; women who chose to pursue the activity were forced to make accommodations to their clothing. This gave new life to arguments for dress reform and placed the wheel woman at the heart of the suffrage movement. While Louise is not known as an activist, her membership in the Buffalo Women's Wheel and Athletic Club demonstrates her belief in women's rights and parallels her fight for equality as a practicing architect.

By 1893 there were no fewer than six bicycle clubhouses in Buffalo: the Buffalo Bicycle Club at 132 College; Comrades Cycling Club; Press Cycling Club at 380 Franklin; Ramblers Bicycle Club at 531 Main; the Wanderers Bicycle Club on Fillmore Avenue; and the Women's Wheel and Athletic Club, which used space at 132 College. The most preeminent men's wheeling club at the time, the Ramblers Club, was cofounded by Richard F. Kelsey, who founded the National Cycling Association before moving to the city. When he joined the editorial staff at the *Buffalo Express*, Kelsey brought his enthusiasm for the bicycle with him and helped create the Ramblers, widely promoting the merits of bicycling in his new home city.[4] The Bethunes' younger partner, Will Fuchs, was an avid cyclist, first riding the ordinary bicycle and then moving on to the safety, and was a longstanding member of the Ramblers.

One of the reasons bicycling was so popular in Buffalo was the condition of the streets. By the early 1890s, Buffalo had the most paved streets in the country, more than Paris and London combined. As the *Buffalo Courier* noted: "In no city has the evolution of the wheel been witnessed more conclusively than in Buffalo, from the old bone shakers used in the early days down to the nearly perfect lightweight of to-day. Old time cyclists have seen this change, and there are wheelmen living in Buffalo to-day who have been devotees of the silent steed from its earliest stages to the present time."[5]

The quality of its paved roads more than made up for the relatively short cycling season due to the abundance of snow for which the city is known. While Buffalonians could only ride six months out of the year, those

Figure 7.2. Will Fuchs (*far right*) with fellow Ramblers Club members, 1880s. Courtesy of Nancy Herlan Brady.

six months provided wheelers with a relatively safe surface on which to ride and perfect their sport. It was also one reason why Buffalo was a favorite city for the League of American Wheelmen, a leading national association for the sport at the time. The league held two conferences in Buffalo, in 1888 and 1901.[6]

The Buffalo Women's Wheel and Athletic Club

Just a few months after the first women's safety bicycle was manufactured, it arrived in Buffalo. The Washington, DC, based Smith National Cycle Company obtained a patent on the drop frame design of the safety in 1887, and its first women's bicycle, the Dart, was produced in early 1888.[7] The drop frame used a diagonal bar in the middle of the frame, as opposed to the horizontal bar just below the handlebars. This allowed women to ride the bicycle in a dress; however, the frames were heavier than the men's safety—by up to fifteen pounds—to maintain the bike's structural integrity. One report stated that Mrs. Smith, the wife of W. E. Smith and owner of the Smith National Cycling Company, visited Buffalo with the Dart.[8] A second source stated that a well-known bicycle enthusiast saw the Dart and had it shipped to his sister, Elizabeth, in Buffalo. According to that article, Elizabeth was the first woman in the region to ride the safety.[9] Regardless of which story is most accurate, it is clear the women of Buffalo were introduced to the Dart shortly after it made its debut. Given the fact that wheeling was already a favorite sport among many men in the city, it was only natural for women to become cyclists when provided with the right vehicle.

The members of the Buffalo Women's Wheel and Athletic Club thought they had founded the first such club in America—and, indeed, the world—but they fell shy of this feat by a few months. The first women's group in the country was founded in the spring of 1888 in Washington, DC, probably because this is the city where the Dart originated and was built. Even so, the creation of the Buffalo club on June 26, 1888, was extraordinary because of its early date and its membership. According to the club manual, founder Mrs. Jennie Stephenson was a pioneer wheelwoman who invited several friends to her house who were interested in wheeling. A plan was hatched among the group, and a second meeting took place on July 3 of that year to establish the club. That inaugural club membership was composed of ten women, including Louise.[10]

Most of these members were professionals, and some of them were local pioneers within their professions. As the club grew, it boasted four physicians, numerous schoolteachers and principals, and, of course, the city's only female architect. Among the physicians were Dr. Ida Bender (1858–1916), who graduated from Normal School in 1878 and taught in Buffalo Public Schools. While teaching, she attended the University of Buffalo School of Medicine and graduated cum laude in 1890. However, Bender never practiced medicine, choosing to stay in the education field. In addition to the wheeling club, she served as the president of the Women's Teachers Association for twenty years and was on the Board of Women Managers for the 1901 Pan American Exposition in Buffalo. She was admired and loved by teachers who worked for her or whom she mentored for her optimism, sense of humor, and generosity, as was evident by the outpouring of grief in the teaching community upon her death.[11] Dr. Annette Rankin was the first woman to graduate from the University of Buffalo (UB) Dental School in 1895; her younger sister, Grace Greenwood Rankin, also attended UB Dental School, graduating three years later in 1898. Dr. Harriott Sheldon and Dr. Lillian Craig Randall (1858–1936; UB Medical School class of '91) opened a practice together in East Buffalo in July 1891. Randall opened Riverside Hospital for Women in 1896. She wrote widely about and lectured on women's health issues. She was president of the Women's Medical Club while a student in 1888. Dr. Ellen Spragge (UB Medical School class of '88) was a successful physician who dedicated herself to fighting for the rights of children. In addition to running her practice and participating in the wheeling club, Spragge volunteered her medical services to the Western New York Society for the Protection of Homeless and Dependent Children in Randolph, New York. She was a tireless advocate and an important fundraiser for the institution.[12]

Motivated by the desire to overcome the prejudice and heckling of women who dared to ride a bicycle, these ladies banded together to bring respectability to wheeling. The women's club was readily embraced by the men's clubs, in particular the Ramblers and the Buffalo Bicycle Club.[13] The women chose to use the latter's clubhouse as their own until they could build their headquarters. The club grew and flourished, creating new divisions for walking, billiards, golf, and bowling, and its members were more than proud that "some of the best-known women in the city" had joined it.[14]

These women knew full well the unprecedented opportunity for freedom the bicycle provided. And they also knew it was incumbent upon them, as leaders in society, to give the pastime respectability so that younger and less-established women could take up the sport. As was noted in *Munsey's* magazine in May 1896: "To men, the bicycle, in the beginning was merely a new toy, another machine added to the long list of devices they knew in their work and play. To women, it was a steed upon which they rode into a new world . . . it was the spinning silver wheels which at last whirled women into the open air, giving them strength, confidence, and a realization that to feel the pulse bounding with enjoyment is in itself a worthy end."[15]

Louise was truly committed to the sport; she was the first to woman to buy a bicycle in Buffalo, in or before 1892, at the cost of $150.[16] She rode her bicycle regularly from home to the office and from the office to the construction site, as was noted in the *Buffalo Courier*'s article "A Clever Woman's Work" in 1896: "She goes from place to place on her bicycle, which she finds a great convenience. Mrs. Bethune is full of ideas, clever and well-read. She devotes herself almost entirely to her work, rarely going out 'on pleasure bent,' and finds her lot a very happy and satisfactory one."[17]

Cycling, Suffragism, and Dress Reform

The founders of the Women's Wheel and Athletic Club were most concerned with the design of their uniform. Said Captain Emma Viliame in 1892, "We think that the wheeling costumes should be nearly as like a riding habit as possible: close fitting and inconspicuous."[18] Given the fact that, at least in the beginning, the club members were composed of established women raised within the confines of Victorian values, bloomers or any other controversial manner of dress were not an option. They were determined to look respectable and composed. Articles from this time described women agitators who dared to wear bloomers or knickerbockers while cycling. Others described the inexperienced women riders who did not adequately prepare to navigate the bicycle and risked inadvertently exposing their undergarments. The Buffalo women wheelers chose neither path; they very carefully considered their attire and the impact their uniform would have on their personal and the club's reputations. Their uniforms were originally bottle green in color and then were changed to serge blue in 1891, with plain skirts composed of three yards of fabric, a meager quantity for the time. The skirts were shorter in the front, had a coattail back, and matching buttons on the side. The jacket had a shirt collar and leg-of-mutton sleeves in the same fabric as the skirt.[19]

The *American Wheelman* best described the composition of women wheelers' uniforms to ensure unnecessary and embarrassing wardrobe malfunctions:

In the first place, her gown is of heavy dark blue serge, so wide that four yards only were required for the entire suit. The skirt is lined with a lighter weight serge of the same color, so that the wind does not catch it and inflate it into a generous and irrepressible balloon.

A divided skirt of still lighter weight serge is worn under the dress, and black tights under the skirt. These three pieces cling to each other with a truly commendable loyalty, so that the dress is prevented from creeping up and making a liberal display of ankle.[20]

One of the club's meetings was entirely dedicated to the style of hat to be worn.[21] It was black, "small, soft and felt, which is comfortable and does not blow off easily."[22] This may be misunderstood as Gilded Age frivolity from our twenty-first-century perspective, but it was serious business. These founding members were making a statement about fairness and equality, and members needed to always look respectable. Keeping hats on, hair in place, shirtwaists tidy, and skirts at the ankle was paramount to reinforcing this respectability. The uniforms of the Buffalo Women's Wheel and Athletic Club members and their counterparts would, ultimately, revolutionize women's dress, challenging the corset and impractically long dress code.

Susan B. Anthony was not the only suffragist to support women bicycling and rational attire. She asked a reporter in 1895, "Why, pray tell me, hasn't a woman as much right to dress to suit herself as a man?"[23] Anthony commented approvingly on the bicycle's role in promoting sensible dress reform and considered the stand women were taking in the matter of dress to be "no small indication that she has realized that she has an equal right with a man to control her own movements." For leaders of the women's movement, such as Anthony and her friend Elizabeth Cady Stanton, the struggle over women's dress was a critical part of the battle for sexual equality and even the right to vote. Stanton forcefully defended a woman's right to dress as she pleased, a right asserted in the context of cycling in an interview in 1895: "Men found that flying coat tails were ungainly and that baggy trousers were in the way [when cycling] so they changed their dress to suit themselves and we didn't interfere. They have taken in every reef and sail and appear in skin tight garments. We did not bother our heads about their cycling clothes, and why should they meddle with what we want to wear? We ask nothing more of them than did the devils in Scripture—'Let us alone.' "[24]

In 1898, Susan B. Anthony expanded on her admiration of the women's wheeling movement to link it to the growing demand for women's right to vote in a letter to the editor of *Sidepaths* magazine: "When bicycles want a bit of special legislation such as side-paths and laws to protect them or to compel railroads to check bicycles as baggage, the women are likely to be made to see that their petitions would be more likely to be respected by the lawmakers if they had votes. . . From such small practical lessons a seed is sown that may ripen into the demand of full suffrage."[25]

Frances E. Willard not only supported the movement; she took it upon herself to learn to ride a bicycle in 1893 at the age of fifty-three. She wrote about this experience in her book *How I Learned to Ride the Bicycle*: "We rejoiced together greatly in perceiving the impetus that this . . . machine would give to that blessed 'woman question.'. . . If a woman ride they must, when riding, dress more rationally than they have been wont to do. If they do this many prejudices as to what they may be allowed to wear will melt away. . . . A reform often advances most rapidly by indirection."[26]

Willard learned to ride at the home of her friend Lady Henry Somerset in England. Lady Somerset was also a wheeler and president of the local women's bicycling club, the Mowbray House Cycling Association, with Willard serving as the club's vice president.[27]

Cycling and Women's Solidarity

At its peak, the Buffalo Women's Wheeling and Athletic Club had over sixty members. Newspaper articles about the club from the time describe women-only banquets, with witty speeches made and impromptu responses stating "whatever else women must take second place to men, they need not as banqueters and after-dinner speakers."[28] One toast given by Louise was titled "I'll put a girdle 'round the earth in forty minutes,"[29] and in 1894 she toasted, "Every woman her own architect."[30] As recorded in the club's summer programs, weekend rides from Buffalo to Niagara Falls, approximately twenty miles, were standard fare.

The press also described a sincere camaraderie and friendship that developed among the members. They were friends and enjoyed each other's company to the point where they added lectures and activities to their winter schedule when cycling was not possible. These lectures included topics on women's health by leading medical figures in Buffalo at the time, including the famous Dr. Roswell Park. This all led to continued interest in the club and in bicycling in general, as many newspaper writers commented: "The interest in women's bicycles grows. No less than seven ladies had appointments last week with one of the local dealers to learn the art of riding, though the weather the earlier part of the week interfered with their plans."[31]

Louise was not just a member; she was one of the club's most ardent wheelers and supporters. When the club was incorporated in 1893, she was one of its trustees.[32] And despite being described in one biography as "stout," she was athletic, and her demonstrated perseverance was evident on a bicycle as well as at the drafting board: "Mrs. Bethune is known as one of the most tireless and persevering riders in the club. No morning is too dark and threatening, no road too hilly, or too sandy, or too muddy, to daunt her courage."[33]

Louise saw herself as a conservative businesswoman, and there is no evidence she supported women's suffrage. In her own words, she was not a political agitator. However, Louise did agitate for increased bicycle riding rights. For instance, in 1892, she led a campaign for Buffalo's prominent Forest Lawn Cemetery to allow bicycles to be ridden within its gates. Like many cemeteries in the late nineteenth century, Forest Lawn was used as a park, and spending time there to visit deceased loved ones or to walk or ride your horse was commonplace. She stated:

Why is it that bicycle riders are not allowed to take their wheels into Forest Lawn Cemetery? . . . Lot owners are not allowed to take their wheels into the cemetery. The rule was passed several years ago, when bicycle-riding was confined mostly to young people, who rode for pleasure, and it was quite proper at that time that the wheels should be excluded from the cemetery. But now it is entirely different. Hundreds of people ride a wheel as a matter of business, and the time for excluding bicycles from the cemetery was passed by. My lot in Forest Lawn is a long distance from the gate, yet if I ride out there on my wheel I have to leave it at the lodge and walk the rest of the way. If I drove a horse I could drive in. In these days when the bicycle very largely takes the place of a horse why should the Cemetery Association discriminate against the bicycle?[34]

Louise persevered, and the Cemetery Association granted permission to the wheelers not long after Louise's editorial appeared. At the March 1896 club meeting, she endorsed a resolution prepared by the Brooklyn Bicycle Club in support of legislation against railroads operating in New York State that were indiscriminately refusing to carry bicycles or charging additional fees to do so.[35] Bicycling rights is the only known issue about which Louise was political and for which she was an agitator. So, while she might not have considered herself a political activist, she did share this one issue with leading suffragists of her time. Of course, not all women's rights advocates were supportive of bicycling. Charlotte Odlum Smith, a nationally recognized advocate for women's labor rights and the president of the Women's Rescue League, vigorously opposed bicycling, stating in 1896: "Bicycling by young women has helped to swell the ranks of reckless girls who finally drift into the standing army of outcast women of the United States more than any other medium."[36]

Louise and her colleagues would prove Charlotte Smith wrong. It was to counter this type of prejudice that led her to take up the sport in the first place.

Wheeling and Architecture

Concurrent with the controversy about women wheelers, concerns were raised that women did not have the intellect or the talent to practice architecture, and it was long thought to be an inappropriate profession for them. But the main opposition was physical: it was widely believed that women did not have the physical strength to perform the work of an architect. The primary opposition to Martha N. McKay's paper, "Woman as Architects," at the Seventh Congress of the Association for the Advancement of Women was that "the idea that women could climb over rafters and ridgepoles as men did, was . . . too ludicrous to be entertained" (see chapter 3).[37] An article titled "Women as Architects" that appeared in the June 1910 issue of *Architect and Engineer of California* listed many reasons why women did not have the innate skill set to work in the profession. It concluded with the declaration that "large drawings necessitate large boards, and the strain of reaching is . . . physically more than any woman should be called upon to bear."[38]

But it is abundantly clear that endless hours of reaching over drafting boards and climbing over rafters and ridgepoles is exactly what Louise did throughout her career. As stated in her entry in "Some Distinguished Women of Buffalo": "Mrs. Bethune has, for some years, taken entire charge of the office work, and complete superintendence of one-third of the outside work."[39] When interviewed, she spoke about the physical strength required to perform the skills of an architect: "A woman would need as a special endowment of great physical strength in order to be able to stand on her feet a good many hours a day without tiring, especially while a student. Three-fourths of the drawings of the young draftsman must be done standing. It is no exaggeration to say that during the first three years of my office studying, I did not sit fifteen minutes consecutively out of the day."[40]

Louise also lamented that early women architects were struggling to compete with their male counterparts because they did not participate in the supervision of construction, as was expected from architects at the time, and which she had done: "They shirk the brick-and-mortar-rubber-boot-and-ladder-climbing period of investigative education, and as a consequence remain at the tracing stage of draftsmanship."[41]

Some early women architects, such as Julia Morgan, wore men's trousers under their dress when supervising construction. Louise may very well have worn a divided skirt (i.e., trousers) under her bicycling uniform and her working clothes while visiting a construction site, as did succeeding women architects. Riding a bicycle and practicing architecture required perseverance and strength, physically and in character.

As the illustration from a 1901 article, "A Woman Who Is the Architect of Her Own Fortunes," demonstrates, the notion of a professional woman at this time was very much associated with the New Woman movement. These "new women" challenged the masculine establishment in their dress and their audacity. The equally revolutionary woman architect—by her mere existence as a professional challenging the conventional wisdom of the time by visiting a construction site or working over a drafting board for hours in a dress and corset—was one physical manifestation for this movement. And the New Woman rode a bicycle.

Figure 7.3. Illustration from the article "A Woman Who Is the Architect of Her Own Fortunes" in the *San Francisco Chronicle* in 1901. This Art Nouveau–inspired drawing demonstrates the influence of the New Woman concept on professional identity.

The True Woman versus the New Woman

> However little she may realize it, every girl who rides her steel horse is a vivid illustration of one of the greatest waves of progress in this century, the advancement of women in freedom and opportunity.[42]

In 1901, the *Atlantic Monthly* published an article by Caroline Tichnor titled "The Steel-Engraving Lady and the Gibson Girl." The tongue-in-cheek piece was an editorial on the conflict between two female prototypes of the Gilded Age: the True Woman, represented by the Steel-Engraving Lady as portrayed in illustrations in popular culture from the 1860s through the 1880s, and the New Woman, epitomized by the Gibson Girl at the turn of the century. In the article, the Steel-Engraving Lady sits demurely in her apartment wearing an elaborate dress and surrounded by the products of her industry, her needlework, and floral arrangements. Without advance notice, the Gibson Girl bounded her way into the scene wearing an ankle-length, unadorned dress with mannish collar and practical footwear; she holds a golf club, having just played the links. The Gibson Girl stated that she has been asked to write a paper on an extinct type and has decided upon the Steel-Engraving Lady as her subject. Tichnor continues to identify the many differences between these disparate models of womanhood. She contrasts their relationship with the outdoors: Steel-Engraving Lady prefers to stay inside, while the Gibson Girl embraces outdoor activity and sports a tan.

Figure 7.4. The New Woman was often portrayed riding a bicycle, as illustrated in the June 1895 issue of *Scribner's* magazine. Image courtesy of the Library of Congress.

Their choice of footwear also speaks to their different characters: the former wears delicate slippers to carry herself with ease, while the latter requires practical shoes to take her through her active day.

Even more substantive topics that are discussed between the two characters include education, vocations, and relationships with men. The Steel-Engraving Lady states that her "theory of education is utterly opposed to yours . . . mine was designed to fit me for my home . . . you are equipped for contact with the outside world, for competition with your brother in business; my training merely taught me to make my brother's home a place which he should find a source of pleasure and inspiration."[43] The article finally ends with the unambiguous statement about the future of

Figure 7.5. An example of a steel-engraved lady illustration from *La Mode Illustrée*, circa 1885. Courtesy of the author.

women in society, "Hail the new woman—behold she comes apace! Woman, once man's superior, now his equal."[44] While we may think of being "superior" as being better, the author's point is that the woman-on-the-pedestal (man's "superior") was actually less "equal" than the New Woman.

Tichnor's Steel-Engraving Lady represented the True Woman, a feminine ideal that emerged in the mid-1800s (see chapter 1). The True Woman was expected to uphold the values of religious piety, purity or virginity until marriage, submission to the men in the woman's life, and domesticity or maintaining the sanctity of home as her sphere of influence.[45] The Steel-Engraving Lady shared with the True Woman an ideal of female beauty, with her "alabaster white skin, glossy smooth abundant hair and dreamy eyes." Of course, very few mid-nineteenth-century women had the luxury to obtain this physical ideal. As wives—even in upper-middle-class families—they had significant household chores, even if the family could afford domestic help. And women from lower- and middle-class families, immigrants, and women of color mostly worked outside of the home, in addition to maintaining their domestic spheres. However unrealistic, the Steel-Engraving Lady provides a point of reference to the modern reader regarding the impact the New Woman had on society when she arrived.

Following the Civil War, universities and colleges began to either admit women into their cloisters or open new women-only institutions. Between 1880 and 1920, the number of four-year collegiate degrees conferred on women increased from 2,500 to 16,000 in the US.[46] In addition, as historian Patricia Marks notes, an imbalance in population created the "redundant women," with more women than men in the population following the high death rate of young men after the Civil War. This created a cohort of women who could not marry, which changed the marital expectations of the middle class. This, in turn, placed additional pressure on the labor market to provide socially acceptable jobs for women, which forced women to consider other professional fields for employment. Eventually, this created a genuine interest among women in pursuing professions beyond the social norm of teaching or nursing.[47] The progression of women completing high school, attending college, and entering the professional workforce resulted in an expectation from some women in the 1890s of a life beyond that of the True Woman.

The New Woman represents women's vastly increased presence in the paid workforce. Yes, like the True Woman, the New Woman was purely an ideal, and an upper-middle-class one at that. While some women, such as Louise, entered the professional ranks, many of the jobs that women held during this time were low paying and involved very long hours in factories, sweatshops, and department stores. And despite the hyperbole in "The Steel-Engraving Lady and the Gibson Girl," most white middle-class women left the workforce when they married.

According to Jean Matthews in *The Rise of the New Woman*, the actual term "New Woman" was coined around 1894, but this type of woman was instantly recognizable. Matthews writes, "As a type, the New Woman was young, well educated, probably a college graduate, independent of spirit, highly competent, and physically strong and fearless." The embodiment of the New Woman was the Gibson Girl, and her vehicle of choice was the bicycle.[48] Named in honor of her creator, the artist and fashion illustrator Charles Dana Gibson—who drew illustrations of women from 1886 to 1910—the Gibson Girl was an immediate and unprecedented sensation. She became the first nationwide standard of beauty, appearing in magazines such as *Scribner's, Colliers Weekly, Life,* and *Harper's* throughout the 1890s up to World War I.

The New Woman's favored ensemble was composed of a white shirtwaist tucked into a plain dark skirt. The skirt was ankle length, slightly shorter than was traditional for women, and was an unadorned A-line in silhouette. The New Woman's attire was the favored costume of the women who were joining the workforce—and it also looked remarkably like the Buffalo Women's Wheel Club's uniform. This functional outfit also reflected the values of the women's rights activists, because these women exuded strength, confidence, and athleticism. While not all women who worked outside of the home were suffragists, their embodiment became a muse for activists of their time. This, in turn, was a contributing factor in Rational Dress Reform and was most associated with the suffrage movement. Rational Dress Reform was initially popularized in the 1850s by Amelia Bloomer, who endorsed women wearing bifurcated garments like men's pants. The movement lost steam with the outset of the Civil War.

Marks cites a turn-of-the-century commentator about women's new fashion, who stated that as men and women differ, so should their dress. But this commentator added, because their activities are becoming more alike, "so women's dress should permit equal freedom of movement and equal health."[49] The shirtwaist, in particular, became iconic and was one of the first articles of women's clothing to be mass produced. It was worn by women in all classes, from the upper-middle-class New Woman to the office worker and beyond. By the turn of the century, there were 450 textile factories making shirtwaists and other garments, employing 40,000 workers, many of whom were immigrants.[50]

Figure 7.6. "The Weaker Sex. II," published in *Collier's Weekly*, July 4, 1903. As the expression of the New Woman, the Gibson Girl projects a new confidence in her relations with men, which some found threatening. Image courtesy of the Library of Congress.

The Growth of Women's Clubs

Memberships in women's clubs among all women, but especially middle-class women, grew exponentially during this period. In 1890, *Harper's Bazaar* published the article "Club Life for Women," which lauded the dramatic increase of women who belonged to clubs throughout the country. The article described the positive effects of women of similar interests and intellect meeting to advance a particular area of interest. It pointed out the differences between modern and earlier women's clubs by stating, "The old fashioned gossip societies have 'had their day and ceased to be.' Women meet at these modern clubs for a higher purpose than to talk about their neighbors."[51]

These clubs were both a response to the private social club life that men had enjoyed for years and a vehicle to broaden women's lives outside of their homes in a socially acceptable manner. Their goal was largely intellectual pursuit and self-improvement. Common topics of concentration were literature, art, history, education, athletics, and civic improvement. Large groups of five hundred members or more would be divided into departments to cover different topics.[52] Mary Livermore, the suffragist, stated it was not "a mere blind craze . . . sweeping women into clubs and leagues. . . . It is the trend of the age; an unconscious protest against the isolation in which women have dwelt in the past; a reaching out after a larger and fuller life; a desire to keep in touch with other women in the evolution of women."[53] Many of these clubs were similar to the Buffalo Women's Wheel and Athletic Club in that their members met to advance a specific topic; they were composed of women with similar backgrounds, education, and interests; and they met in public or semipublic and socially acceptable locations. For example, many women's clubs met in community libraries. During the 1890s–1900s there were approximately twenty women's clubs in existence in Buffalo; most were small and probably met in other clubhouses or private homes.

Louise was a member of several other national women's clubs, including the Daughters of the American Revolution (DAR). Founded in 1890, this organization was formed because "women felt the desire to express their patriotic feelings and were frustrated by their exclusion from men's organizations formed to perpetuate the memory of ancestors who fought to make this country free and independent."[54] She was also a member of the National Society of New England Women, which was founded in 1895.

Whether the intent of these women's clubs was progressive, provocative, or conservative, the members well understood the importance of their existence, if only to grow accustomed to the sound of their own voices. As Matthews states, members acquired the self-confidence to speak in public and saw themselves as agents of personal growth and transformation.[55]

In the end, the New Woman Movement was one very prominent sign that women were, by necessity or inclination, redefining their sphere beyond the boundary of the home. As Lillian Bett stated in 1895: "The new woman has been the subject for illustration and description more or less earnest. She is described as smoking, drinking, and demanding what she calls liberty. There is a new woman, the product of evolution, the result of domestic, social and commercial changes. . . . This is the new woman, the flower of this marvelous century, not a caricature drawn by the would-be wit, or by the unthinking man who cannot see below the surface nor beyond the range of his personal experience."[56]

To be sure, Bethune and the pioneering professional women of her generation were most certainly not New Women—but they weren't True

Women, either. They were that vital bridge between the two movements. Through their excellence in their work, bravery in assuming positions on controversial topics such as appropriate dress and recreation, and principle in the company they kept and clubs they joined, these early professionals charted a path that younger women would follow in growing numbers.

Louise Bethune, Feminist

Was Bethune a feminist? Until now, the common assumption was that she was not. However, in her life and work, Louise promoted many causes that were central to the women's rights movement.

Figure 7.7. Members of the Buffalo Women's Wheel and Athletic Club. Collection of the Buffalo History Museum, general photograph collection, Sports and Recreation—Bicycling.

The term "feminist" was unknown during most of Louise's life. It began to circulate after 1910, according to historian and feminist scholar Nancy Woloch, and was applied to a smaller group of women who made a series of demands that went beyond the suffrage movement. Woloch noted that all feminists were suffragettes, but not all suffragettes were feminists.[57] Certainly, if Louise had even heard the term, as defined by Woloch, she would not have considered herself one. However, in asking the question using a contemporary definition for feminist—the belief in full social, economic, and political equality for women—the answer is different.

The women's movement pursued seven separate goals: personhood or legal status, the right to education, professional legitimacy, participation in clubs and hobbies, pay equity, dress reform, and suffrage. The Married Women's Property Act of 1848 in New York State addressed women's legal status, granting them the right to own property and profits made from this property following marriage; it became the model for similar laws in subsequent states in the 1850s.[58] Both Louise and her mother Emma were direct beneficiaries of this law. Without it, Louise would not have been able to marry Robert and maintain her career.

Louise was always unequivocal about her strong belief in the right for women to receive an education equal to men. She advocated for coeducational architectural programs (see chapter 8), regularly spoke to high school girls about the architectural profession, and consistently supported women's educational programs. This was underscored at a banquet for the Women's Wheel and Athletic Club where she "happily responded to [the toast] 'Every Woman Her Own Architect,' making a point that our daughters, with their college educations, are to be the best builders."[59]

As the first professional woman architect, Louise was often profiled as a shining example of professional legitimacy. Her participation in the Women's Wheel and Athletic Club demonstrates Louise's support for pursuing meaningful friendships with other women around intellectual and athletic pursuits. Louise was a staunch and unequivocal advocate for pay equity, which was the women's equality issue for which she cared most. Every profile on Louise after 1891 mentioned her advocacy for pay equity. Her activity as a bicyclist and a superintendent of construction necessitated modifications to her clothing. And her mere participation in these activities challenged the Gilded Age notion of what a woman in a dress could do.

When Louise spoke to the Women's Union in 1891, she stated that as a businesswoman she could not be an agitator. When she said that her public persona needed to be conservative rather than aggressive and her strength was in her adaptability, not in reform, she was probably speaking specifically about women's suffrage. However, even regarding this issue, there are no existing references to her speaking out directly against women winning the right to vote. She simply stated that as a businesswoman, she could not afford to alienate potential clients through overt political protesting.

Two years later, in the spring of 1893, this issue arose again at a speech made before the same group by Buffalo-based Mrs. Henry L. Lyon, a women's education advocate. Speaking about "what kind of education best fits women for the duties of life,"[60] Lyon argued that girls should have a complete and thorough education, whether they wished to pursue a profession or marry and devote themselves to domestic duties. Lyon believed that, regardless of whether a woman chose to work outside the home, she might be required to do so if her husband died or the family encountered some other financial hardship. Therefore, a complete education would provide her with the skills to earn an income.

The next day, the *Buffalo Enquirer* reported that many of the attendees had disagreed with Lyon's argument, including Louise, saying that Louise believed that a woman could not choose a profession, leave it, and return to it after several years, expecting to resume it at her former level of competence and responsibility. Louise was referring to the many years of training needed to earn a professional degree and then working in a practice to become self-sufficient.

Taking her comments out of context, the *Enquirer* declared, "Mrs. Bethune has since given [Lyon's] theories a severe blow by endorsing the bachelor girl, the educated, self-supporting girl." The reporter used Louise's statements to argue that women professionals would need to choose between either remaining single or getting married and then regretting their retirement from professional life. Incredibly, the *Enquirer* concluded that women should, therefore, abandon professional life entirely and be trained only for domestic duties, which would require limited education.[61]

Louise was so upset by the *Enquirer*'s misrepresentation of her comments that she issued a rebuttal on April 13. In her response, Louise stated that she had been responding to the question, "What occupations are open to the woman thrown suddenly upon her own resources?" While in support of women who wish to pursue a profession, Louise was also advocating for general education for all women, regardless of their choice in life, to ensure self-reliance:

> To say that professional life, once dropped, can with difficulty be renewed under such circumstances (as the loss of a husband and breadwinner) is not in any sense to disagree with Mrs.

Lyon, but is simply one more argument in favor of a broader education . . . for every woman who elects to become a home maker. . . . I am, and have been for many years, most heartily in sympathy with Mrs. Lyon's views as I understand them, and have never expressed myself otherwise.[62]

This was a common situation for Louise—one that occurs even today—where her life and statements were represented (or misrepresented) to argue against women's equality. Louise was an intellectual, opinionated, and strong, but reserved and conservative by nature. She was not prone to ostentatious or overtly public demonstrations of her opinions. And to succeed in the conservative and pragmatic building industry, she couldn't align herself with the radical feminists of her day. That has led many to infer she was antagonistic toward feminism and the more general topic of women's equality, one of the major issues during her lifetime.

But Louise left many clues in her interviews and actions revealing her opinions regarding women's equality that support the idea that she believed women were equal to men. She believed women should receive an education equal to men, were as capable as men in professional life, should be paid equally to men, and should be free to pursue intellectual, athletic, and social pursuits equal to men. Louise's opinion on the controversial issue of women's suffrage is not known. But, regarding her more general philosophy on women's equality, Louise Bethune was direct, unapologetic, and constant.

The Disbanding of the Women's Wheel and Athletic Club

By the mid-1890s, the Buffalo Women's Wheel and Athletic Club was continuing to grow by attracting new and younger members, but in 1897 the founders decided to disband: "After a long and honorable, though unostentatious career, the Buffalo Women's Wheel and Athletic Club, which was, as far as was known, the first woman's wheel club to be formed in the world was last night disbanded."[63]

The stated reason for this decision was that they had accomplished their goal of ensuring the social recognition of women riding a bicycle. Women wheelers were no longer frowned upon, and the club was enjoying press and acceptance in the city in equal terms with the men's clubs.

Yet, other factors contributed to the closing of the club. Despite their best efforts, the women were unsuccessful in building a home. From 1892 to 1895, Louise led the initiative to raise funds to design and build a club-house of their own. According to *American Wheelman*, Louise did design the new building, but the required funding was never raised and the project was ultimately abandoned. Louise then turned her attention to renovating space in the Mayfair Hotel for the club, but this, too, did not materialize. By 1896, they were meeting at the Chapter House, home of the Women's Teachers Association, no doubt arranged by the WTA president and wheeler Dr. Ida Bender.[64] Their own clubhouse would have provided them with a structure, literally and figuratively, which would have continued to galvanize the group long after the ability or inclination to ride had waned for its founding members, just as physical clubhouses do for other associations.

Its membership also was changing. As new and younger members joined the group, it was evident they were less concerned with social acceptance and more interested in simply advancing themselves in the sport. For example, the 1893 captain of the club's wheeling section, the unmarried Kitty Klipfel, was of the new guard of members who were bicycling with men as equals. She enjoyed the "proud distinction of being the champion lady rider of Buffalo."[65] She regularly competed with men in distance racing meets, such as the Rambler Souvenir Century Run.[66] For women such as Klipfel, social acceptance was a concern of the recent past. She was more interested in performance, so she rode the lightest bicycle she could obtain and wore the outfit that would best support her sport.[67] In 1894, the club announced it was again modifying its uniforms back to the bottle green color and exchanging the skirts for bloomers: "With the exception of a few members, [the club] has adopted the bloomer costume for riding. The ladies have ordered the reformed costumes and before the snow flies a majority will be wearing the new style dress. Captain Kitty Klipfel organized the move-ment and she says bloomers are the only practical styles."[68] Older members probably found this change shocking—or amusing—but it was of a piece with the new emphasis over sport and comfort rather than respectability.

Finally, the founding members were aging. When the club was created, Louise was thirty-two years old. By 1897, she was forty-one years of age. The founding members were ready to move on, and the new members had new ambitions. And because they had no home to continue to draw them together, they decided to disband on a high note. The Women's Wheel and Athletic Club of Buffalo last met on January 5, 1897, congratulating itself on an accomplished mission. The *Buffalo Times* summarized its impact at the time: "It is the claim of the Woman's Wheel and Athletic Club that it popularized the bicycle among conservative women in Buffalo. It did this, and more. Its members introduced seemly and sensible cycling costumes, they walked, they bowled and they created an interest among women in all healthful exercise. There is always room for such a club. Although it has seen the completion of its mission, there is even more—the demands of good exercise, and for those who will lead the way."[69]

While women would not gain the vote for twenty more years—seven years after her death—Louise was a crucial participant in two movements, proving herself equal in the masculine worlds of architecture and wheeling, which paved the way to this achievement.

Chapter 8

A Question of Equality

The Woman's Building

The future of woman in the architectural profession is what she herself sees fit to make it.

—Bethune, "Women and Architecture"

Figure 8.1. Louise Bethune, circa 1892. Courtesy of the author.

One of the most significant milestones in Louise Bethune's career was, in fact, a nonevent. In 1891, Louise chose not to participate in the competition for the Woman's Building at the World's Columbian Exposition, despite being invited by her longtime professional colleague Daniel Burnham, the chief of construction for the fair. While the men were handpicked and offered commissions commensurate to their work, the architect of the Woman's Building was expected to enter a design competition at her own expense. The winning entrant would receive a commission, but only of one tenth the amount offered to the male architects. Louise rejected these terms, but this act of principle robbed her of the opportunity to work alongside her nationally more prominent AIA colleagues on the most architecturally ambitious project of their careers. However, it provided Louise the platform to voice her strong belief in pay equity for women. And given the fact that Sophia Hayden, the winning architect of the Woman's Building, never practiced after the opening of the project, it demonstrates Louise's wisdom and strength of character in not participating.

Few events fully describe the many nuances surrounding the women's movement and the fight for gender equality at the turn of the nineteenth century than the development of the Woman's Building for the World's Columbian Exposition. In many respects, it was the culmination of years of perseverance to celebrate women's skills and products independently of men. Yet, the drama and politics surrounding the effort are indicative of the societal fissures that existed in Gilded Age America, particularly for women. And to Louise Bethune, the most senior practicing woman architect at the time, the women-only building design competition was a misguided process, which led to disastrous results. Her refusal to submit an entry to the competition made national news, and her stand for "equal pay for equal remuneration" defined her position on women's equality.

Setting the Stage for the Columbian Exposition

Before World War I, international fairs were important vehicles for women to promote their capabilities, domestic or otherwise. Architectural historian Mary Pepchinski states that, during this time leading up to the emergence of the women's movements in North America and Europe, "a new type, the Woman's Building, made its appearance at the World Exhibitions."[1] Despite outward appearances, these projects did not challenge societal views of women but, rather, reinforced them.[2] This was certainly the case with the

Columbian Exposition Woman's Building, where three divergent positions on women's role in society and their perception of equality were on display.

Between the Great Exhibition in London in 1851 and World War I, Europe and the United States hosted nineteen international fairs, to "demonstrate to the world the state of 'civilization,' as it was reflected in the fine arts and in industrial technology."[3] The first exposition to feature a building devoted to women's interests was in Vienna in 1873. The second was at the Philadelphia Centennial of 1876, which was also America's first significant exposition. Elizabeth Duane Gillespie, a great-granddaughter of Benjamin Franklin, led the Women's Executive Centennial Committee, which helped raise funds for the fair, with the condition that there be a display of women's work in the Main Exhibit Hall. However, upon fulfilling its fundraising commitment, the committee was informed there was no available space in the Main Hall for the women's area. They were advised to consider constructing their own building instead, which was estimated to cost $30,000. However, they were also informed there was no available funding to support the additional building so they would need to raise the funds themselves,[4] which they accomplished in four months.[5]

Hermann Schwarzman, the chief architect of the Centennial, was commissioned to design the building. Later, Gillespie would state her deep regret that she had not suggested a woman architect: "We never thought of employing a woman architect and thus made our first great mistake." And further, "I fear we hindered this legitimate branch of women's work instead of helping it."[6] Empress Theresa of Brazil, whose husband was guest of honor at the Centennial, opened the Woman's Pavilion on May 10, 1876, to an all-women audience with the intent of celebrating the sisterhood of women shared around the world.[7]

But it was at the hundredth anniversary of the signing of the US Declaration of Independence celebrations on July 4, 1876, when the real drama unfolded between two factions of the women's movement. While the Women's Executive Centennial Committee had made its own statement through its women's building, the National Woman Suffrage Association—led by President Elizabeth Cady Stanton, Matilda Gage, and Susan B. Anthony—requested to be included in the July 4th program to read the Women's Declaration of Rights. After the request was denied, at Independence Hall, Susan B. Anthony and five colleagues forced the issue by presenting the Women's Declaration to the presiding officer, who allowed it to be read. Anthony read the statement and her colleagues distributed copies to the audience. As Stanton remarked, "And thus in the same hour, on opposite sides of old Independence Hall, did the men and women express their opinions on the great principles proclaimed on the natal day of the Republic."[8] As Mary Cordato observed, "In contrast to the Woman's Building, the activities of The National Woman Suffrage Association represented a propaganda appeal for equal rights. . . . Suffragettes hoped to show the world 'that the women of 1876 know and feel their degradation no less than did the men of 1776.' "[9]

The exhibits in the Woman's Pavilion—and *The New Century for Women*, a newsletter that was published by the Women's Centennial Committee and distributed from the Woman's Building—demonstrated a belief in women's equality by highlighting their contributions to society.[10] However, the Centennial Committee preferred to stay within the lines of acceptable societal norms. While they promoted rational dress, new occupations for women, and improved education, they were not interested in raising controversy, but awareness instead. These opposing views played out during the planning for the Woman's Building of the 1893 Columbian Exposition with some of the same players. This time, architects Louise Bethune, Minerva Parker Nichols, and Sophia Hayden would be caught in the middle of the showdown.

The Woman's Building of the World Columbian Exposition

> Comment on the success or lack of success of the Woman's Building designed by Miss Hayden is unfair to her and to the general architectural profession.
>
> —"Chicago," *American Architect and Building News*

At the dedication ceremony of the Columbian Exposition on October 22, 1892, Daniel Burnham, chief of construction, remarked:

> In August 1890, the World's Columbian Exposition was to decide upon a site for this great exposition. Without hesitation they promptly invited the most eminent of American landscape architects to join them and give advice. The suggestions of these men were approved and adopted. In December it became necessary to select the architects of the buildings. Again the

corporation entrusted the work of choosing an expert, and since that time no single important step of the World's Columbian Exposition has been taken without the advice of an expert man. When before has any community so entrusted its interests to its strongest sons?[11]

He then stated, "I now have the honor to present to you the master-artists of the Exposition." The president of the board of the Exposition replied, "Mr. Burnham and gentlemen: It becomes my agreeable duty . . . to receive from you these buildings which represent your thoughts and skill and labor as master-artists of construction." Following the president's lengthy speech on the brilliance of the architects and beauty of the buildings, eighty medals were distributed to the architects and artists involved in the exposition buildings.[12] Sophia Hayden, architect of the Woman's Building, attended the opening ceremony after a prolonged absence from the site. She, too, was offered a medal for her contribution to the exposition and her design was praised along with the work of the male architects. The Woman's Building was her first architectural commission—but it was also her last.

Just as they had been for the Philadelphia Centennial, the women of Chicago's elite were very much involved in fundraising for the project. However, they were determined not to suffer the same fate that occurred in 1876. Led by Myra Bradwell and Emma R. Wallace, prominent public service activists advocated for the local fair committee to create a woman's auxiliary in recognition of their work. This led to the creation of the Chicago Women's Department. These women were mostly from wealthy families with vast experience in fundraising for philanthropic causes. Some were suffragists, but that was not their primary interest.[13]

Another group of Chicago women were also galvanized in anticipation of the fair. These were largely professionals who were dedicated to the suffrage movement and equal rights for women. They chose to commemorate Queen Isabella of Castile to honor her patronage role of Christopher Columbus's voyage, thereby using this as a vehicle to celebrate women's accomplishments.[14] Both groups wanted a women's building; however, they had different intended goals. The Women's Department saw the building as home for exhibits that celebrated the industry of women and to promote philanthropy. The "Isabellas" thought it should serve as a clubhouse and assembly space for women regarding women's issues. They also believed that women's work should be on display at the exposition, but they agreed with Susan B. Anthony that their exhibits should not be segregated to one building but should be displayed along with the men's work. In other words, they thought that women should compete on equal terms with men.[15]

As with the Philadelphia Centennial Woman's Pavilion, here again were two divergent perspectives on the role of women in society and on the meaning of women's equality. Nancy Cott writes that the nineteenth-century women's movement had three different aims. The first was a focus on service to society and the increased opportunities for women in charitable work and seeking civic reforms. These benevolent women were interested in addressing societal problems but not changing the social order. The second was focused on women obtaining equal civic, legal, and economic rights. They sought to improve the existing social order through gender equality. The third focus was on women's total emancipation. They sought to radically transform society.[16] Where the Women's Department played in the first arena, the Isabellas were advocates of the second and third ones. Or, as Jeanne Weimann wrote, "the Women's Department and the Isabella Association represented dramatically the split in the women's movement between those who wanted women to work for general reform, and those who wanted to work primarily for this one equal right."[17]

Through the efforts of Susan B. Anthony and influential women in Washington and Chicago, the Fair Bill that President Harrison signed was amended to include a board of female managers. This is ironic, because Anthony had been advocating for women to hold membership along with men on the fair's National Commission, the organizing body of the Columbian Exposition. The notion of a separate body to organize women's activities or exhibits was counter to Anthony's ethos. Upon the creation of the Board of Lady Managers—as it was called—the Women's Department and the Isabellas battled over its direction and control. After months of hearing campaigns, the National Commission selected the board's membership by addressing the wishes of both groups; the board was composed of national members from all over the country, as suggested by the Isabellas, along with nine members from Chicago. However, eight of these members came from the Women's Department and only one from the Isabellas. This imbalance would continue throughout the planning process of the fair. By the time the fair was opened, the Isabellas' presence was no longer evident in a meaningful way.[18]

At the first meeting of the Board of Lady Managers on November 18, 1890, Bertha Honore Palmer was elected president. Mrs. Palmer was a wealthy and influential Chicago socialite. Her husband, Potter Palmer, was second vice president of the National Fair Commission and on the committees for grounds and buildings, and fine arts. One of the first matters for the board to address was the question of a Woman's Building. There was no funding for this structure and there were competing views about its purpose. The decision was made that it would be used as a clubhouse and assembly space for women, as well as serving as the administrative headquarters for the board. It would also feature exhibits of women's work, which would be curated to demonstrate the progress of women since 1492.[19] The idea of a design competition for the Woman's Building came from Frances Shepard of the Daughters of the American Revolution, who proposed a resolution "that competitive designs for this building be invited from the women architects of this country as well as from men."[20] The resolution was adopted unanimously by the board. They would need to work with Daniel Burnham to implement this strategy.

The Architects Meet in Chicago

The board of directors of the fair made two key decisions regarding its landscape and design. First, they chose nationally renowned landscape architect Frederick Law Olmsted and his partner Henry Codman to design the fairgrounds, and then they selected the successful Chicago firm of Burnham & Root to lead the project, with Daniel Burnham as chief of construction and John Root as consulting architect. Upon reviewing the magnitude of the project and the deadline for completion, the committee on grounds and buildings decided to not hold competitions for the building assignments to architects but to select a few leading architects to "constitute a Board of Consulting Architects, acting in harmony, apportioning out the work among its members, and consulting at various stages until the plans were perfected."[21] This approach was in harmony with the AIA philosophy regarding design competitions at the time. *Harper's Monthly* noted that Burnham "was from the start strongly in favor of ignoring the long-established custom of competition" and appointing the architects, and that it was his "persistence and earnestness" that swayed the committee.[22]

Burnham initially chose nationally recognized architects for these commissions, as befitting a national event such as the fair. Four of the firms were from the East: Richard Morris Hunt; George B. Post; McKim, Mead & White, all of New York; and Peabody & Stearns of Boston. The fifth was the Kansas City firm of Van Brunt & Howe. The fact that no Chicago-based firms were selected generated an outcry from critics. In response, Burnham invited the local firms of Adler & Sullivan, William Le Baron Jenney, Henry Ives Cobbs, S. S. Beman, and Burling & Whitehouse to participate. The selected architects met on January 10, 1891, in Chicago to commence the work.[23] They were paid $10,000 per firm: $3,000 upon the completion of the schematic designs, $6,000 upon completion of the design development documents, and $1,000 when the buildings were completed. Daniel Burnham and his exposition staff would complete the more arduous construction documents in Chicago.[24]

Tragically, Burnham's business partner, John Root, died suddenly shortly after the board of architects' meeting, on the night of January 15, from a sudden onset of pneumonia. This unforeseen loss deeply impacted Burnham. He would be forced to carry the burden of the completion of the exposition and the expectations of his city and country on his own. Root's death also deeply impacted the architect's selection process for the Woman's Building. As a progressive within the AIA and long-standing supporter of women architects, Root's absence would be felt throughout the design and implementation process for the project.

The Woman's Building

On January 13, 1891, just two days before he died, John Root received a letter from Bertha Palmer stating: "Mr. Waller alarmed me last evening by saying that he understood that Mr. Hunt was to build our building. Of course, we will not have a man called in until the woman architects have tried and failed to produce a suitable plan."[25]

From the outset it was clear that the Woman's Building would be treated differently than the other buildings of the fair. The Board of Lady Managers would be the primary decision makers and would dictate the terms of the selection of architect, followed by the artwork, and then the exhibits when the building was complete. It appears that John Root held more sway than Daniel Burnham over Palmer, because of his elevated social standing in Chicago, his education, and reputation as a skilled designer.[26] According to the *Inland Architect*, Root had successfully suggested appointing a woman architect for the commission.[27] However, after his death, the idea of a design competition gained traction with the Board of Lady Managers. In her correspondence with Burnham, Palmer stated that "the announcement of the competition and the sending in of a number of good designs by competent women would attract attention to our work, and also be an advertisement for all women who entered the competition." She also noted, erroneously, that there were no women architects who had "such a reputation for planning public buildings as would justify us in giving our building to her with the same assurance of success as in the case of a male architect" and that "the best design might come from the most unexpected source."[28]

Given the fact that Louise practiced almost exclusively in Western New York, it is understandable that Bertha Palmer would not have known of her work and abilities. However, Daniel Burnham and John Root were well aware of Louise's portfolio. As one of her sponsors when she was admitted into the Western Association of Architects in 1885, Burnham helped manage any potential opposition from his WAA colleagues on the grounds of her gender. Root had nominated Louise for her 1888 admission to the AIA at the Fellow level. Since 1885, she had attended the annual WAA and AIA conventions, and all three were very active within both organizations. If John Root had successfully convinced Bertha Palmer to appoint a woman architect, Louise would have been the top candidate.

The drama around the selection process for the architect of the Woman's Building took place within weeks of Root's passing. Without his close friend and trusted business partner at his side and the largest commission of his career upon him, Burnham had a lot to manage. The Woman's Building was just one of many issues competing for his attention. Burnham advised against holding a design competition, probably for the same reasons he had opposed them for the other exposition buildings.[29] In the end, he acquiesced to Palmer's request, but insisted that she write the specifications for the building for the competition brief, which he administered. Palmer and her allies would form the design jury and Burnham would deliver their building as designed by their architect.[30]

The *Inland Architect* mentioned three practicing women architects whom Burnham personally invited to enter the design competition: Louise, Sallie T. Smith in Birmingham, Alabama (see chapter 4), and Minerva Parker (Nichols) in Philadelphia. Smith was in practice with her father and had been a member of the WAA but did not join the AIA after the merger of the associations. She was serving as an Alternate Lady Manager from Alabama. Before the competition was announced, Smith wrote the Exposition Commission stating, "I am one of the few women architects of this country and would like an equal showing with the men." According to Weimann, further inquiry revealed that she "misrepresented herself" and, disheartened in not receiving the commission, did not submit an entry to the competition.[31] While it's not clear what is meant by "misrepresent," it's likely that they meant that she "misrepresented" herself as a partner in a firm or as a member of the professional association (she had been a WAA member but not an AIA member).

Originally from Chicago, Minerva Parker was the granddaughter of early Chicago architect Seth A. Doane. She graduated from the Franklin Institute Drawing School in Philadelphia in 1885 and then worked for architect Edwin W. Thorne, taking over his office in 1888 when he retired. By 1891, Parker had built a solid reputation as a residential architect in the Philadelphia area. Parker was commissioned in 1890 by the Isabellas

MINERVA PARKER NICHOLS.

Figure 8.2. Architect Minerva Parker Nichols. Frances E. Willard and Mary A. Livermore, eds., *A Woman of the Century: Fourteen Hundred-Seventy Biographical Sketches Accompanied by Portraits of Leading American Women in All Walks of Life.*

to design the Queen Isabella Pavilion, to be located at the Columbian Exposition. The Isabellas requested the Moorish-style design as a reference to Queen Isabella's Spanish nationality. This building was never realized due to philosophical differences with the Board of Lady Managers, which may also have impacted Parker's opportunity to receive the Woman's Building commission. Parker submitted her Queen Isabella Pavilion as her competition entry, which was also not consistent with the Beaux Arts aesthetic of the fair architecture.[32]

Louise refused to submit a design, just as the *Inland Architect* predicted she would.[33] As the journal noted:

> It seems to have struck some brilliant mind that the proper way to procure plans [for the women's building] would be by a competition among women architects. . . . One [woman architect, Louise] is a member of the American Institute of Architects. This . . . architect will certainly ignore any competition scheme . . . they are, at best, unprofessional, and . . . the best architectural talent can only be secured through selection. . . . The result will be to the almost certain discredit of woman architects.[34]

Daniel Burnham circulated the design competition through the fair's department of publicity and promotion. The deadline was March 23, 1891. Applicants were supposed to be restricted to members of the architectural profession. Submissions were to be sealed and would be juried anonymously. The design of the 200-by-400-foot, two-story building was not to exceed $200,000 in construction costs and was to adhere to the classical style of the other fair buildings. The winning applicant would receive a $1,000 honorarium plus expenses; prizes of $500 and $250 would be awarded to the second- and third-place applicants, respectively. Thirteen women entered the competition, with only Parker being a practicing architect.[35] Burnham requested that Bertha Palmer attend the opening of the submissions; Palmer brought Frances Shepard and Amy Starkweather, the superintendent of the Woman's Building. Burnham insisted the three women select the first-, second-, and third-place winners at the meeting.

First place was awarded to Sophia Hayden, the first woman to graduate from the Massachusetts Institute of Technology's (MIT) four-year architectural program. She had recently graduated and was teaching mechanical drawing at the Eliot School in Jamaica Plain, Massachusetts. Lois Howe, a graduate from the MIT two-year architectural program and Hayden's friend, won second prize. Howe had first heard of the competition and enlisted Hayden to also submit a design. At the time, she was working as a junior architect in the firm of Francis Allen in Boston. Third place was awarded to Laura Hayes, who had no architectural training and was working as Palmer's personal assistant. Her third-place finish led to further questions regarding the credibility of the competition.

Both Hayden and Howe were trailblazers as university-trained female architects. Sophia Hayden was born in 1868 in Santiago, Chile, the daughter of a New England dentist, Dr. George Henry Hayden, and a Spanish woman. At the age of six, she moved to Jamaica Plain, Massachusetts, to live with her grandparents. In 1886, Hayden entered MIT and became the first woman to complete the four-year degree, receiving a Bachelor of Science in architecture, with honors. She was often described as gifted: reserved, modest, and someone with quiet determination, a valuable trait for a pioneer in any field. For her master's thesis, Hayden had designed a fine arts museum, in the Beaux Arts style taught at MIT. When she learned of the Woman's Building design competition from Lois Howe, they both decided to enter and "see what fortune would attend two institute girls." She used her thesis project as the foundation for her entry. While not working in a firm at the time of her submission, she had always intended to practice architecture.[36]

Lois Howe was born in 1864 in Cambridge, Massachusetts, where she grew up. After two years at the School of the Museum of Fine Arts in Boston, Howe enrolled in the two-year architectural program at MIT. In 1891, Howe wrote a letter to the building and grounds committee of the Columbian Exposition, offering her services to design the Woman's Building. A recommendation from renowned architect Robert Peabody, a member of the Architectural Board, accompanied her letter.[37]

On March 25, 1891, Burnham sent a telegram to Hayden congratulating her on her victory and requesting her to travel to Chicago immediately to commence work. She was situated at the fair site office in a room next to Burnham and Charles Atwood, the newly appointed consulting architect from New York. She was assigned two draftsmen to assist her in completing the plans. All seemed to progress as a normal project, with the architect developing the design through careful analysis and making modifications as necessary, due to changes in the program or recommendations from Burnham and Atwood. The condensed schedule placed additional stress on the project and Hayden's team, which was not driven by Burnham, but by Palmer, who wanted to see immediate progress on the building.[38]

SOPHIA G. HAYDEN.
Architect of the Woman's Building.

Figure 8.3. Sophia Hayden. *Harper's Weekly*, June–November 1892.

Figure 8.4. Lois Howe. Courtesy of MIT Institute Archives and Special Collections.

On May 26th, after completing the quarter-inch scaled drawings, Hayden departed Chicago for Boston, leaving the construction details to Burnham. The chief of construction seemed genuinely impressed with Hayden, stating, "I sincerely congratulate you upon the success of your plans, which is further evidenced by the construction."[39] Her decision to leave during its construction was consistent with the other architects' buildings, which were all detailed and built under Burnham's direction. However, given Palmer's tight grip on the design process, the decision proved fateful for Hayden. In December 1891, Burnham requested Hayden's return to Chicago to "inspect the work, and give us any further ideas you may desire carried out."[40]

Bertha Palmer had been busy during Hayden's six-month absence. Through Frank Millet, director of decorations, Palmer had issued a design competition for the sculptures for the Woman's Building. Hayden might have known about the national competition, but she was not consulted in the selection of artist. Throughout 1891–1892, Palmer crisscrossed Europe and the United States acquiring artwork for the Woman's Building and securing gifts from wealthy European and American donors. As art historian Wanda Corn notes, Palmer was "the sole coordinator of the decorations for the Woman's Building."[41] She saw herself as the primary decision maker in the design of the building, not Sophia Hayden.

Upon her arrival to the construction office, Hayden saw for the first time the models for the sculptures that would adorn the cornice of the building by Alice Rideout, a sculptor from Marysville, California. Rideout would also create *Place in History*, a relief sculpture in the cornice of the south façade. Hayden had hoped to design the interiors of the building, but gave up on the idea. In fact, Palmer had already assigned its interior design to Candace Wheeler, a decorator who, with Louis Comfort Tiffany, had decorated the interior of the Palmer mansion in 1884.[42] Admittedly, Wheeler was an experienced and highly competent decorator who was well accustomed to completing large-scale projects under tremendous pressure. She also shared Palmer's views of the role of women in society. While she believed in the importance of promoting women's skills and economic equality, she firmly believed that traditional femininity should be preserved and used the Woman's Building decorations to metaphorically promote this ideal, describing the interiors as "a man's ideal of woman—delicate, dignified, pure, and fair to look upon."[43]

At the Board of Lady Managers meeting in September 1891, Palmer invited the members to contribute ornamental materials such as marble columns, carved balustrades, and porcelain tiles. Many accepted the offer and soon the board office was accepting building materials from state commissions. Hayden was tasked with the review of these materials to determine if each object was usable, but as she noted, "it was too late to give these details the study that would have been necessary" to effectively incorporate them into her design.[44] Under normal circumstances, this type of work would have been part of the design development phase and not an afterthought during construction. At this late stage, Burnham would be involved, because the construction and schedule would have been impacted. And there were still many design decisions to be made. In April, while Hayden was rejecting some of these materials, she was still designing the 180-foot-long balustrade for the roof garden. Tensions increased when Palmer heard about Hayden's rejection of donations to the building from Laura Hayes and from the board members.

By the summer of 1892, Hayden had reached a breaking point. She wrote to Palmer, requesting an interview, but Palmer was traveling and did not reply to Hayden's request for a month. By then Hayden had left her post; during the summer she entered Burnham's office and had a nervous breakdown. She was ushered off the site and spent time in a rest home for "melancholia."[45] Hayden's collapse provided the excuse to question the feasibility of women working as architects. The *American Architect and Building News* stated:

Reports have been circulated to the effect that as a result of overwork she had broken down mentally, and that grave fears were entertained as to what the outcome might be. The reports might have been exaggerated, though the fact that Miss Hayden did break down is undoubtedly true, the state of her health being such that it was a question for some time whether brain fever might be the result. It is said that Miss Hayden had an especially aggravating experience with her superiors, the "Lady Managers" in their desire to incorporate into her building all sorts of bits of design and work, whether they harmonized in any particular with it or not, simply because they had been the work of women. It is reported that the Lady president has been of all others especially trying in this respect, forgetting in her zeal for women in general, what was due to the architect as architect. It may be that Miss Hayden's experience has been unusual, but the planning and construction of any building with the accompanying dealing with clients is always liable to be "especially trying" and it seems as if it was a question not yet answered how successfully a woman with her physical limitations can enter and engage in the work of a professional which is a wearing one. If this building of which the women seem to be so proud . . . is to mark the physical ruin of its architect, it will be a much more telling argument against the wisdom of women entering this especial profession than anything else could be. The provocation for worry may have been great, or this especial woman may have been exceptionally weak and nervous.[46]

While advocating for the role of architect as the lead artistic and technical author of any building, the author questioned whether women could handle the many demands placed on architects. The newly graduated architect Hayden's level of experience was not discussed.

Minerva Parker immediately came to her defense. Blaming the conditions of the design competition process in the first place, Parker described Hayden as a victim of her very success, stating, "What other building, whether given by appointment or by competition, could have fallen into the hands of an architectural student without experience or practice?"[47] She went on to chastise any critic who would use one woman's experience to question the validity of all women architects. This was noted by the *American Architect and Building News*, which commended her response stating, "Miss Hayden has been victimized by her fellow-women to such an extent that her health has been seriously . . . impaired, but we fancy the results would have been much the same had the work been as unwisely imposed upon a masculine beginner who had acquired only the same imperfect training and guided by the same immaturity of judgment and experience."[48]

Louise's Position on Women in Architecture

On March 6, 1891, Louise gave a lecture to the Buffalo Women's Education and Industrial Union titled "Women and Architecture." She spoke at a coterie, or small monthly gathering that was not well attended. However, her talk was published in the *Inland Architect* and became the seminal resource for understanding Louise's opinions on architecture and women in the profession and society. Louise drew from this lecture for profiles written on her, and the lecture was published in newspapers nationally. Praising Louise, the *Buffalo Courier* wrote, "It is unfortunate that the lecture was not packed. It is seldom that a lecture is delivered by a woman in such an easy, graceful manner, and at the same time with such force, always concise and to the point."[49]

Louise covered three topics: the role of women in architecture compared to women in other professions, the contemporary role of women in architecture of the 1890s, and the future of women in the profession. One of the most controversial comments she made that day was in reference to women's activism: "If in what I say of the future your personal prejudices are offended, pray remember that you have bound me by no previous confession of faith. The objects of the business woman are quite distinct from those of the professional agitator. Her aims are conservative rather than aggressive; her strength lies in adaptability, not in reform, and her desire is to conciliate rather than to antagonize."[50]

Louise's position against agitation and favoring adaptability over reform was consistent with other professional women of the time. As Judith Paine noted, any woman who "departed from the Victorian code . . . risked being labeled improper, peculiar, or both. These stigmas were especially dangerous to acquire in architecture, the practice of which depends upon securing commissions."[51]

Founded in 1884 by Buffalo socialite and activist Harriet Townsend, the Women's Educational and Industrial Union aimed to promote education and social reform for women, regardless of social status. Its motto was "Each for all and all for each." Louise had some history with the union; in 1886 they had purchased an historic mansion on Niagara Square and retained Bethune & Bethune to complete its renovations. However, the work was conducted by Robert Bethune on a pro bono basis, where the fees were drastically reduced or donated. (Louise did not perform pro bono work.) By 1891, the union decided to expand with a new building. This time they solicited Richard Waite, the Bethunes' former employer, as the architect, also working pro bono. Why would a women's organization whose sole purpose is to educate and advocate for working women not employ the first woman architect to design their building? The answer is fee. Louise demanded to be paid for her work. Understanding Louise's audience that day and the context in which she spoke—a few weeks after the announcement of the design competition for the Columbia Exposition and just after the union had selected a male architect to design their new headquarters—may explain her strident tone.

Unlike many early women architects, Louise did not receive the patronage of Buffalo's affluent women. There certainly were opportunities. Before the Women's Education and Industrial Union, the Buffalo Female

Academy commissioned a design for their Chapter House in 1884. While the association prided itself that theirs was the first clubhouse built by all women, they did not hire Louise but Rochester architect James G. Cutler. The YWCA funded a new building in 1888 but commissioned Edward Kent as the architect. The woman's social group, the Twentieth Century Club, hired Green & Wicks in 1893 to renovate and design their clubhouse, and in 1906, Buffalo Seminary, an exclusive private girls' school, commissioned Boston architect George F. Newton. Louise had female clients, but they did not belong to the social set who often supported women architects that Minerva Parker Nichols and, later, Julia Morgan enjoyed. Louise was firmly in the professional women's camp and this repeated snub may have impacted her attitude toward agitating in the first place.

Louise's partnership with two men enabled the firm to pursue architectural projects through conventional means. Additionally, because Robert performed pro bono work, the firm benefited from the good will generated by this work, while Louise was able to stand on principle and demand payment for her work. Louise's lack of interest in advocacy for women's rights, combined with her indifference in assisting various charities to advance their missions (often requiring pro bono work from professionals), may have contributed to the relationship between Louise and the union and other affluent women's social clubs. Without any surviving documentation, this relationship appears to be based on either antipathy from both sides or, at the very least, each pursued respectful, but distinctive, parallel paths.

Louise's position on women's equality can best be understood from her support for "equal remuneration for equal service," in particular regarding the Woman's Building. Her objections to the competition—besides the AIA's position against architects participating in design contests—were twofold. First, she objected to the fact that the male architects on the architectural board were appointed, while the women had to enter a competition to win the position. And second, the architect of the Woman's Building would receive a compensation of "about one-tenth" of that of her male counterparts for the same service. Based on this inequity, she did not submit an entry. Louise described the competition as the brainchild of the Board of Lady Managers, stating: "The board desires a woman architect, and the chief of construction has issued a circular inviting competition, notwithstanding the fact that competition is an evil against which the entire profession has striven for years, and has now nearly vanquished; it is unfortunate that it should be revived in its most objectionable form on this occasion, by women, and for women."[52]

Louise's remarks that day demonstrated a woman who was confident in her own abilities, her equality compared to her male colleagues, and her belief that "the future of woman in the architectural profession is what she herself sees fit to make it." Louise believed that her role as the first woman architect should include developing pathways for other women to pursue architecture, which may also have contributed to her decision to not enter the design competition. However, her closing comments regarding the Woman's Building competition were especially poignant and insightful: "It is an unfortunate precedent to establish just now, and it may take years to live down its effects."[53]

The Legacy of the Woman's Building

The Woman's Building was the first structure to be completed on the exposition grounds. The building was the site for the World's Congress of Representative Women, held in May 1893. The event was attended by suffrage luminaries such as Susan B. Anthony and Elizabeth Cady Stanton, where relevant and sometimes controversial papers were read on topics such as dress reform, education for girls, legal rights of women, and the vote.

Through the efforts of the architects of the fair, the AIA was successful in lobbying Congress to pass the Tarsney Act that established limited competitions for federal commissions. Although short-lived—the law was repealed in 1912—it demonstrates the influence these men gained from their work at the fair. In 1901, Senator James McMillan invited Daniel Burnham and Charles McKim to sit on the Senate Park Commission. Through this effort, they designed the master plan for the capital, based on the Court of Honor of the Columbian Exposition.[54]

World's fairs continued to erect women's buildings, but they were never as politically charged as the one at the Columbian Exposition. In 1895, for example, the Cotton States and International Exposition in Atlanta had a Woman's Building. Architect Elise Mercur from Pittsburgh submitted the winning design entry out of thirty others. In 1901, Buffalo hosted the Pan American Exposition. There was a women's building on its grounds, but it was used predominantly as a clubhouse for women visitors; an existing building was used for this purpose. Louise's good friend and fellow wheeler Dr. Ida Bender was the chair of education on the board of women managers, so any discussions on erecting a new building would have included Bethune. But she would have been too busy to assist anyway because she was working on the most important commission of her career, the Hotel Lafayette.

Lois Howe went on to have a prolific career. In 1901 she became the second woman to be admitted to the American Institute of Architects. Howe's career spanned forty-three years, from 1894 to 1937, during which she developed an expertise in residential housing, especially public housing. She entered a partnership with Eleanor Manning in 1913. The firm took a third partner, Mary Almy, in 1926. Approximately 426 commissions can be attributed to Howe and her partners. Minerva Parker married Unitarian minister William Nichols in 1894, the same year that she completed her most important commission, the New Century Club, in Philadelphia. This led to the commission for the New Century Club in Wilmington, Delaware. In 1896, the couple left Philadelphia and settled in Prospect Park, New York. Parker Nichols retired from her formal practice, yet periodically designed buildings after this time. She left a legacy of more than fifty buildings.[55] Sophia Hayden never worked again in the architectural profession. In 1900, she married artist William Blackstone Bennett in Winthrop, Massachusetts. She spent the rest of her life there, living quietly as an artist.[56]

Louise's refusal to participate in the World Columbia Exposition was often repeated in every subsequent account of her career, as was her belief

WOMAN'S BUILDING. DESIGNED BY SOPHIA G. HAYDEN, UNITED STATES.

Figure 8.5. The Woman's Building, Columbian Exposition, 1893. Sophia Hayden architect. Courtesy of the author.

in pay equity for women. On Sunday, November 9, 1913, just a month before she died, Louise was featured in the *Buffalo Sunday Morning News* article "Women in Buffalo's Professional and Business Life": "Mrs. Bethune has always been a strong believer in women's emancipation through equal pay for equal service. Because of her strong belief in the justice of this principle, she refused to submit plans in the competitive contest for the woman's building at the Columbia exposition, compensation for which was to be less than half that paid the men who submitted drawings."[57]

At the heart of the dramas surrounding the Woman's Building was a conflict among women on their future role in society: the wealthy women of influence who wished to maintain the status quo versus the more progressive suffragists who sought progressive change and women's equality. The question of professionalism was also poorly addressed at a time when architecture was maturing from a craft to take its place beside law and medicine as an expertise-driven occupation. At best, it was a missed opportunity; at worst, it was a setback for women architects.

Chapter 9

The "Triumphant" Hotel Lafayette—and Beyond

To Mrs. Louise Bethune . . . undoubtedly belongs the foremost place
among professional women of the city.

—"Women in Buffalo's Professional and Business Life"

Figure 9.1. Louise Bethune around the time she was designing the 1912 addition
to the Hotel Lafayette. Zina Bethune Archive on Louise Bethune, circa 1860–1962.
Courtesy of the University Archives, University at Buffalo.

The Gilded Age of America is often characterized as a period when the country emerged from the shadow of Great Britain and became a global economic leader. It was a time of exponential expansion in industry, transportation, invention, population, and wealth, at least for some. It was also a period when America began to look for expressions of identity that reflected its history and its newly earned status as a global player. Architects, landscape architects, and artists formed two distinct movements as part of this search for a new American identity. One was an avant-garde approach, which drew from nature, native materials, poetry, and new technologies to develop an aesthetic unique to its place and time. This new movement was primarily based in Chicago and became known as the Chicago School. Its leaders included Louis Sullivan and Dankmar Adler. The second, a much more widely accepted movement, looked to Europe and the great societies of Western civilization for expressions that best represented America's new position. This movement would become known as the American Renaissance.

The American Renaissance was marked by both a newly found deep interest in the young country's history and also in foreign cultures.[1] As stated by architectural historian Richard Guy Wilson, the term American Renaissance applies to the "identification of many Americans—painters; sculptors; architects; craftsmen; scholars; collectors; politicians; financiers, and industrialists—with the period of the European Renaissance and the feeling that the Renaissance spirit had been captured again in the United States."[2] The similarities are striking. The newly minted industrialists identified with the merchants of the Renaissance, and they sought to demonstrate their taste and sense of belonging through architectural design and art. They commissioned primary and secondary residences with extravagant budgets and sponsored cultural, educational, and institutional buildings.

Buffalo was deeply impacted by this movement. Its rich business and industrial leaders commissioned new mansions along Delaware Avenue—also known as Millionaire's Row—and other affluent streets within Olmsted's parkway system. They also made significant investments in new institutional and commercial buildings from local and nationally notable architects in a concerted effort to raise the standing of Buffalo as a sophisticated city, on par with New York, Boston, and Chicago.

In the first decade of the twentieth century, after the economic recovery from the 1893 Depression, Bethune, Bethune & Fuchs grew by realizing more prestigious projects with sophisticated designs, benefiting from the city's growth in wealth and interest in modern design. Starting with their work at the Hotel Lafayette, their architectural vocabulary reflected the American Renaissance aesthetic. Louise Bethune's interests outside of work also began to reflect the zeitgeist of the time. She joined the Daughters of the American Revolution (DAR), New England Historical Society, and the Buffalo Genealogical Society. However, this burst of productivity in her work would sadly be followed by a series of physical illnesses that would force Louise to leave the firm and the work she loved and spend her final two years convalescing and diminished.

Bethune's Magnum Opus: The Hotel Lafayette

The opening of the Hotel Lafayette, on June 2, 1904, was a momentous occasion for the city of Buffalo; the *New York Times* celebrated the new building, describing it as "one of the most perfectly appointed and magnificent hotels in this country."[3] The building was initially conceived in 1899 as a luxury hotel to meet the anticipated demand from the 1901 Pan American Exposition that was to take place in the city, and to serve Buffalo's rapidly expanding status as a center of commerce. However, the project faced numerous financial obstacles that jeopardized its completion. The grand opening, and its immediate success, inspired new business ventures for Bethune, Bethune & Fuchs and became their most important project.

Lafayette Square was (and remains) an important gathering place in Buffalo. It was part of Joseph Ellicott's 1804 radial plan for the city. It was called Courthouse Park until 1825, when the Marquis de Lafayette visited Buffalo while touring the country and gave a speech at the site; it was then renamed in his honor. The square hosted events of local and national significance from the start. In 1848, the Free Soil Convention took place in the square and the adjacent French Church, which had been a community meeting space and place of worship for more than sixty years and would become the site of the Hotel Lafayette. Its members opposed the expansion of slavery in the western states, and many of the attendees would become members of President Lincoln's cabinet and continue to fight slavery in the US.[4] In 1879, the Ladies Union Monument Association raised funds to erect the Civil War Soldiers and Sailors Monument in Lafayette Square. In 1881, the Ninth Congress for the Advancement of Women was held in the Buffalo Library, facing the square. The square was the site for rallies in support of both world wars and is still the location of public rallies and concerts.

The site was also personally significant for Louise. Richard Waite's architectural office was in the German Insurance Building, facing the square, and the Blanchard family lived in an apartment on 394 Main St., a half block from Lafayette Square from 1874 to 1879, when Louise was finishing high school and while she worked for Waite. And in 1888, she attended the national convention of the American Institute of Architects as a new member at the Central Library on Lafayette Square, where the AIA and WAA negotiated their merger.

Given the importance of the square and that particular site, the financial difficulties in bringing the Hotel Lafayette to fruition resulted in two years of anxiety, ridicule, and frustration for Buffalonians. In March 1899, a group of Buffalo businessmen gathered to determine the viability of erecting a hotel to compete with the well-established Iroquois Hotel, which was located at Main and Washington Streets. The upcoming 1901 Pan American Exposition presented the immediate need; however, there was a general belief that the growing city could support another luxury hotel. Local architect H. H. Little was retained to develop concept plans and elevations. In addition to the amenities expected in a luxury facility, there was a keen desire for the building to be "completely fireproof." Buildings during this era, in particular hotels, were often destroyed by fire; erecting fireproof buildings was one of the primary concerns of architects of Louise's generation. The initial budget was $800,000. The architect produced concept floor plans and renderings of the exterior in the Romanesque style for review.[5] The original financial partners in the project were local, including Joseph A. Oaks and Charles A. Pooley. In October 1899, it was reported that the owners had selected new architects, Bethune, Bethune & Fuchs.[6]

However, on April 1, 1900, a new financial partnership was announced that included Oaks, Pooley, Walter Clapp, and Henry Wills; both Clapp and Wills were from Boston. The name Hotel Lafayette was unveiled, and Henry Ives Cobb was listed as the architect.[7] Cobb was originally from Boston and was educated at MIT and Harvard, and then relocated to Chicago. Upon graduation, he worked for Peabody & Stearns in Boston for a short period. In 1881, he won the commission for the Union Club in Chicago and moved there. Among his notable Chicago projects were the Potter and Bertha Palmer Residence in 1882, the Wellington Hotel in 1890, the Newberry Library in 1893, and the Fisheries Building at the World Columbian Exposition in 1893. The choice of a nationally recognized architect demonstrates the partners' ambitions for the building. The $925,000 Hotel Lafayette project was to be complete by April 1, 1901, in time for the opening of the Pan American Exposition.

At first, the project advanced quickly; the land was acquired and existing buildings, including the French Church, were demolished by June. Cobb released a rendering of the nine-story building, in a Venetian Renaissance Revival style, of light gray brick and terra cotta.[8] By July 21, 1900, excavation was complete and the foundations were started. And then the project came to a halt. By the fall, rumors were circulating that the partners were having financial difficulties, and by late fall, the partnership had failed.

On June 7, 1901, J. A. Oaks announced he was assembling a new financial partnership to complete the project and address the "hole in the ground," as the site was now known locally. Bethune, Bethune & Fuchs were renamed as its architects. The Bethunes knew both Oaks and Pooley,

Figure 9.2. Rendering of the Hotel Lafayette by Henry Ives Cobb, June 1900. Collection of the Buffalo History Museum. *Pan-American Magazine* 2, no. 3 (June 1900): 4.

the directors of the short-lived Jav-O Cereal Coffee Company, for whom they had designed a factory in 1898. They had also designed Oaks's residence in 1899 at 281 Parkside Ave. (see chapters 3 and 6). Finally, the firm's partners had some hotel-design experience, albeit limited; they had made the plans for the remodeling of Buffalo's Agency Building to a hotel in November 1900.[9] And, while it had occurred years earlier, both Robert and Louise worked on the Pierce Palace Hotel design while apprenticing for Richard Waite in 1876–1881.

By August 7, 1901, the Monument Square Hotel Corporation was formed with Buffalo partners J. A. Oaks, C. J. Spaulding, and H. H. Persons. The partners announced that construction would begin on September 1 and be complete in one year.[10] The cost for the project was estimated at $600,000, and the first-class hotel would be fireproof and have 250 rooms.[11] But again, the project failed due to insufficient finances. On March 20, 1902, the corporation defaulted on its mortgage payments, and foreclosure proceedings were filed.[12] It took wealthy Rochester businessman Walter B. Duffy to save the project. Although the property was scheduled to be auctioned on June 5th, Duffy paid off the mortgage and acquired the property that July.[13] Duffy decided to continue the project as conceived by the Monument Square partners and use the designs of Bethune, Bethune & Fuchs and not start anew. While the design was not complete, the exterior materials of red brick and terra cotta had been selected, as had the size of the building and the budget of $700,000. Delays in obtaining the iron were expected to delay the onset of construction by more than eighteen months.[14]

"It's a Beauty"

The New Hotel Lafayette: Pictures from the architects' drawing showing the design of the building which is to occupy the site at the corner of Washington and Clinton streets in this city. It's a beauty.

—"Buffalo's Fine New Hotel"

With the Hotel Lafayette, Louise finally was given the opportunity to demonstrate her design abilities on a project that was worthy of national attention. It was her redemption for the missed opportunity from the Women's Building. All subsequent interviews and profiles proudly described the Hotel Lafayette and Louise's prominent role as its designer. It was her only architectural project that received national coverage in the press. When she died in 1913, her many obituaries stated that Louise "took special pride in the work of planning the Lafayette Hotel."[15]

Both Louise and Robert were deeply involved with the Hotel Lafayette project. Robert acted as the spokesperson for the firm to the press and ran the business side of the project. He and J. A. Oaks made at least one trip to New York in late March 1902 to view similar hotels.[16] Louise described her role in January 1909 as "superintending the alterations and additions to the Lafayette Hotel."[17] Taking the role of lead designer and construction supervisor was a bold step for a woman of this era.

There is no account from Bethune, Bethune & Fuchs regarding their choice of French Renaissance for the hotel's exterior design. However, it was probably not selected because of either pressure from the community or suggestions made from Oaks, Spaulding, and the other business partners, because neither of the previous architects chose it. H. H. Little's design was reported to be Romanesque, and Henry Ives Cobb's design was a Venetian

Figure 9.3. Rendering of the Hotel Lafayette by Bethune, Bethune & Fuchs Architects, October 1902. This was the first view of the hotel for the public and the rendering is still one of the most used images of the hotel to this day. Courtesy of the author.

variation of Italian Renaissance Revival. Lafayette Square had an eclectic mix of buildings in revival styles, Second Empire and Romanesque, so any of the revival styles would have fit the bill. However, styles in the French tradition were more prominent on Lafayette Square than the others.

Just as important, luxury hotels and mansions in Buffalo and New York were often designed in French styles. French Renaissance would have been considered complementary to Buffalo's Iroquois Hotel. The Iroquois's predecessor, the Richmond Hotel, had burned down in 1887 in a horrific fire that resulted in the deaths of fifteen employees and guests. It was renamed and rebuilt in 1890 by the Buffalo-based firm Eisenwein & Johnson in the Second Empire style.[18] One of the Lafayette's managers, George Sweeney, also ran New York's Hotel Victoria. Richard Morris Hunt had designed it as a luxury apartment building, and it was converted to a hotel in 1879. The building was designed in the Second Empire style and was the size of an entire block on Twenty-Seventh Street, between Fifth Avenue and Broadway. The Bethunes worked closely with Sweeney and stayed at the Victoria on numerous occasions.

Additionally, from the 1870s through the 1890s, an increasing number of residential buildings were constructed in the French styles, including many of the townhouses built for Gilded Age millionaires, who chose Second Empire, French Renaissance, and Beaux-Arts Classicism for their buildings. Richard Morris Hunt; McKim, Mead & White; John Kellum; and Carrere & Hastings were busily incorporating the modern French vocabulary for the New York townhouses of the Vanderbilt, Astor, Stewart, Slone, and Tiffany families, to name a few.[19] Employing the French style in the hands of skilled architects was de rigueur.[20] By the early twentieth century, a series of luxury hotels began to pop up in New York, and because the French styles were the well-established architectural vocabulary for New York's elite, they became the prominent style for these hotels. One example is the Hotel Broztell, at 7 East Twenty-Seventh St., which was designed by architect/engineer/author William Birkmire and opened in 1905. Although very different in scale and proportion, the choices in material and detail at the Broztell bear a strong resemblance to the Hotel Lafayette.

A pamphlet for the Hotel Lafayette was published shortly after it opened. It described the exterior "of dark red vitreous brick and trimmings of semi-glazed white terra cotta" and the "marquise carriage porch and window balconies" of wrought iron.[21] The exterior façade at the first floor was composed entirely of terra cotta. The arched openings over the storefront windows and doors had a Romanesque aesthetic that was common in the Italianate and French Renaissance styles. The beveled corner of the building that faced the intersection of Washington and Clinton Streets was the focus of the building, serving as the main entrance. The choice suites were located on the upper floors. The most important of these suites was located on the second floor and was accentuated by a wrought-iron terrace, overlooking Lafayette Square. The second-floor windows were capped with pediment details. Windows running along the perimeter, upper floor, and second floor were detailed with terra cotta quoining. The frieze detailing the roofline provided the greatest ornamentation, with terra cotta corbels and classical egg-and-dart sculpture. Three lion's heads, a common detail in French Renaissance buildings, kept watch over the main entry. The windows in the field of the building elevation were relatively unadorned, with only a keystone embellishing the header.

The interior made quite a stir. Described as the "Waldorf Astoria of Buffalo" when it opened, the decor was praised, noting there was "nothing like it between New York and Chicago."[22] The prominent design firm of Duryea & Potter, from New York, is credited with the decorations in the public space.[23] The lobby was finished in Numidian marble and mahogany. The white marble tile floor and the abundance of windows on Washington and Clinton Streets would have brightened an otherwise darker, yet rich, palette. The coffered ceiling was the most decorative aspect of the lobby. As reported during the opening, the "entire ceiling is treated in harmonizing shades of gold. The decorative frieze above the wainscoting is carried out on gold-leaf tapestry. A bronze piacque effect is produced between each panel, giving the profile of General Lafayette and his associated officers."[24]

The Corinthian capitals of the marble columns met the wood-beamed ceiling with plaster cartouche ornamentations. The initials "LH," which were carved in the plaster and brass light fixtures were a delicate touch that was carried throughout many of the rooms on the first floor. The ladies reception room sat adjacent to the lobby and had the same finishes. Great attention was paid to detail in the other public rooms on the first floor, although the marble was replaced with scagliola, a form of plasterwork mixed with dyes and glues to imitate marble or granite. Scagliola was a cost-effective method of maintaining the rich aesthetic in the public spaces of the hotel. Today, much of this portion of the hotel no longer exists because it was replaced by an Art Moderne design during the renovations of the 1940s.

The outer restaurant was "an artistic blending of brown and green, relieved by decorations in gold."[25] Facing Washington Street, the room was distinctive for its liberal use of English oak in the wainscoting, pilasters, and coffered ceiling. The plaster ornamentation—the egg and dart and palmette in the pilaster capital, and the cartouche in the beams—were relatively understated when compared to the other rooms. The lightly colored vaulted ceiling of the grill room added to the sense of intimacy of the space and brightened it as well. This offset the dark mood set by the Flemish oak wainscoting and pilasters, and dark red floor tile. As reported at the opening, in this room, the "decorations are on genuine leather, representing different studies of Falstaff . . . the drapings are of leather, and the windows have obscure leaded glass."[26] Although similar architectural finish materials were used in the outer restaurant and the grill room, the effect was different in each, with the outer restaurant exuding a more formal atmosphere and the grill room being much less so.

The hotel boasted state-of-the-art amenities of the day: telephones and running water throughout; bathrooms in many of the private rooms; and, as every advertisement stated, it was "COMPLETELY FIREPROOF."[27] The success of the hotel led to the need for an addition. By 1909, plans began for the hotel's expansion by the firm, which was completed in 1912. Louise supervised this project and replicated many of the finishes of the original building.

Several spaces were removed as part of the 1912 expansion. The first was the grand staircase, which led the to the Ladies Parlor, the Banquet Room, and the private suites on the second floor. Flanked by four Numidian marble Corinthian columns in the main lobby, it was called an "architectural triumph," which must have been very satisfying for the architects.[28] The main corridor terminated at the Tea Room, which was located just behind the grand staircase. This space was less a room and more a well-appointed alcove, just off the kitchen. The oval plaster ceiling articulation and two-bay niche with backlit stained glass skylight were the primary architectural features. Finally, the Writing Room was located adjacent to the Grill Room, and was surrounded by wainscoting and pilasters decorated with scagliola.

While they were finalizing plans for the Lafayette addition, on October 12, 1910, Louise was asked to accompany George Sweeney, his wife, and business partner, Harry Yates, to inspect two hotels in Chicago, the Blackstone and the La Salle, which had both recently opened. Louise took several guided tours of the facilities with the hotel superintendents, taking copious notes and offering technical advice along the way. Louise's comments on the buildings were based on design and technical matters, demonstrating her interest and expertise in both areas.[29]

The Lafayette addition doubled the size of the hotel. It also relocated the front entrance from the intersection entry to the Clinton Street side of the building. Among the most noteworthy spaces in the new addition were the Orchard Restaurant, the Auto Club of Buffalo, and Peacock Alley.

Figure 9.4. Lafayette Square with the newly opened Hotel Lafayette. Image courtesy of the author.

Figure 9.5. Hotel Lafayette today. Photo by Douglas Levere, University at Buffalo.

The promoters described the Orchard Restaurant as "dainty."[30] The white and gold ornamental room with crystal light fixtures was designed to be used primarily for ladies' dining. (Today it is known as the Crystal Room.) As opposed to the Orchard Restaurant, the Auto Club Room was polychromatic; it was designed to house the Auto Club's business office. Peacock Alley was designed to be a multifunction space. Envisioned as a place for receptions, dining, displaying art, and for use as a corridor, and—most importantly—promenade, this space was in some respects the lifeblood of the hotel from which all emanated.[31]

In the wide corridor, the main features were the Corinthian pilasters, copied from the 1904 building, scagliola finished walls, and a spectacular 7-foot-high-by-116-foot-long painting from 1885 by American painter Abbott Fuller Graves, named *Périgny sur Yerres*, a town in Southern France.[32] The integration of art and architecture was a dominant theme during the American Renaissance, in particular showcasing American history in painting and sculpture. Graves began his formal training as a painter in Boston and then continued in Paris and Italy. Many of his paintings were lush floral landscapes, often including female figures. The allegorical depiction of young women was common in the American Renaissance. The young, naïve, and beautiful female figure was often used to represent the American values of virtue and liberty.

The integration of artwork was even more evident in the new Lafayette Room, which was the former Grill Room. This time, the room became the primary dining facility for the hotel and was redecorated with an overtly patriotic tone. As described when it opened:

> The decorative scheme of this essentially English room commemorates America's emancipation from British rule. The massive carved oak fireplace from Knole House, Sevenoaks, the ancient seat of the Archbishops of Canterbury, has its large center panel occupied by a fine painting of the coat-of-arms of the Marquis de La Fayette. This biazon was obtained by owners in Paris and is thought to be the only authentic copy in this country. The lofty frieze, which occupies the elliptical lunettes between the groins, commemorates other Revolutionary patriots who were the young Lafayette's instructors in the principles of liberty, equality and fraternity and the devastating terrors of war. The frieze panel next [to] the large fireplace has as chief motif the coat-of-arms of General Washington, whose stars and stripes suggested the national flag of the United States. Other patriots

Figure 9.6. Hotel Lafayette Lobby when it was opened in 1904. Bethune, Bethune & Fuchs Architects. Image courtesy of the author.

of Revolutionary days whose ancestral arms occupy prominent place in the decorations are Franklin, Jefferson, Otis, Hancock and Schuyler . . . a veritable Hall of American Armory.[33]

Given Bethune's patriotic inclinations, this would have immensely satisfied her. The Hotel Lafayette was successful for decades and underwent several additions. Will Fuchs designed a ballroom addition in 1916–1917 (following the deaths of Louise and Robert); Eisenwein & Johnson designed the south addition in 1924–1926; the Lobby and the Crystal Ballroom were renovated in the Art Moderne style in 1942 and 1946, respectively. In 1962, the Yates family sold the property. It changed ownership again in 1978 and was operated as a rooming house until 2010, a neglected and diminished reminder of Buffalo's once proud place of prestige in the country. However, the building's fate was about to change. In 2010, the Hotel Lafayette was listed on the National Register of Historic Places, the only building by Louise Bethune to receive this distinction. In 2012, Buffalo developer Rocco Termini invested $35 million with the use of historic tax credits and the careful direction of Jon Morris from Carmina Wood Morris Architects to fully restore the building. Today, Louise's opus can be experienced as she had intended, and Lafayette Square is once again the busy center of a city emerging with its own renaissance.

Figure 9.7. Lafayette Room (former Grill Room), Hotel Lafayette. Courtesy of the author.

Figure 9.8. Peacock Alley, Hotel Lafayette, 1911. Courtesy of the author.

Figure 9.9. Peacock Alley today, Hotel Lafayette. Photo by Douglas Levere, University at Buffalo.

Figure 9.10. *Périgny sur Yerres*, painting by Abbott Fuller Graves in Peacock Alley at the Hotel Lafayette. Photo by Douglas Levere, University at Buffalo.

Aftermath

The Lafayette Hotel project was the most prestigious of Bethune's career. It was the only nationally recognized building in the firm's portfolio. The ambitious client provided a budget to ensure a quality in details and finishes that Louise rarely enjoyed. The success of this project brought other clients with noteworthy commercial commissions; many of these commercial projects were designed in the French Renaissance style, in keeping with the Hotel Lafayette.

Bethune, Bethune & Fuchs were listed as the architect for the new Hotel London in London, Ontario, in 1906. It was reported that Buffalo-based entrepreneurs were financing the seven-story hotel. The design of the $100,000 structure was based on the Hotel Spalding (later Hotel Woodstock) in New York, which is a blonde brick and terra cotta French Renaissance building. It appears this building was never realized. Other commercial buildings in Buffalo, however, were. Louise designed three of them: the Wilson Building, Bricka & Enos Department Store, and Denton, Cottier & Daniels Music Store. The factory work continued, and they also designed department stores; the firm drew practical lessons from their experience in factory and hotel design in these designs during the final stage of Louise's productive career.

The first decade of the twentieth century saw the development of the factory from a masonry, dark, and monolithic structure to an open, light-filled

VIEW OF NEW WAREHOUSE, IROQUOIS DOOR COMPANY

Figure 9.11. Rendering of the Iroquois Door Company Building, 1904. Courtesy of the author.

one with a regular floor plan that allowed for flexibility in use. Advances in reinforced concrete made this innovation possible. These industrial buildings would profoundly influence European architects in the 1920s, who would usher in a monumental shift in architectural sensibilities known as the International style specifically and the modern movement in general. American architect Albert Kahn is widely credited with the initial design of the daylight factory. The building type was engineering-driven, meant for the purely practical reasons of maximizing space and daylight for workforce productivity. Kahn's 1903 Building No. 10 for the Packard Motor Company in Detroit was very influential in establishing this new style. The reinforced concrete frame supported and distributed the loads, allowing for generous column bays and, therefore, vast expanses of open spaces. Because the perimeter building skin was also non-load-bearing, exterior elevations could be composed of expansive windows, virtually flooding the floor with natural light.

Just a year after Kahn's Packard building, Bethune, Bethune & Fuchs designed the Iroquois Door Company on Exchange Street in the heart of Buffalo's industrial district. In *A Concrete Atlantis*, architectural historian Reyner Banham described the building as a "model of puritanically stern, rectangular discipline, achieved by using concealed metal angles for the spans and plain stone sills under the windows."[34] The building was designed to be as practical and efficient as possible, with absolutely no ornamentation or definition of the brick façade to reflect the column grid. Windows span the structural bays. Surrounded by similarly unadorned factories and warehouses, the building's severe and simplistic façade was designed completely in context to its industrial environment and purpose. The three-story building was so successful that it was expanded with a new story in the 1920s. The simple structure and façade would influence the firm's commercial work for the remainder of the decade.

Its neighbors were the Larkin Soap Company's factory buildings. Frank Lloyd Wright's Larkin Administration Building also opened in 1904. The revolutionary design of that building provided a new way of thinking about the workplace. The new space celebrated the worker, with natural light, large expanses of workspace for the Larkin clerks, and inspirational quotations on the walls on the virtue of work. It was also a very muscular building, entirely at home in its industrial context.

The Bethune firm created similarly functional buildings for other clients. The $20,000 blonde brick warehouse for Jacob Dold demonstrates an aesthetic that combines the utilitarian needs of the warehouse in concert with the urban needs of a mercantile zone of the city.

The relatively modest 1906 Wilson Building was a mixed-use structure, with elements from the Hotel Lafayette that can be found in its

Figure 9.12. Elevation of the Jacob Dold Warehouse. Bethune, Bethune & Fuchs Architects, 1904. Courtesy of the Author.

Figure 9.13. Jacob Dold Warehouse Building today. Douglas Levere, University at Buffalo.

French Renaissance design. The construction of the Wilson Building was announced in mid-1905, and the building opened at the end of the year. It is an example of the changing fabric of Buffalo's architecture before World War I. The two-story commercial and office building was built in brick and terra cotta and was designed to house five stores, and offices on the second floor. The Main Street symmetrical façade was broken into five bays, with a continuous frieze and parapet detail over the center and end bays. The frieze, similarly, provided the greatest ornamentation, with terra cotta corbels. The lion's heads reappeared, four sculptures this time, watching over Main Street. The second-floor windows were articulated with terra cotta quoining. The center bay was articulated with a door and pediment and Doric columns on the second floor.

After the building opened, it was used to hold a series of exhibits, fundraising sales, and festivals. One example of this was the exhibit of New England relics by the National Society of New England Women, in which Louise served as a member and treasurer. She may very well have planned

Figure 9.14. Wilson Building, 1905, photo circa 1920. Collection of the Buffalo History Museum, general photograph collection, Streets—Main and Tupper.

the exhibit. Another event was an Easter sale in support of the Western New York branch of the International Sunshine Society.

The Daniels Building (1908) was monumental in scale and is noteworthy for how it integrated the new construction technology developed for factory design in a commercial building. The music store Denton, Cottier & Daniels was established in 1827, and its founder, James D. Shepard, is credited with bringing the first piano to Buffalo.[35] It was considered the oldest music store in America and the largest between Chicago and New York.[36] In addition to simply selling musical instruments—in particular pianos—to Buffalo families, the company also promoted cultural entertainment in the city, selling tickets to local concerts and providing practice space in the store for those learning an instrument. Professional musicians touring through the area were often found practicing there on the day of their performance.

Figure 9.15. Rendering of the Daniels Building, Bethune, Bethune & Fuchs Architects, circa 1907. Courtesy of the author.

The Daniels Building opened in 1908 at the corner of Court and Pearl Streets, and was described in the press: "The building is not only a testimonial to the material growth and progress of Buffalo but also an adornment architecturally to the city and a monument to the love of music among the people of this city."[37]

The site was deliberate and fortuitous. By not having a Main Street address, the company was "breaking away from the idea of a one-street town and to step forth as a leader in a greater Buffalo, whose activities and prosperity are not dependent upon a single thoroughfare."[38] The company saw itself as a leader in the community and a pioneer of its development. The corner lot location provided Bethune, Bethune & Fuchs with the opportunity to impact two street façades significantly. The five-story yellow Kittanning brick-and-cream terra cotta building was in a very restrained French Renaissance style. However, the detail was considerably more streamlined than previous buildings. And the large proportion of glass in the twenty-one-foot bay storefront was reminiscent of the façade of the Iroquois Door Company warehouse from 1904. The amount of glass was noted at the time in the local press: "The Daniels Building . . . has proportionately more glass space and window light than any other building in Buffalo, and is equaled by few if any in this respect in the country."[39]

Certainly, the building glazing is similar to the work of Chicago School architects such as Louis Sullivan and John Root from the 1890s. But the lack of ornamentation, aside from the corbels in the frieze, the terra cotta keystones topping the fifth-story arched windows, and the capital of the pilasters, was remarkable and hints at the modern movement that was to come following the Great War. The first floor held the sheet music department, administrative offices (with skylight), and special ticket office to purchase tickets to musical events throughout the city. The second through fourth floors were showrooms for both upright and grand pianos, with an entire floor devoted to Steinway pianos; the fifth floor held a workshop for tuners, polishers, and the storeroom. Programmatically, the building shares much in common with the Iroquois warehouse. The music store was, after all, a sales and storage facility for large and heavy musical instruments. And the need of the customers for natural light when purchasing pianos and sheet music or playing the instruments in the store was very similar to factory workers requiring natural light to enhance their productivity. It was quite natural for the architects to draw from their industrial design experience for this project.

In addition to the proportion of glass for this mercantile use, the building also was designed with a steel-frame construction and monolithic concrete floor slabs. Indeed, the Daniels Building was the first steel mercantile building in Buffalo, with the steel coming from the local Lackawanna Steel Company, a major supplier. The need for a fireproof facility was still a concern and necessity in 1908. For insurance, the stairways were constructed of iron and slate. When it opened, it was considered a symbol of an important company and for the city in which it was founded, "the new store marks an advance over all that has gone before. It typifies the new city, the Greater Buffalo, and the Daniels Building stands as a symbol of the energy, the sagacity, the success of the firm which has been a part of Buffalo for well nigh a century."[40]

Many of the design elements of the Daniels Building were also used in the Bricka & Enos Department Store Building that opened one year later. Bricka & Enos was a Buffalo-based furniture store. Founded in the 1880s, they built a following by offering store credit for furniture sets.[41] By 1908 they were a multistore institution ready to expand again. They relocated to a new commercial building designed by Bethune, Bethune & Fuchs for the John Greiner Estate, at 621–623 Main. The four-story, midblock structure was designed in the French Renaissance style. The materials were yellow brick with terra cotta details. Because the building was intended to be a four-story department store, the windows encompass most of the façade and remain the same scale throughout. Many of the details from the Wilson Building and, therefore, the Hotel Lafayette are utilized here. The building is capped by a terra cotta parapet detail and the frieze at the roofline is defined by corbel ornamentation. The arched windows on the fourth floor have a keystone detail and are joined with the third-floor windows by exterior trim. Like the Hotel Lafayette, the second-floor windows are the most richly detailed, with terra cotta quoining and capped by a cartouche. The first floor was quite modern, with no ornamentation at all, simply a glass storefront.

Standing adjacent to the very ornate Neo-Classical Market Arcade Building, the Bricka & Enos Building looks modern and unadorned. Buffalo architects Green & Wicks designed the indoor shopping arcade in 1892. Today, the two buildings are connected, sharing an address and internal connecting elevator, with the former Bricka & Enos Building now holding a restaurant on the first floor and offices, including an architectural firm, on the second through fourth floors. The Bricka & Enos Department Store was the last building credited to Louise, aside from the 1912 addition to the Hotel Lafayette.

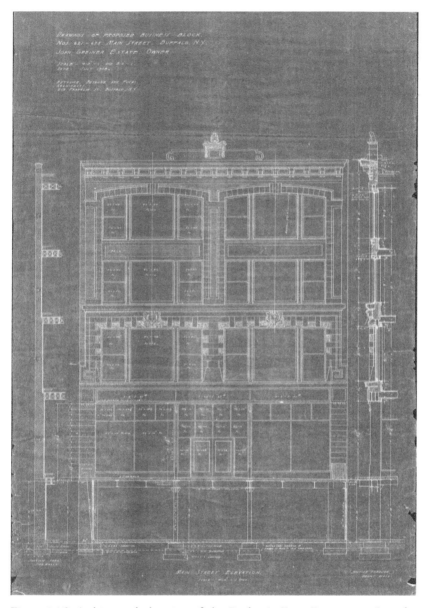

Figure 9.16. Architectural elevation of the Bricka & Enos Department Store by Bethune, Bethune & Fuchs Architects, 1908. Zina Bethune Archive on Louise Bethune, circa 1860–1962. Courtesy of the University Archives, University at Buffalo.

Figure 9.17. Former Bricka & Enos Building today. Douglas Levere, University at Buffalo.

Personal Pursuits and Life After Architecture

In 1897, Louise contacted Williams H. Manning, a distant Blanchard relative living in West Somerville, Massachusetts, regarding her family history. She noted, "I am a business woman with very little time or money to spend on genealogy but my interest is great."[42] In January of that year, the Buffalo Women's Wheel and Athletic Club had disbanded, and by November, Louise was pursuing genealogy as her primary pastime activity. She was not alone in this fascination. Starting with the centennial of the American Revolution in 1876, Americans became interested in their ancestry and the history of the country.[43] Genealogy clubs and historical societies started cropping up in communities throughout the country. The Buffalo Genealogical Society was founded in 1899; Louise was an early member and served as its registrar in 1903–1904 and president in 1907–1908. During this decade, Bethune conducted extensive research on the Blanchard, Williams, and Bethune families.[44]

In concert with her genealogical research, Louise successfully applied for membership to the Daughters of the American Revolution in 1904 through Ebenezer Williams, her maternal great-grandfather. This led to her involvement with the Society of New England, for which she served as treasurer. It was at this time that Bethune discontinued her activities with the professional architecture associations. She ended her AIA membership in 1904, which has led to the erroneous but widespread belief that she also retired in 1904. On the contrary, this decade was her most prolific professionally. However, she had scaled back her AIA national activities after the merger of the WAA and AIA, and the Woman's Building competition, which occurred within two years of each other. Regionally, the passage of the New York State Architect's Licensing Bill in 1906 was the culmination of what she had hoped to achieve through her AIA and WAA memberships. Because she was now interested in her researching her family's history, she decided to focus any energies and time outside of the office on these pursuits.

Louise's genealogical correspondence is filled with anecdotes from a successful woman who was fitting a personal passion in the schedule of a more-than-full-time occupation and the running of a busy firm.[45] Many letters opened with apologies for tardy replies due to her job responsibilities. The last of these was written on July 14, 1910, to Alexander Mackenzie in Toronto, in which she noted, "This is our very busiest season always and this year we are especially rushed."[46] She was working on the addition to the Hotel Lafayette at that time. However, the following month, Robert wrote Mackenzie: "Mrs. Bethune has been ill for several months and is now just beginning to recover although she is still confined to her bed with a trained nurse."[47]

Sometime between 1911 and 1913, Louise wrote the essay "It Is to Laugh" for family and close friends, describing the period when she was convalescing. Many of the stories are peculiar and the structure of the essay is rambling, demonstrating an incoherence that can be attributed to her illness. However, there are also interesting anecdotes that describe the stress Louise was under just before she became sick. She was managing the practice, serving as the design and technical lead on the Hotel Lafayette addition, and overseeing her rental property, performing the maintenance duties herself.[48] According to her essay, Louise had just recovered from five months of bronchitis when, in January 1910, she suffered a fall outside of her home and broke her coccyx, the lowest bone of the spine. It took five months to heal, and she attributed her subsequent illnesses to this episode.[49] She was well enough—or forced herself to be well enough—to travel to Chicago with George Sweeney and Harry Yates on a business trip in October 1910, as discussed earlier in this chapter. However, after her return home she became sick again with a bladder infection, which required bed rest. Then while she was recovering from the Chicago trip she received yet another call from Sweeney, who had come to Buffalo from New York to consult with her and Yates on the design of the Hotel Lafayette expansion. Although she was barely able to sit in bed, she willed herself up, put on a red wrap dress and fur coat, and took a painful taxi ride to her office for the meeting; she was taken home by an employee afterward. This project meeting led to yet another recovery period in bed.[50]

Louise's condition took a turn for the worse in August 1911, when she wrote a colleague that she was recovering from a protracted illness. All subsequent correspondence referenced her illness, and what had been frequent episodes of ill health now became permanent convalescence. By April 1912, she noted that she had been seriously ill for over a year. At that time, she could sit up for two or three hours at a time but had to walk around the house on crutches.[51] Lifting heavy books was nearly impossible, yet she expressed confidence that she would recover and resume her studies, at least.[52] Yet in a letter dated March 2, 1912, Louise wrote a somber note, "Have been a hard working professional woman for thirty-five years but think I shall only putter from now on."[53]

During this period of convalescence, Louise was very diminished but still had the ability and empathy to help others in need. In a letter to her friend, Miss Woodcock, who was about to be institutionalized for a nervous condition, she shared her own experience with depression: "I know well what it is to have a heart that feels like a stone bruise." She encouraged her friend to sleep outside if she could while at the institution, as Louise did often during the summer.[54] Shortly thereafter, in a letter to her uncle, Charles Williams, about a family member's upcoming nuptials she wrote, "My prolonged illness has cost me so much that gifts are about out of the question with me."[55]

On January 24, 1913, Bethune responded to a letter stating that she "was in the hospital, literally on my back, and with iritis [inflammation that affects the colored ring around your eye's pupil] and conjectavitis [sic] in addition to various other afflictions brought on by years of overwork."[56] Disturbingly, she also stated, "I have had a long illness but for some time have sat up a few hours a day and have several times thought I would take up my genealogical correspondence again, but found myself too weak to handle my letter files, [to] verify references."[57]

Louise's genealogy correspondence stopped with the January 1913 letter, so there is no record of her activity or correspondence during her last year. Luckily, on November 9, 1913, the *Buffalo Sunday Morning News* published an article titled "Women in Buffalo's Professional and Business Life." Its date of publication is particularly poignant because it occurred just one month before Louise died. Louise was described as the most prominent woman in business, despite her diminished condition, and the fact that she had been sick for two years and had not worked professionally in that time. However, that was not the only professional acknowledgment that Bethune received during the decade, because both she and Robert were also included in *The National Cyclopedia of American Biography* in 1904 and *Who's Who in New York* in 1909. Interestingly, Louise was also included in the 1904 anthology *Women in the Fine Arts, from the Seventh Century B.C. to the Twentieth Century A.D.*, but did not respond to the author's request to contribute additional information to the book. This may have been because of work demands or a lack of interest in participating in a professional (she had resigned from the AIA at this time) or gender-specific publication.[58]

Robert and Charles nursed Louise while she was ill, so her death, on December 18, 1913, of kidney disease, was probably expected. This sad event made local news and it was picked up by the national press and, of course, architectural newsletters. Her passing inspired these publications to take stock of the advancement of women in architecture since the ground-breaking opening of her office in 1881. Sadly, these advances were not as significant as many had hoped, herself included. Noting that Louise had achieved a position that few other women equaled as architects, the *Western Architect* noted, "It is therefore, not because of a lack of example that the woman architect has not become a feature in architectural practice."[59]

Louise had filed her will on January 4, 1908, listing three beneficiaries: her mother, Emma Blanchard; Robert; and Charles. To her mother, Louise bequeathed most of her estate, probably to ensure that her mother would be financially secure should Louise die first. Emma inherited Louise's personal property in Mattapoisett, Massachusetts; her rental property at 331 Tonawanda Street, Buffalo; as well as clothing, jewelry, and her savings outside of money connected to the firm. Robert inherited Louise's financial interest in the firm, her architectural library, and papers. Robert and Charles jointly inherited the family residence at 904 Tonawanda Street. At the time the will was written, both Robert and Will Fuchs were still in debt to Louise for their shares of the firm, which shows that she was the primary property holder in the family and the major financial partner of the firm.[60]

Following Louise's death, Robert and Will continued to run the firm. One of their projects was the Frontier Theater, in 1913, which was located on Rhode Island and West Streets in Buffalo. But Robert did not survive Louise for long; he died after a five-week illness resulting in a failed gall-bladder surgery on July 17, 1915.[61] Both Louise and Robert were cremated and laid in the same burial plot at Buffalo's Forest Lawn Cemetery. When they were buried, only Robert's name was listed on the headstone. This might have been a family tradition because Emma and Dalson Blanchard, buried alongside Robert and Louise, also shared one headstone, with only Dalson listed. Or Charles may have had private reasons for not listing the names of his mother and grandmother on their headstones.[62]

While the prolific E. B. Green practiced from 1881 until 1945, it was during the 1920s that Buffalo saw a new generation of architects rise to prominence. Over time, Louise's name would slip into obscurity, as the firm's buildings were slowly but steadily demolished throughout much of the twentieth century and the city marched toward modernity. The Hotel Lafayette was one of just thirty or so Bethune buildings to survive the wrecking ball. Until the 1950s, it was a successful hotel, known for its elegance and prime location. Sadly, the building's reputation declined in the 1960s, and by the turn of the twentieth century the hotel was rundown in appearance.

Figure 9.18. Louise Bethune late in life. Zina Bethune Archive on Louise Bethune, circa 1860–1962. Courtesy of the University Archives, University at Buffalo.

In many ways the hotel's arc mirrored that of Buffalo, having been built during the city's golden era and then suffered a fifty-year decline from the 1960s to 2010. The restoration of the Lafayette Hotel in 2012, 108 years after it first opened, coincided with the third wave of interest in Bethune's work and legacy—the first occurring during her lifetime, the second in the 1970s–1980s, and the third beginning in 2001. This building, of which she was most proud, provides another vehicle to tell Louise Bethune's story to a new audience eager to learn more about the first professional woman architect.

Conclusion

The Forgotten Woman Architect—Rediscovered

In this book, I've explored Louise Bethune's life and work, and her relationship to the key architectural and social movements that shaped her. I examined her key role in the architectural firm that she founded, going well beyond simply designing buildings to supervising budgets and onsite work—a highly unusual role for women of the day. Further, I dug into her personal and professional lives to question the perceived wisdom that she stood in opposition to the more progressive women who were agitating for social change. Rather than proselytizing in the public square, Louise let her work and deeds speak for her support of women's right to work outside the home and to be equitably recompensed for their efforts. In her architecture, family life, and public and private behavior she spoke to a new generation of professional women, opening the doors not only to the practice of architecture but to their broader engagement with the world beyond domestic life.

Bethune's Architectural Legacy

As with other architects, Louise's firm's remaining buildings are the best representation of her legacy. Today, approximately 30 Bethune, Bethune & Fuchs buildings remain standing out of their 180 known structures. Many of these existing buildings are private residences primarily located in Buffalo's fashionable Elmwood Village neighborhood. You can traverse the streets adjacent to Frederick Law Olmsted's Emerald Necklace and see the firm's houses commissioned by Thorn, Reiman, Noye, Comstock, Warren, and

Davidson, to name a few. The most noteworthy residence still standing is the Spencer Kellogg House on Summer Street, which is now a multifamily dwelling.

Additionally, two Bethune, Bethune & Fuchs factories—the Iroquois Door Company Building and the Sabins storage facility on Sycamore Street—and several commercial structures are still standing. Of these, the Jacob Dold Warehouse on Swan Street was restored in 2014 for mixed commercial and residential use; the R. K. Smither Building on Niagara Street is also being restored for similar occupancy. For years, the original Jehle's Grocery Building on Ashland Street has been the home of a thriving neighborhood restaurant, acclaimed for its physical charm and contribution to street life in Elmwood Village. And, in 1996, the Bricka & Enos Building, along with its neighbor, Buffalo's famous Market Arcade, were restored, with the individual buildings united into one complex.

The Hotel Lafayette is by far the most significant Bethune structure. Its restoration in 2012 by developer Rocco Termini and Carmina Wood Morris Architects was enormously important for Buffalo. The first building in New York State to be saved through state and federal historic tax credits, its restoration coincided with the most substantial economic expansion the Queen City of the Lakes had witnessed in decades. Embracing Buffalo's extraordinary architectural legacy through the restoration of its historic buildings is part of the economic equation. Celebrating that rich past is now viewed as a crucial ingredient in advancing the city. Bethune's restored opus has come to embody the Lady Architect's finest work during the Queen City's finest years and symbolizes what is to come.

Most of the rest of Louise's work was destroyed during the 1950s–1970s, when Buffalo, like many cities in North America, entered a period of physical expansion. Rather than restore or preserve many older buildings, it was common to destroy and replace them with more contemporary designs. Louise's Lockport Union High School, her firm's most complex educational structure, suffered the fate of the wrecking ball in 1956. Her Elmwood Music Hall, the former Seventy-Fourth Regiment Armory, was demolished in 1938, even though, as the *Buffalo News* noted, for the first three decades of the twentieth century "the place always had something going on, whether it was Boy Scouts, suffragettes, prohibitionists, or speeches from a long line of presidential candidates and New York governors—including both Presidents Roosevelt."[1]

The Horatio G. Brooks Mansion in Dunkirk, the Buffalo Livestock Exchange, and the Denton, Cottier & Daniels Music Store were also torn down during the sixties and seventies. The Buffalo Weaving & Belting Factory did escape demolition and was still in use at the turn of the twenty-first century. However, it succumbed to a fire in 2002.

Bethune's Personal Legacy

Following the deaths of Louise and Robert in 1913 and 1915, respectively, their son Charles served in World War I. He married Wilhelmina Dubke (1886–1967) in 1916. They had one child, in 1919, Charles William Bethune Jr., whom they called William (Billy). Charles had a very successful medical career in Buffalo, serving as the head of urology at Sisters Hospital for thirty-five years and then becoming an examining physician for child labor with the County Health Department. Like his parents before him, he was very active in his professional associations, heading the Board of Censors of the Erie County Medical Society for over thirty years. He was also very active on many local and state medical societies.

Figure C.1. Dr. Charles W. Bethune in the 1920's. Zina Bethune collection on Louise Bethune, circa 1860–1962. Courtesy of the University Archives, University at Buffalo.

Figure C.2. Zina Bethune, Louise and Robert's great-granddaughter (1945–2012). Photo courtesy of Sean Feeley.

Their son, William, grew up to become a sculptor and painter. He married actor Ivy Vigder in 1940, and they lived in New York City. They had one child, Zina, in 1945. William died in 1950 at the young age of thirty-one, when Zina was a child of five years and before he had a chance to pursue his art fully. His father died shortly after that, in 1952.

Zina Bethune, like her great-grandmother, was a trailblazer who overcame adversity and followed her passions to chart her course. After the deaths of her father and grandfather, she was raised by her mother in New York City and had strong and loving support from her grandmother, Wilhelmina Bethune. Zina referred to her grandmother as her emotional anchor, and she spent vacations in Buffalo as often as possible. It was from her grandmother that she learned of Louise's career and legacy.[2]

As a child, Zina studied ballet with George Balanchine and the New York City Ballet. She pursued a career in theater and dance, despite battling scoliosis, lymphedema, and hip dysplasia throughout her life. At the age of twenty-four, she formed Zina Bethune and Company in New York

City. In 1980, she founded a multimedia performance company, Theater Bethune, in Los Angeles. Zina also was passionate about children's education in the arts and founded Infinite Dreams, a nonprofit company that tutored eight thousand children with disabilities through dance. In 2006, she was bestowed the first USA Today Hollywood Hero Award for her work with mentally and physically disabled children. Like her great-grandmother, Zina overcame personal and physical hardship and, through perseverance and hard work, forged her path and career until her untimely death in 2012.

Women in Architecture: A Continuing Struggle

Louise Bethune's life spanned an era that saw seismic shifts in most aspects of American society. In her fifty-six years, she witnessed the inventions of the telephone, the automobile, the airplane, and the harnessing of electricity to light her city and power its factories. In her childhood, President Lincoln issued the Emancipation Proclamation, and throughout her youth and adult life, the country slowly yet systematically settled western America. Although it was more common for men than women, Bethune was part of a movement of inventors and entrepreneurs who saw new opportunities in emerging fields, and she seized opportunities to make her way and chart her course. Although women still did not have the vote, the long fight for suffrage would be won within a decade of her death.

The architectural profession also changed dramatically during Bethune's lifetime. Thirteen architects in New York City founded the AIA the year after she was born. By the time of her death, the AIA boasted 1,040 members, two of whom were women: Lois Lilley Howe and Henrietta C. Dozier.[3] By Bethune's death in 1913, there were twenty-four schools of architecture and licensing laws in many states, including her own.

However, the advancement of women in the profession took much longer to achieve. Within a few years of Louise's resignation from the AIA (in 1904), male architects were still debating whether women should be members. In 1907, Ida Annah Ryan's application for admission was questioned by some, who did not know there were already women members, three at that time, and did not believe women should be admitted.[4]

However, despite this obstacle, women would follow Bethune into architecture and make impressive contributions to the built environment. Julia Morgan (1872–1957) was the first woman admitted to the famed École des Beaux-Arts in 1898 and practiced in Oakland, California. During her remarkable forty-seven-year career, she designed close to seven hundred buildings.[5] For forty-six years, Mary Colter (1869–1958) worked as the primary architect and designer for the Fred Harvey Company, one of the most successful hospitality companies in the southwest at the time, in particular serving the National Parks. She designed twenty-one buildings for the company, in the Grand Canyon and along the major routes of the Atchison, Topeka, and Santa Fe Railway. Her designs combined an arts and crafts philosophy with Native American aesthetic and building technique to create an architectural vocabulary that was authentic and true to its place.[6] And Ethel Bailey Furman (1893–1976) is widely considered to be the first female architect in Virginia and the first Black woman architect in the United States, with a legacy of over two hundred buildings in the Richmond area.[7]

Each decade of the twentieth century saw women architects in the United States making significant contributions to the built environment, in their firms or as members of larger studios. However, as Louise had predicted, the number of women architects never rose in equal numbers comparable to other professions, such as medicine or law. Despina Stratigakos noted in *Where Are the Women Architects?* that the United States occupational census reported 379 women architects in 1939, 300 in 1949, 260 in 1960, and 400 in 1975.[8] One hundred and one years after Louise began her career as an intern for Richard Waite, the sluggish growth of women in the profession led *New York Times* architectural critic Ada Louise Huxtable to complain in 1977: "[The woman architect] has been excluded from the male clubbiness so characteristic of the profession, and once in a firm, is limited in her contacts with clients and site supervision. She has never been admitted to the architect 'star system.' . . . Architecture is apparently going to be the last 'liberated' profession—behind medicine and law."[9]

Huxtable was not alone in her frustration. The women's liberation movement of the 1960s eventually impacted the architectural profession in the mid-1970s, almost a decade after Title VII of the 1964 Civil Rights Act passed. Growth in the number of women entering the architectural profession began. And, along with that, came an interest in the history of women architects and dissatisfaction with their treatment by male peers. Activism during this era was manifested in two ways: critical writing of practitioners, such as Ellen Perry Berkeley's "Women in Architecture" article, which ran in architectural publications, and women in architecture groups. Groups such as the Organization of Women Architects (OWA) in the Bay Area, the Chicago Women in Architecture, and the Alliance of Women in

Women in Architecture Exhibit; New York; 1974
Adriana Barbasch, Architect

Figure C.3. Adriana Barbasch, AIA (1929–2018) at an exhibit on women in architecture in New York City in 1974. Courtesy of the author.

Architecture in New York City offered support for women to get licensed through educational seminars, and they organized exhibits on women architects and offered career counseling workshops.

It was because of this activism that the AIA was forced to confront the inequity its women members claimed. In 1970 just 1 percent of AIA members were women.[10] As Gabrielle Esperdy notes, the organization was confronted in 1973 for being "an exclusive gentleman's club" at its national convention. AIA New York, AIA New Jersey, and the Boston Society of Architects jointly introduced the "Status of Women in the Architectural Profession" resolution: "In society at large we are in the midst of a struggle for women's rights brought into sharp focus by the current feminist movement. A.I.A. and the architectural profession have not responded to this climate change."[11] This led to the AIA's formation of the "Women and Minorities"

Subcommittee, which studied the topic and released an "Affirmative Action Plan" in 1975. The report listed grievances of women that included sexual harassment, structural obstacles hindering promotions, and a sense of being unwelcome in the institute. The report called for every AIA chapter to conduct a self-analysis to identify any practices of discrimination, stating that not acting would harm the organization and the profession.

It was also amid this activism that Louise Bethune was "rediscovered." In the 1950s to 1970s, a few publications focused on her life and work. These were Madeleine Stern's short biography in *We the Women: Career Firsts of the 19th-Century America* in 1962 and George E. Pettengill, Hon. AIA's article in the March 1975 issue of *AIA Journal*, titled "How A.I.A. Acquired Its First Woman Member, Mrs. Louise Bethune." Gwendolyn Wright acknowledged Bethune in her chapter on early practitioners in Susana Torrey's *Women in American Architecture: A Historic and Contemporary Perspective* in 1977. And Bethune was a secondary character in Jeanne Madeline Weimann's 1981 recount of the Woman's Building competition at the World Columbian Exposition titled *The Fair Women*.

Starting in the 1980s, AIA member Adriana Barbasch spent years researching Louise's life and career. She was approached by AIA New York State in 1986 to write a brochure on Bethune. This request began a twenty-year initiative that resulted in a foundation of research on her career, from which all subsequent biographers have drawn. Barbasch wrote "Louise Blanchard Bethune" in Berkeley and McQuaid's *Architecture: A Place for Women*, which was published in 1989. It was through Barbasch's efforts that AIA New York State and the AIA College of Fellows in 2001 placed a memorial to Bethune in Forest Lawn Cemetery, near her unmarked grave. And in 2013, I worked with AIA Buffalo/WNY and AIA NYS to dedicate a foot marker on her grave to honor her. Additional publications on Bethune have followed, including *Louise Blanchard Bethune: America's First Professional Woman Architect* by Johanna Hays in 2014 and *Storming the Old Boys Citadel: Two Pioneer Women Architects of Nineteenth Century North America* by Carla Blank and Tania Martin in 2014.

As late as the 2000s, women were still breaking norms and becoming "firsts" in architecture. In 1971, Buffalo's Carol Case Siracuse, AIA, and two colleagues were the first women graduates of Princeton University's School of Architecture. In 1992, L. Jane Hastings, FAIA, became the first woman chancellor of the AIA College of Fellows. And in 1993, Susan A. Maxman, FAIA, became the first woman president of the AIA. In 2004, Zaha Hadid became the first woman to receive the Pritzker Prize, the equivalent of the

Nobel Prize in architecture. Yet, as Despina Stratigakos notes, "looking at the [twentieth] century as a whole, the progress that women had made collectively in the architectural profession towards achieving equality with their male colleagues was surprisingly limited."[12]

From the late 1980s onward, women's enrollment in the architectural profession grew. However, many chose not to become licensed, and many left the profession. A 1991 AIA study reported that just 8 percent of licensed architects were women. By 2010, that percentage had grown; women comprised 18 percent of AIA members and 20 percent of all licensed architects. While this had been a growing concern among leaders in the profession, women's inequity in architecture did not gain national attention until 2011, when several simultaneous initiatives put women in architecture back in the spotlight.

In 2011, Despina Stratigakos and I worked with Mattel to launch Architect Barbie I Can Be, as the toy's career of the year. As an initiative to expose little girls to the architectural profession, news reports about the project revealed the inequities women have endured for decades. This led to AIA San Francisco creating "the Missing 32%" research project the following year, which sought answers to the question of why so many women leave the profession and why so many do not pursue licensure. The Missing 32% formed Equity by Design (EQxD). This organization continues to research the issues facing equity within the architectural profession and holds biannual symposia on this topic.

In 2013, Harvard Graduate School of Design students Caroline James and Arielle Assouline-Lichten led an online petition to retroactively recognize Denise Scott Brown for her contribution in her husband Robert Venturi's 1991 Pritzker Prize. This petition sparked a conversation about the gender inequities in the star system and credit for authorship in architecture that had been ignored for decades. While this petition was unsuccessful, it galvanized an army of activists to begin recognizing women. Finally, in 2014, the AIA posthumously awarded Julia Morgan (1872–1957) the Gold Medal, the first woman to receive its highest honor. And in 2016, Denise Scott Brown and Robert Venturi were the first partnership to receive this award.

Also in 2016, the AIA created the Equity and Inclusion Task Force to study the inherent inequities in the profession for women, people of color and the LGBTQ community. The AIA is actively engaged in changing the profession to realize Bethune's goal of equal pay for equal service. Actually, the entire country is still working to achieve this goal, as is evident in the passage of the Lilly Ledbetter Fair Pay Act of 2009, which increases the time a plaintiff can file a claim against an employer for an act of discrimination, including unfair wages.

The number of licensed women architects has grown during this period. In 2018, 25 percent of all licensed architects were women, an increase of 5 percent from 2010. Momentum is building in favor of women architects reaching a footing in the profession equal to their male counterparts. Louise Bethune's descendants in architecture are the beneficiaries of her prophecy made in 1891: "The future of woman in the architectural profession is what she herself sees fit to make it."[13]

Appendix

Bethune, Bethune & Fuchs Buildings

No.	Year Completed	Name of Building	Client	Location	City, State	Description	Cost	Reference	Notes	Lead Designer	Extant
1	1883		Charles F. Bingham	7th St.	Buffalo, NY	uncertain	$7,000	SE 8 (Aug. 30, 1883) 307/AP 30			0
2	1883		G. F. Fields	Delaware Pl.	Buffalo, NY	Barn/Stable	$6,000	SE 8 (Aug. 30, 1883) 307/AP 35	40 × 101 brick		0
3	1883	Guard of Honor	Charlotte Mulligan	620 Washington	Buffalo, NY	Club House for Boys	$12,000	SE 8 (Aug. 2, 1883) 211/AP 40		RAB	0
4	1883	Noye House	Mrs. R. K. Noye	31–35 Richmond Ave.	Buffalo, NY	house	$15,000	SE 8 (Aug. 30, 1883) 307/AP 37		LBB	1
5	1883	PS 8 (old PS 16)	BPS	Utica & Masten	Buffalo, NY	public school	$50,000	SE 8 (Aug. 30, 1883) 307/AP 24		RAB?	0
6	1883	Smither Store	Robert Smither, druggist	596 Niagara St.	Buffalo, NY	3-story frame; flat & store	$7,000	SE 7 (Feb. 30, 1883) 254/AP 30			1
7	1883	Tyler House	M. W. Tyler	39 Richmond Ave.	Buffalo, NY	house	$8,000	SE 7 (Feb. 30, 1883) 254/AP 31		LBB	1
8	1883	Blanchard Building	Emma Blanchard	Fargo Ave.	Buffalo, NY	new building at rear of residential lot		City of Buffalo Council Proceedings, 1883, p. 439	wood frame building 105' southwest of Fargo Ave. L. and E. M. Blanchard listed on petition	LBB	0

9	1884	PS 39 (old PS 24)	BPS	487 High St.	Buffalo, NY	public school	$40,000	*IABN* 8 (Oct. 1886) 42/AP25			0
10	1885	Cosack & Co. Lith.	H. T. Koerner	92–100 Lake View Ave.	Buffalo, NY	factory	$22,000	*AABN* 17 (Feb. 28, 1885), p. 107	3-story; 60' × 264'		0
11	1885	Kellogg House	Spencer Kellogg	211–215 Summer St.	Buffalo, NY	house	$16,000	*AABN* 17 (Feb. 28, 1885), p. 107	brick + $3,500 for barn	LBB	1
12	1885	Webster House	E. Webster & Son	430 Prospect Ave.	Buffalo, NY	semidetached house	$18,000	*AABN* 17 (Feb. 28, 1885), p. 107			1
13	1885	Hickman House	A. A. Hickman	1268 Main St.	Buffalo, NY	house	$5,000	*AABN* 17 (Feb. 28, 1885), p. 107		LBB	0
14	1885	Potter House	Dr. J. H. Potter	177 Dearborn St.	Buffalo, NY	house	$4,000	*AABN* 17 (Feb. 28, 1885), p. 107		LBB	1
15	1885	Baldauf House	Mrs. E. Baldauf	Hodge Ave.	Buffalo, NY	house	$4,500	*AABN* 17 (Feb. 28, 1885), p. 107		LBB	0
16	1885	Mitchell House	W. G. Mitchell	197 Prospect Ave	Buffalo, NY	house	$3,500	*AABN* 17 (Feb. 28, 1885), p. 107	AIA Application	LBB	0

continued on next page

No.	Year Completed	Name of Building	Client	Location	City, State	Description	Cost	Reference	Notes	Lead Designer	Extant
17	1885	Pierce House	Mrs. John Pierce	Hodge Ave.	Buffalo, NY	house	$3,500	*AABN* 17 (Feb. 28, 1885), p. 107		LBB	0
18	1885	Davidson House	Mrs. Davidson	354 Ashland Ave.	Buffalo, NY	house	$2,500	*AABN* 17 (Feb. 28, 1885), p. 107		LBB	1
19	1885	Thorn House	George L. Thorn	40 Bidwell Parkway	Buffalo, NY	house	$3,500	*AABN* 17 (Feb. 28, 1885), p. 107		LBB	1
20	1885	Public School 38 (old PS 18)	BPS	Vermont St. 350 Pl. 28	Buffalo, NY	public school	$30,000	*AABN* 17 (Feb. 28, 1885), p. 107			0
21	1885	Police Station 11	BPD	Broadway & Williamsville	Buffalo, NY	police station	$15,000	*AABN* 17 (Feb. 28, 1885), p. 107	2-story, brick, 40' × 85'		0
22	1885	Kellogg & McDougall	Kellogg & McDougall	Ganson St.	Buffalo, NY	factory	$15,000	*IABN* 8 (June 1885), p. 79	5-story, 40' × 150'		0
23	1885	Waterman House	George L. Waterman	484 Howard	Buffalo, NY	house	$10,000	*IABN* 8 (June 1885), p. 79	frame. AIA Application	LBB	0
24	1885	Reynolds House	Miss Reynolds		Buffalo, NY	house	$5,000	*IABN* 8 (June 1885), p. 79	frame		0

25	1885	Graves House	Roger W. Graves	310 W. Utica	Buffalo, NY	house	$4,500	*LABN* 8 (June 1885), p. 79	frame		1
26	1885	Riley House	Michael Riley	116 Georgia	Buffalo, NY	house	$3,000	*LABN* 8 (June 1885), p. 79	frame		0
27	1886	Women's Union Gymnasium Addition	The Women's Education and Industrial Union		Buffalo, NY	gymnasium and offices	$100	*Buffalo Weekly Express* (Aug. 5, 1886), p. 5	renovation to Babcock Property for gymnasium and offices	RAB	0
28	1886	Druar House	John Druar		Buffalo, NY	house		*LABN* 8 (June 1885), p. 79	brick		0
29	1886	74th Regiment Armory and Drill Hall	74th Regiment Army		Buffalo, NY	armory and drill hall	$40,000	*LABN* 8 (June 85), p. 79	3-story brick, 120' × 285' later Elmwood Music Hall		0
30	1886	Addition to Homeopathic Hospital	Homeopathic Hospital	12th St. / Maryland St.	Buffalo, NY	addition	$8,000	*LABN* 7 (Apr. 1886), p. 48	addition 1-story		0
31	1886	Bennett Stable	David S. Bennett	64–78 Tracy St.	Buffalo, NY	stable	$4,000	*LABN* 7 (Apr. 1886), p. 48	frame		0
32	1886	Beemer Stores	M. B. Beemer	145, 147, 149 Seneca St.	Buffalo, NY	stores	$25,000	*LABN* 7 (May 1886), p. 69	4-story brick		0
33	1887	Police Station #8	BPD	482–486 William St.	Buffalo, NY	station and stable	$16,000	*LABN* 7 (Aug. 1886), p. 11			0

continued on next page

No.	Year Completed	Name of Building	Client	Location	City, State	Description	Cost	Reference	Notes	Lead Designer	Extant
34	1887	Livery Stable	White Brothers	13th St.	Buffalo, NY	stable	$10,000	IABN 7 (Aug. 1886), p. 11	brick		0
35	1886	Buffalo Hammer Company Shop	Buffalo Hammer Company	1548 Niagara St.	Buffalo, NY	store	$15,000	IABN 7 (Aug. 1886), p. 11	brick		0
36	1886	Addition to Police Station #5	BPD	Niagara St.	Buffalo, NY	addition	$3,000	IABN 7 (Aug. 1886), p. 11			0
37	1886	Store for W. Guenther	W. Guenther		Buffalo, NY	store	$10,000	IABN 7 (Oct. 1886), p. 42			0
38	1886	Odd Fellow's Hall			Vittoria, Ont.	hall	$5,000	B(NS) (5 July 3, 1886)			0
39	1887	Lautz House	Carl Lautz	31 Dodge St.	Buffalo, NY	house	$4,000	IABN 7 (Oct. 1886), p. 42			0
40	1887	Bell House	George Bell	427 Prospect Ave.	Buffalo, NY	house	$4,000	IABN 7 (Oct. 1886), p. 42			0
41	1887	Collignon House	Mrs. Collignon	Ellicott St.	Buffalo, NY	house	$17,000	IABN 7 (Dec. 1886), p. 87			0
42	1887	Cutler House	Abner Cutler	Jewett Ave.	Buffalo, NY	house					0
43	1887	Police Station #2	BPD	400 Seneca / Louisiana	Buffalo, NY	Police Station		AIA Application			0

44	1887	Hoffman Millinery House	Hoffman	201 Genesee	Buffalo, NY	store		AIA Application			0
45	1887	Public School 40 (old PS 31)	BPS	Oneida St.	Buffalo, NY	school	$30,000	IABN 7 (Dec. 1886), p. 87			0
46	1887	Public School 4	BPS	325 Elk	Buffalo, NY	school addition	$5,907	AIA Application	renovations		0
47	1887	Brooks House	Horatio G. Brooks	529 Central Ave.	Dunkirk, NY	house	$35,000	AIA Application IABN 8 (June 1885), p. 79	brick	LBB	0
48	1887	Meyer House	A. J. Meyer (Alphonso J.)	795 Genesee St.	Buffalo, NY	house		AIA Application	City Treasurer		0
49	1887	Chapel for Baptist Society	Baptist Society		Buffalo, NY	church		AC 8 (Nov. 19, 1887)	frame		0
50	1887	Rano Residence	Alderman C. O. Rano	Dearborn	Buffalo, NY	house		Buffalo Times (Sept. 28, 1887), p. 1		RAB	0
51	1887	Public School for District No. 11	Hammondsport PS		Hammondsport, NY	school		AC 8 (Dec. 24, 1887)	stone w/ cut stone trim		0
52	1888	Factory Bldgs. for Volker & Felthausen Manufacturing Co.	Volker & Felthausen Manufacturing Co.	189 Tonawanda	Blackrock, NY	factory		AC 9 (Jan. 7, 1888)/AE 2 (Feb. 1888)	brick 30' × 80'		1
53	1888	Addition to Public School 33	BPS	757 Elk (Elm) St.	Buffalo, NY	school	$45,000	AE 2 (Aug. 1888)	2-story brick		0

No.	Year Completed	Name of Building	Client	Location	City, State	Description	Cost	Reference	Notes	Lead Designer	Extant
54	1888	Public School 26	BPS	101 Milton St.	Buffalo, NY	school	$45,000	AE 2 (Aug. 1888)			0
55	1888	Episcopal Church	Kensington Episcopal Society	Shawnee & Marigold	Buffalo, NY	church	$4,000				0
56	1888	Addition to Public School 20	BPS	East and Amherst St.	Buffalo, NY	school addition	$9,500	Proceedings of Buffalo Common Council, Mar. 26, 1888			0
57	1889	Factory Bldg. for John C. Jewett Manufacturing Co.	John C. Jewett Manufacturing Co.	27 Chandler	Buffalo, NY	factory	$150,000	Buffalo Morning Express and Illustrated Buffalo Express (Nov. 28, 1889), p. 5	brick		1
58	1889	Hamburg High School	Hamburg PS		Hamburg, NY	school/unbuilt	$10,000	AE 3 (Aug. 1889)	brick		0
59	1889	Six houses	John Robinson	15th St.	Buffalo, NY	houses	$15,000	E&BR 20 (Oct. 26, 1889)/AE 3 (Nov. 1889)	Six 2-story buildings	LBB	0
60	1889	Apartment House	N. G. Benedict	319–321 14th St.	Buffalo, NY	apartment building	$7,000	AE 3 (Nov. 1889)			1
61	1889	Lockport High School	Lockport PS		Lockport, NY	school	$100,000	IABN 14 (Oct. 1889), p. 43			0

62	1889	Bard House	C. R. Bard		Allegany, NY	house	$5,500	AE 3 (Nov. 1889)	frame	LBB	
63	1889	Nisell House	Miss Nisell	329 Porter Ave.	Buffalo, NY	house	$3,500	AE 3 (Nov. 1889)	alterations/ demolished	LBB	0
64	1889	Boehme House	Charles J. Boehme	41 Fargo Ave.	Buffalo, NY	house	$8,000	AE 3 (Nov. 1889)	2.5 story	LBB	0
65	1889	Byrne House	M. J. Byrne	Connecticut St.	Buffalo, NY	house		AE 3 (Nov. 1889)	2 story	LBB	0
66	1889	Crocker House	L. B. Crocker	Lake View	Buffalo, NY	house	$6,000	AE 3 (Nov. 1889)	house across the street from J. T. Noye	LBB	0
67	1889	Bath Houses	City of Buffalo	Michigan St. and Porter Ave	Buffalo, NY	bathing houses		*Proceedings of Buffalo Common Council,* July 15, 1889	2 buildings		0
68	1889	Elk Street Market	Elk Street Market	Elk St.	Buffalo, NY	market	$12,000	AE 3 (Nov. 1889)	alterations and enlargement		0
69	1889	Hotel for W. J. Connors	W. J. Connors		Buffalo, NY	hotel	$5,000	AE 3 (Nov. 1889)	2 story (40' × 60')		0
70	1889	Stable for White Brothers	White Brothers	Jersey St.	Buffalo, NY	stable	$30,000			RAB	0
71	1889	Apartment House			Bridgeport, CT	hotel		AE 3 (Nov. 1889)			0
72	1889	Apartment House	Philip Houck	141 Genesee St.	Buffalo, NY	hotel	$14,000	AE 3 (Nov. 1889)	brick & stone		0
73	1889	2 houses for T. O'Brien	T. O'Brien	570 Genesee St.	Buffalo, NY	houses	$3,500	AE 3 (Nov. 1889)	2-story frame	LBB	0
74	1889	Veterinary Stable	William Somerville Jr.	59–61 Franklin St.	Buffalo, NY	stable	$1,500	AE 3 (Nov. 1889)	brick		0

continued on next page

No.	Year Completed	Name of Building	Client	Location	City, State	Description	Cost	Reference	Notes	Lead Designer	Extant
75	1889	Stores and Flats—addition	R.K. Smither	588–592 Niagara St./Jersey	Buffalo, NY	stores and flats		*AE 3* (Nov. 1889)/ *AE 4* (Mar. 1890)	brick & stone; original 1889 and addition 1890		1
76	1889	Block of stores	Michael Newell	184 Main St. (at Exchange St.)	Buffalo, NY	stores and flats		*AE 3* (Nov. 1889)	Buffalo Medina Sandstone		0
77	1889	Martin House	Miss Martin	Bouck Ave. (or Lafayette Ave.)	Buffalo, NY	house		*AE 3* (Nov. 1889)	house		0
78	1889	Storage Building for Mease & Snyder	Mease & Snyder	Niagara St. near Georgia St.	Buffalo, NY	storage	$15,000	*AE 3* (Nov. 1889)	5-story brick		0
79	1889	Baseball Grandstand and Fence	Buffalo Baseball Club		Buffalo, NY	grandstand and fence	$20,000	*AE 3* (Nov. 1889)			0
80	1889	Fuchs Building	Fuchs Estate	Main and Mohawk	Buffalo, NY	office building		*Buffalo Courier* (Feb. 21, 1889), p. 6	building renovation		0
81	1890	Comstock House	George W. Comstock	45 Lexington Ave.	Buffalo, NY	house	$6,200	*Buffalo Morning Express and Illustrated Buffalo Express* (Jul. 24, 1889) & May 4, 1890	Frame; Warren sold property to Comstock in July 1889 for $1	LBB	1

#	Year	Name	Client	Address	City	Type	Cost	Notes	Source	Attribution	Count
82	1890	Warren House	Melvin F. Warren	41 Lexington Ave.	Buffalo, NY	house	$6,500	frame	*Buffalo Morning Express and Illustrated Buffalo Express* (Jul. 24, 1889) & May 4, 1891	LBB	1
83	1890	Abel House	Charles Lee Abell	(43?) Lexington Ave.	Buffalo, NY	house			*AE 3* (Nov. 1889)/*AE 4* (June 1890)	LBB	1
84	1891	Chase House	John Lord Chase	67 Lexington Ave.	Buffalo, NY	house		frame	*Buffalo Courier* (Oct. 3, 1891), p. 6	LBB	1
85	1890	Stores and Flats	Mrs. Elizabeth Baldouf	1057 Main St. at North	Buffalo, NY	stores and flats			*AE 3* (Nov. 1889)/*AE 4* (June 1890)		0
86	1890	Erie County Savings Bank	Erie County Savings Bank	Niagara, Pearl and Church Sts.	Buffalo, NY	bank			*AABN 28* (May 10, 1890)	WF	0
87	1890	East Aurora Bank	East Aurora Bank		East Aurora, NY	bank		not built	*AE 4* (June 1890)/BREN (Nov. 1890)		0
88	1890	Enlargement to Niagara Storage Warehouse	Mease & Snyder	220-224 Niagara St.	Buffalo, NY	warehouse	$20,000		*AE 4* (June 1890)/BREN (Nov. 1890)/ E& BR 22 (June 7, 1890)		0

continued on next page

No.	Year Completed	Name of Building	Client	Location	City, State	Description	Cost	Reference	Notes	Lead Designer	Extant
89	1890	Store and dwelling	Ed Smith	955 Seneca at Exchange	Buffalo, NY	store and house	$10,000	AE 4 (June 1890)			0
90	1890	Hall House	John Hall		Buffalo, NY	house		AE 4 (June 1890)	W. L. Wallace (NY) architect. R. A. & L. Bethune supervising architect	W. L. Wallace	NA
91	1890	Erie County Penitentiary	Erie County	Root St.	Buffalo, NY	women's prison	$60,000	BREN (Nov. 1890)/ BREN (Nov. 1890)/ RE& BN 2 (Mar. 1891) ER 23 (Apr. 11, 1891)	brick, stone, and iron 100 new cells for women inmates		
92	1890	5 houses for N. J. Connors	N. J. Connors	Hudson & 7th St.	Buffalo, NY	houses		E&BR 22 (June 21, 1890)	5 houses, 2 stories	LBB	0
93	1890	Buffalo Livestock Exchange	Buffalo Livestock Exchange	1167 William & Depot	Buffalo, NY	factory	$60,000	BREN (Nov. 1890)/ RE&BN 2 (Mar. 1891)	brick		0
94	1890	Tillinghast House (?)	James D. Tillinghast	685 Delaware Ave.	Buffalo, NY	house	$5,000	AE 4 (June 1890), p. 138	barn?		0

95	1890	Chippewa Market	City of Buffalo	Chippewa St.	Buffalo, NY	market		*Proceedings of Buffalo Common Council,* Sept. 29, 1890	repairs and alterations		0
96	1890	Stable Police Station 8	BPD	William and Watson Sts.	Buffalo, NY	stable			BREN (Nov. 1890)		0
97	1890	Business Block	August Beck	186 Genesee St. at Elm	Buffalo, NY	commercial		RE&BN 2 (Mar. 1891)/ ER 23 (Apr. 11, 1891)	5-story, brick and stone (50' × 40') stores and residence		0
98	1890	Beck House	August Beck	Elm St.	Buffalo, NY	house	$12,000	RE&BN 2 (Mar. 1891)	residence		0
99	1890	Connors Residence	W. J. Connors	Corner White's Corner Rd. and Tiff St.	Buffalo, NY	house	$10,000	*Buffalo Morning Express and Illustrated Buffalo Express* (Oct. 19, 1890), p. 11	residence	RAB & W. Fuchs	0
100	1891	Stable	Joseph Leonard	33 Elm St.	Buffalo, NY	stable	$7,000	ER 23 (Apr. 11, 1891)	3-story brick		0
101	1891	Stable	Capt. Thomas J. Cavanaugh	12th St.	Buffalo, NY	stable		*Buffalo Courier* (Oct. 3, 1891), p. 6			

continued on next page

No.	Year Completed	Name of Building	Client	Location	City, State	Description	Cost	Reference	Notes	Lead Designer	Extant
102	1891	Trevor House	Francis. N. Trevor	453 Willow	Lockport, NY	house	$10,000	RE&BN 2 (Mar. 1891)		LBB	maybe
103	1891	Sutherland House	(?) Sutherland Sisters	3101 High St.	Lockport, NY	house	$10,000	RE&BN 2 (Mar. 1891)	frame	LBB	0
104	1891	Store and dwelling	Charles Whitmore		Lockport, NY			RE&BN 2 (Mar. 1891)	frame		0
105	1891	Stockton House	Dr. Stockton	436 Franklin St.	Buffalo, NY	house	$14,000	RE&BN 2 (Mar. 1891)	brick	LBB	1
106	1891	Addition to Moore & Snyder Storehouse Warehouse	Moore & Snyder	Maynard St.	Buffalo, NY	warehouse	$14,000	RE&BN 2 (Mar. 1891)			0
107	1891	Renovation of 5 houses for Louise Bethune	Louise Bethune	Huron between Franklin and Pearl Sts.	Buffalo, NY	houses		RE&BN 2 (Apr. 1891)	brick	LBB	0
108	1891	Clinton Market	City of Buffalo	Clinton St.	Buffalo, NY	hay market		*City of Buffalo Council Proceedings*, Apr. 6, 1891			0
109	1891	Office Building for J. B. Greene	J. B. Greene	Main St. & North Division	Buffalo, NY	office building		*Buffalo Commercial* (Jan. 3, 1891)	14-story brick; probably not built	LBB & RAB	0
110	1892	Potter Residence	George Starr Potter	1119 Delaware Ave.	Buffalo, NY	house				LBB	1

No.	Year	Name	Owner	Address	City	Type	Source	Notes	LBB	Value
111	1892	Davidson Residence	James Davidson	601 Central Ave.	Bay City, MI	house			LBB	maybe
112	1892	Storage	Niagara Storage Co.		Buffalo, NY	storage warehouse	*Buffalo Courier* (Oct. 3, 1891), p. 6	6-story brick		0
113	1892	Burns House	H. V. Burns	Howard Ave.	Buffalo, NY	house	*Buffalo Courier* (Oct. 3, 1891), p. 6		LBB	0
114	1892	Murray House	John K. Murray	Pittsburgh, PA	Buffalo, NY	house	*Buffalo Courier* (Oct. 3, 1891), p. 6	May not have been built	LBB	0
115	1892	Lehner House	Andrew Lehner Jr.	Locust St.	Buffalo, NY	house	*Buffalo Courier* (Oct. 3, 1891), p. 6		LBB	0
116	1892	Bruch House	Jacob Bruch	Tupper St.	Buffalo, NY	house	*Buffalo Courier* (Oct. 3, 1891), p. 6		LBB	0
117	1892	Kelner House	John S. Kelner	Virginia St.	Buffalo, NY	house	*Buffalo Courier* (Oct. 3, 1891), p. 6		LBB	0
118	1892	Williams House	Hon. B. H. Williams	17 W. Utica St.	Buffalo, NY	house	*Buffalo Courier* (Oct. 3, 1891), p. 6	Williams and Potter were law partners	LBB	0

continued on next page

No.	Year Completed	Name of Building	Client	Location	City, State	Description	Cost	Reference	Notes	Lead Designer	Extant
119	1892	Whaley House	Frank Whaley		East Aurora, NY	house		*Buffalo Courier* (Oct. 3, 1891), p. 6		LBB	0
120	1892	Market-Clerk Ben Sabins Store		586 Michigan, Buffalo, NY			$7,000	*Buffalo and Illustrated Buffalo Express* (Sept. 4, 1892), p. 10			0
121	1892	Crooker House	James F. Crooker	Point Breeze	Youngstown, NY	house		*Buffalo Courier* (Oct. 3, 1891), p. 6	Crooker and family moved here when he worked for NYS	LBB	
122	1892	PS 48	BPS	E. Summer St.	Buffalo, NY	school		*Buffalo Courier* (Oct. 3, 1891), p. 6	"radical ventilation system"		0
123	1892	Police Station #10	BPD	Niagara St.	Buffalo, NY	police station		*Buffalo Courier* (Oct. 3, 1891), p. 6			
124	1892	Wilgus House	Edward Wilgus	495 Ashland Ave. (corner at Auburn)	Buffalo, NY	house		*Buffalo Courier* (Oct. 3, 1891), p. 6		LBB	1
125	1892	Woodlawn Beach Resort	Woodlawn Beach and Cottage Company	Woodlawn Beach	Blasdell, NY	hotel and pavilions		*Buffalo Courier* (Oct. 3, 1891), p. 6			0

126	1892	Clubhouse	Buffalo Women's Wheel and Athletic Club	N/A	Buffalo, NY	clubhouse	N/A	*American Wheelman* (Nov. 1892), p. 343.	never built	LBB	0
127	1894	Wetmore House	Samuel Wetmore	30 Woodlawn Ave. at Otis Pl.	Buffalo, NY	house	$7,000	*ER* 30 (Nov. 24, 1894) 433 & *AABN* 46 (Dec. 8, 1894)	frame	LBB	0
128	1895	Shea's Theater	Fuchs Bros.	515 Washington St.	Buffalo, NY	theater	$150,000	*ER* 31 (Feb. 2, 1895), p. 179 *Buffalo Courier* (Jan. 29, 1895)	Property donated by Fuchs Bros.; possibly unbuilt		0
129	1895	Store for Charles Berrick	Charles Berrick	86 Ellicott St.	Buffalo, NY	store		*ER* 31 (May 25, 1895)	4-story brick		0
130	1895	Masten Park High School	BPS	NA	Buffalo, NY	high school competition		*Buffalo Courier* (May 29, 1895), p. 5	M. E. Beebee & Son Architects selected; R. A. Waite and BB&F shortlisted.		NA
131	1895	Messersmith House	H. Messersmith	392 Summer St.	Buffalo, NY	house	$10,000	*IABN* 6 (July 1895), p. 63	3-story brick	LBB	1

continued on next page

No.	Year Completed	Name of Building	Client	Location	City, State	Description	Cost	Reference	Notes	Lead Designer	Extant
132	1895	Business Block	E. G. & W. L. Fuchs	505–515 Washington St.	Buffalo, NY	business	$30,000	ER 32 (July 6, 1895)	4-story brick		0
133	1896	Store for Morris Guske	Morris Guske	192–198 Seneca St.	Buffalo, NY	store	$14,000	ER 33 (Feb. 1896)	brick		1
134	1896	Alterations to block for M. H. Birge	M. H. Birge	Main St. near Seneca	Buffalo, NY	business	$12,000	ER 34 (June 27, 1896)			0
135	1896	Addition to Police Station #9	BPD	Seneca & Babcock Sts.	Buffalo, NY	police station	$10,000	ER 34 (Oct. 3, 1896)			0
136	1896	Flats for J. T. Burke & E. C. Coalsworth	J. T. Burke & E.C. Coalsworth	Franklin St.	Buffalo, NY	residences	$20,000	ER 34 (Nov. 7, 1896)	4-story brick		0
137	1896	Connors Athletic Club	W. J. Connors Social and Athletic Club	Louisiana St. between South and St. Clair	Buffalo, NY	gymnasium and club (may not have been built)		*Buffalo Morning Express and Illustrated Buffalo Express* (May 6, 1896)	35' × 100'; club in front and gym at back		0
138	1896–97	Store & Factory for Sarah Howard	Sarah Howard	208–212 Terrace	Buffalo, NY	store & factory	$18,000	ER 35 (Dec. 26, 1896)	4-story		0
139	1897	Hotel for Louis Eckert	Louis Eckert								

140	1897	Buffalo Public School #12		Spruce at Broadway	Buffalo, NY	new brick school	$42,000	City Records: Common Council Proceedings, 1897, p. 1786	4-story		0
141	1897	Buffalo Savings Bank	Buffalo Savings Bank		Buffalo, NY						0
142	1898	Cataract Power and Conduit Co. Buffalo Terminal House	Cataract Power	2280–2286 Niagara St.	Buffalo, NY	transformer house		Buffalo Times (Aug. 6, 1898), p. 5			1
143	1898	Grandstand	James Franklin	East Ferry St./Olympic Park	Buffalo, NY	grandstand		City Records			
144	1898	Store and Residence for Louis Kirkover	Louis Kirkover	Clinton and Baitz SW	Buffalo, NY	store and dwelling	$5,000	City Records	2-story brick		0
145	1898	Factory for J. A. Oaks	J. A. Oaks	Grote NW/Central Switch	Buffalo, NY	factory	$5,000	City Records	2-story frame		0
146	1898	Oaks House	J. A. Oaks	281 Parkside Ave.	Buffalo, NY	house	$10,000	City Records	2-story frame	LBB	0
147	1899	Store and House	William H. Baker	213 Franklin St.	Buffalo, NY	house and store	$9,000	City Records	2-story brick		0
148	1899	Bald Meat Market	Bald Meat Market	1762 Main St.	Buffalo, NY	market	$6,500	City Records	2-story brick		1
149	1899	Becker Property	John Becker	555–557 Washington	Buffalo, NY	office building		City Records	renovation		0
150	1899	Buffalo Electric	Buffalo Electric	38–40 Court St.	Buffalo, NY		$2,000	City Records			0
151	1899	Jehle Grocery	Fred Jehle	309–311 Bryant	Buffalo, NY	store and house		City Records	2-story brick		1
152	1900	Champlin	O. H. P. Champlin	36–46 Carroll at Ellicott	Buffalo, NY	factory	$50,000	City Records	6-story brick		0

continued on next page

No.	Year Completed	Name of Building	Client	Location	City, State	Description	Cost	Reference	Notes	Lead Designer	Extant
153	1900	Elliot House Addition	Mrs. Belle E. Elliot	454 Michigan Ave.	Buffalo, NY	addition	$3,000	City Records	2-story brick restaurant run by Elliott		0
154	1900	Renovation of Loomis Estate	Loomis	115 Franklin St.	Buffalo, NY	renovation	$1,200	City Records			0
155	1900	Prospect Building (Birge Bldg.)	People's Bank	316 Pearl St.	Buffalo, NY			City Records			0
156	1900	Reiman House	Mary A. Reiman	186 Ashland Ave.	Buffalo, NY	house	$7,000	City Records	2-story frame	LBB	1
157	1900	Willman Estates		586 Washington St.	Buffalo, NY	stores	$34,000	*Buffalo Commercial* (Aug. 8, 1900)	4-story brick store and flats		0
158	1900	Agency Building	John H. Smith		Buffalo, NY	renovation for hotel		*Buffalo Commercial* (Nov. 23, 1900)	probably not built		0
159	1900	BPS #8 building addition	Buffalo Public Schools	East Utica and Masten	Buffalo, NY	addition		*Buffalo Review* (July 11, 1900)			0
160	1901	BPS Central High School Addition	Buffalo Public Schools	Court and Franklin	Buffalo, NY	brick addition		City Records, *Council Proceedings* (1901), p. 1037	brick addition, never built		0
161	1902	Dold Warehouse	Jacob Dold	145 E. Swan St.	Buffalo, NY	warehouse	$20,000	City Records			1

#	Year	Name	Builder/Owner	Location/Description	City	Type	Cost	Source	Notes	Status
162	1902	Quarantine Hospital	Board of Public Works	addition to existing hospital	Buffalo, NY			*Buffalo Evening News* (Dec. 31, 1901), p. 7	Not built; BB&F not paid despite claim, *Buffalo Evening News* (Nov. 25, 1902), p. 9; settled at $500.	0
163	1902	Kensington Bicycle Company	Kensington Bicycle Company	addition for manufacturing automobiles	Buffalo, NY			*Buffalo Evening News* (Mar. 13, 1900), p. 7	Not built; company foreclosed in 1905	0
164	1902	Granger House	William H. Granger	210 Delaware Ave.	Buffalo, NY	renovation of house	$5,500	City Records	renovation of brick house	0
165	1902	Rendell Store/Dwelling	Elias D. Rendell	Louisiana/SE at Seneca	Buffalo, NY	store and house	$9,800	City Records	2-story brick store and house	0
166	1902	Girvin House	Mr. H. J. Girvin	85.5 17th St.	Buffalo, NY	house		scans of drawing, archive	frame	LBB
167	1903	Buffalo Weaving Co.	Buffalo Weaving Co.	234 Chandler St.	Buffalo, NY	factory	$17,000	*Buffalo Enquirer* (July 18, 1903), p. 9	3 brick bldgs.	0
168	1903	Stable	John H. Schmitz	65–67 Military	Buffalo, NY	church stable	1500	City Records		
169	1903	Blackrock Market	Richard Humphrey	Niagara and Tonawanda St.	Buffalo, NY	market		*Buffalo Evening News* (June 22, 1904), p. 17	not built	0

continued on next page

No.	Year Completed	Name of Building	Client	Location	City, State	Description	Cost	Reference	Notes	Lead Designer	Extant
170	1904	Lafayette Hotel	Walter Duffy/ J. A. Oaks	Washington/ Clinton	Buffalo, NY	Hotel	$700,000			LBB	1
171	1904	Iroquois Door Co.		659 Exchange St.	Buffalo, NY	Factory			3-story		1
172	1906	Wilson Building	Walter T. Wilson	Seneca and Larkin	Buffalo, NY	warehouse	$18,500	*Buffalo Commercial* (Mar. 23, 1904), p. 10	3-story brick		0
173	1907	Bethune Residence	Self and Son	904 Tonawanda St.	Buffalo, NY	house		*Buffalo Commercial* (Nov. 23, 1900)	2-story frame, two family, Tonawanda near Crowley; Charles had his medical office there		
174	1908	Daniels Building	Denton, Cortier & Daniels		Buffalo, NY			*Buffalo Enquirer* (July 10, 1906), p. 9			0
175	1907	St. Francis Hotel			London, Ont.	hotel	$130,000		BB&F unsure if built		0
176	1908	Bricka & Enos Building	John Greiner Estate	621–623 Main St.	Buffalo, NY				3-story terra cotta bldg.		1
177	1909	Bowling Alley	C. P. Annent & Brother	F. F. Brown Estate	Buffalo, NY	Bowling Alley	$30,000	*Buffalo Times* (Oct. 2, 1909), p. 9	2-story, 12 lanes		
178	1912	Lafayette Hotel Addition		Washington/ Clinton	Buffalo, NY	hotel			Bethune Archives	LBB	1

| 179 | 1913 | Frontier Theater | | Rhode Island and West St. | Buffalo, NY | movie theater | | *Buffalo Enquirer* (Dec. 22, 1913) | Bethune & Fuchs (LBB had retired) | 1 |

32

Notes

Introduction

1. "A Clever Woman's Work," *Buffalo Enquirer*, February 9, 1892, 4.

Chapter 1. Becoming Louise

1. Frances E. Willard and Mary A. Livermore, eds., *A Woman of the Century: Fourteen Hundred-Seventy Biographical Sketches Accompanied by Portraits of Leading American Women in All Walks of Life* (New York: Charles Wells Moulton, 1893), 81.

2. National Archives, "Signers of the Declaration of Independence," n.d., https://www.archives.gov/founding-docs/signers-factsheet, accessed May 9, 2021.

3. Bethune DAR Records. He began his service in 1775 under Colonel Patterson of Berkshire, Massachusetts, and fought in eleven states and Canada, including at the Battle of Bunker Hill. Later in 1876, Ebenezer fought and was captured by the Iroquois in the Battle of the Cedars, eighty-nine miles from Montreal; he was exchanged after ten days in prison. At the Battle of Yorktown, he was selected as one of two captains to lead the central storming party at the final attack on Lord Cornwallis. He continued fighting for Washington near the Hudson, until the British evacuated New York on November 25, 1783; Williams accompanied the US Army in its victory march into New York City following the British defeat. Finally, he was present when Washington took leave of his officers, on December 4, 1883.

4. Blanchard Genealogy Records, Letter to Mrs. Louise Bethune from Mrs. Louise F. Williams Teeple, December 1897.

5. Ibid.

6. Miss Sarah (Stedman) Williams (1764–1850) meeting Capt. Ebenezer Williams in 1786–1787, recounted by their daughter, Mrs. Louise F. Williams Teeple in 1897. Blanchard Genealogy Records.

7. National Archives, https://www.fold3.com/search?keywords=Ebenezer+ Williams&general.title.id=467:Revolutionary+War+Pensions, accessed on May 8, 2021.

8. Ibid.

9. Bethune's distant cousin was Amy Ella Blanchard (1856–1936), an author of children's literature. While they were contemporaries, it is uncertain that they knew each other personally. However, Bethune thought enough of the connection to include an entry on the author in her Blanchard Genealogy Records, stating, "She has for years been ranked with the most popular writers of books for girls of which she has written a large number." See Amy Ella Blanchard, Blanchard Genealogy Records.

10. Cayuga County, New York, Town of Senett, "Military Tract of Central New York," n.d., https://www.cayugacounty.us/918/Military-Tract-of-Central-New-York, accessed May 23, 2021.

11. History of Manlius, NY, http://history.rays-place.com/ny/onon-manlius-ny. htm, accessed May 23, 2021.

12. Willard and Livermore, *A Woman of the Century*, 81.

13. Ufuk Akcigit, John Grigsby, and Tom Nicholas, "The Rise of American Ingenuity: Innovation and Inventors of the Golden Age," Harvard Business School Working Paper, No. 17–063, January 2017.

14. Peter L. Bernstein, *Wedding of the Waters* (New York: W. W. Norton, 2006), 347.

15. Ibid.

16. Judith Wellman, *The Road to Seneca Falls: Elizabeth Cady Stanton and the First Woman's Rights Convention* (Chicago: University of Chicago Press, 2004), 68.

17. Elizabeth Cady Stanton, Susan B. Anthony, and Matilda Joslyn Gage, *History of Woman Suffrage*, vol. 1 (New York: Fowler & Wells, 1881), 67.

18. Wellman, *Road to Seneca Falls*, 68.

19. Tracy A. Thomas, *Elizabeth Cady Stanton and the Feminist Foundations of Family Law* (New York: New York University Press, 2016), 24.

20. Library of Congress, American Women, "Married Women's Property Laws," n.d., https://guides.loc.gov/american-women-law/state-laws#s-lib-ctab-19233885-1, accessed January 18, 2021.

21. Leroy Harrington, "Forestville, Its Environs, Past and Present," prepared and read at a meeting of the Chautauqua County Historical Society, June 4, 1949, 13.

22. US Census Bureau, "Decennial Census of Population and Housing," n.d., https://www2.census.gov/library/publications/decennial/1860/population/1860a-26. pdf, accessed May 25, 2021.

23. Willard and Livermore, *A Woman of the Century*, 81.

24. Ibid.

25. Ibid.

26. US Civil War Draft Registrations Records, 1863–1865, for Dalson Blanchard, June 31, 1863, Ancestry.com, https://www.ancestry.com/familytree/person/ tree/88183930/person/30564543027/facts, accessed May 25, 2021.

27. Period research shows that people who came from well-educated families were more innovative than others and were identified early and mentored. These inventors were likely to have moved to a region more conducive to innovation, and these places were more often densely populated and wealthy. Additionally, the more inventive states grew faster; innovation correlated to population growth. And finally, innovation strongly correlated with social mobility. See Akcigit, Grigsby, and Nicholas, "Rise of American Ingenuity," 3.

28. "In Memory of the Dead," *Buffalo Enquirer*, August 22, 1891, 5. After he passed away, Dalson's fellow district school principals issued a resolution saluting his irreproachable integrity, honesty, and honor, a testament to the high esteem he enjoyed among his colleagues.

29. *National Cyclopedia of American Biography* (New York: James T. White, 1904), 9.

30. "The Public Schools," *Buffalo Commercial*, September 6, 1886, 3.

31. Cynthia Van Ness, "Population Growth and Decline over the Years," http://www.buffaloah.com/h/bflopop.html, referenced August 18, 2018.

32. "People and Events," *Omaha Daily Bee*, February 9, 1914, 4.

33. "Women in Buffalo's Professional and Business Life," *Buffalo Sunday Morning News*, November 9, 1913, 19.

34. *Buffalo Central School: 1874–'75*, 23.

35. "Women in Buffalo's Professional and Business Life," *Buffalo Sunday Morning News*, November 9, 1913, 19.

36. Willard and Livermore, *A Woman of the Century*, 81.

37. Ibid.

38. Sarah Allaback, *The First American Women Architects* (Urbana: University of Illinois Press, 2008), 20.

39. Louise Bethune, "Women and Architecture," *Inland Architect and News Record* 17 (March 1891): 21.

40. Horace Mann, "Woman," *New-York Daily Tribune*, December 9, 1852, 3.

41. Bethune, "Women and Architecture," 21.

42. Allaback, *The First American Women Architects*, 21.

43. Bethune, "Women and Architecture," 21.

44. Allaback, *The First American Women Architects*, 159.

45. Ibid., 83.

46. Alice Severence, "Talks by Successful Women IX—Miss Gannon and Miss Hands on Architecture," *Godey's Magazine* 83 (September 1896): 314.

47. The American Institute of Architects (AIA) briefly considered opening a school of architecture themselves but decided that architecture schools offered by an established university were a better option for the profession. Mary N. Woods, *From Craft to Profession: The Practice of Architecture in Nineteenth-Century America* (Berkeley: University of California Press, 1999), 67.

48. Ada Louise Huxtable, "The Last Profession to Be 'Liberated' by Women," *New York Times*, March 13, 1977, 93.

49. Susana Torre, *Women in American Architecture: A Historic and Contemporary Perspective* (New York: Watson-Guptill, 1977), 52.

50. Allaback, *The First American Women Architects*, 24.

51. Mary Louisa Page, Illinois Distributed Museum, https://distributedmuseum. illinois.edu/exhibit/mary-louisa-page/.

52. Bethune, "Women and Architecture," 21.

53. Bethune commented on her advocacy for women to be admitted into architecture schools in her 1891 address, "Women and Architecture."

54. Willard and Livermore, *A Woman of the Century*, 81.

55. Phebe Hannaford, *Daughters of America: Or Women of the Century* (Boston: B. B. Russell, 1883), 286.

56. "Woman's Work," *Buffalo Daily Courier*, July 13, 1884, 3.

57. Allaback, *The First American Women Architects*, 97.

58. "Women in Art," *American Builder and Journal of Art*, September 1, 1872, 52.

59. "Woman's Work," *Buffalo Daily Courier*, July 13, 1884, 3.

60. Ibid.

61. AIA Archives.

62. Willard and Livermore, *A Woman of the Century*, 81.

63. Bethune, "Women and Architecture," 21.

64. "Women in Buffalo's Professional and Business Life," *Buffalo Sunday Morning News*, November 9, 1913, 19.

65. In "Women as Architects," Bethune notes the expense of the books she purchased as an apprentice.

66. Bethune, "Women as Architects," 3.

67. City of Buffalo, *Our Police and Our City* (Buffalo: Author, 1893), 705–710.

68. Martin Wachadlo and Christopher Brown, "Richard A. Waite: A Forgotten Master," *Western New York Heritage* 6 (Winter 2004).

69. Ibid.

70. City of Buffalo, *Our Police and Our City*.

71. Deborah S. Gardner, "The Architecture of Commercialism: John Kellum and the Development of New York, 1840–1875," PhD diss., Columbia University, 1979, 4.

72. "Two Popular Architects," *American Architect and Building News*, March 1, 1879.

73. "A Jewel Palace," *New York Times*, November 12, 1870, 2.

74. Gardner, "The Architecture of Commercialism," 4.

75. Stephen N. Elias, *Alexander T. Stewart: The Forgotten Merchant Prince* (Westport: Praeger, 1992), 171.

76. Wachadlo and Brown, "Richard A. Waite."

77. Ibid.

78. The 1904 City of Buffalo Directory lists William T. Waite (Richard's brother) as the architect whose office is in the German Insurance Building. Prior listings include Richard A. Waite and William T. Waite in business together.

79. "Odd Oscar: How the Apostle of Aestheticism Lectured," *Hamilton Spectator*, May 31, 1882.

80. Roy Nagle Collection, Buffalo History Museum.

81. "The Cary Hotel," *Buffalo Morning Express and Illustrated Buffalo Express*, January 30, 1882, 4.

82. Willard and Livermore, *A Woman of the Century*, 81.

Chapter 2. Family and Firm

1. "Real Estate Transfers," *Buffalo Commercial*, November 9, 1881, 3.

2. United States Census Report 1880, schedule 1, 193. The other members of the household were Emma Blanchard's sister, S. M. Lawrence, and a servant, Mina Mier.

3. Buffalo City Directories, 1888–1895.

4. "School Principal Dead," *Buffalo Times*, Tuesday, August 18, 1891, 1.

5. "Death of D. W. Blanchard," *Buffalo Courier*, Tuesday, August 18, 1891, 8.

6. *Proceedings of the Common Council of the City of Buffalo*, 1885, 39.

7. Buffalo City Directories, 1888–1895.

8. Emma is no longer listed in the Buffalo City Directory and Bethune mentions in correspondence that his mother now lives in Mattapoisett.

9. Angus's second child was Norman (1822–1892), who became a surgeon and the founder of the Trinity College Medical School in Toronto. Norman's grandson, Dr. Henry Norman Bethune (1890–1939), was a celebrated Canadian surgeon, inventor, communist, and political activist who rose to international fame during the Spanish Civil War and in China in the 1930s.

10. Henry F. Withey and Elsie Rathburn Withey, *Biographical Dictionary of American Architects (Deceased)* (Los Angeles: New Age, 1956; facsimile edition, Hennessey & Ingalls, 1970), 377.

11. Richard Edwards, *New York's Great Industries: Buffalo and Vicinity* (New York: Historical, 1884), 143.

12. Charles Moore, "Leverett A. Pratt," in *History of Michigan Volume II* (Chicago: Lewis, 1915), 818.

13. Ron Bloomfield, "Leverette A. Pratt and Walter Koeppe in the Drafting Room, May 8, 1895,"in *Legendary Locals of Bay City Michigan* (Charleston: Arcadia, 2012), 78.

14. Bethune refers to meeting Robert, a fellow student, at Waite's office. *National Cyclopedia of American Biography*, vol. 12, 9.

15. Willard and Livermore, *A Woman of the Century*, 81.

16. Certificate of Marriage of Jennie L. Blanchard and Robert A. Bethune, Erie County Records.

17. "Local Observations," *Buffalo Courier*, December 11, 1881, 3.

18. Lydia Edwards, *How to Read a Dress: A Guide to Changing Fashion from the 16th to the 20th Century* (London: Bloomsbury Press, 2017), 108.

19. "False Statements," *Buffalo Times*, September 4, 1886, 5.

20. These photos may have been staged, which was not uncommon at the time.

21. She would also become a treasurer for the Society of New England Women, member of the New England Historic Genealogical Society, and a member of the Daughters of the American Revolution. Louise attended the Society of New England Women monthly meetings until the year she died.

22. "Louis XIV Rex," *Buffalo Evening News*, February 14, 1888, 1; "It Was a Triumph," *Buffalo Evening News*, February 7, 1890, 15; "The Press Club Ball," *Buffalo Evening News*, April 10, 1893, 17.

23. "Republican Protest," *Buffalo Morning Express and Illustrated Buffalo Express*, October 10, 1882, 4.

24. Zina Bethune Archive on Louise Bethune, University at Buffalo Special Collections.

25. "Dr. Charles W. Bethune," *Buffalo Courier Express*, October 3, 1952, 7.

26. Buffalo City Directories, 1905–1913. The Buffalo City Directory listed Robert's home as his office address of 215 Franklin St. from 1907 to 1909, while Louise and Charles lived at 904 Tonawanda St. However, personal letters written during this time do not suggest that Robert and Louise lived apart. Robert's home address was listed as 904 Tonawanda after 1910.

27. Bethune Genealogy Records, Grosvenor Special Collections, Buffalo and Erie County Library.

28. Louise Bethune, "It Is to Laugh," Zina Bethune Archive on Louise Bethune, University at Buffalo Special Collections.

29. "Bethune's Prompt Action Prevented a Panic," *Buffalo Times*, January 30, 1905, 9.

30. WAA letters. AIA Records.

31. Ibid.

32. Edwards, *New York's Great Industries*, 143.

33. Louise Bethune, "It Is to Laugh," Zina Bethune Archive on Louise Bethune, University at Buffalo Special Collections.

34. Last Will and Testament of Jennie Louise Bethune, Surrogate Court, filed January 16, 1914, County of Erie, State of New York.

35. Buffalo City Directory, 1881. The 1882 city directory lists R. A. Bethune Architect with no mention of L. Bethune.

36. Woods, *From Craft to Profession*, 111.

37. Ibid.

38. Bernard Michael Boyle, "Architectural Practice in America, 1865–1965: Ideal and Reality," in *The Architect*, ed. Spiro Kostof (Oxford: New York University Press, 1977), 314.

39. "Woman's Work: Women as Architects," *Buffalo Daily Courier*, July 13, 1884; "A Clever Woman's Work," *Buffalo Enquirer*, February 9, 1892.

40. AIA Archives, Robert Bethune. Other references Robert listed in his WAA application included the Buffalo Board of Police (including Mayor Jonathan Scoville

and Commissioner Michael Newell), the building committee of the Homeopathic Hospital, Spencer Kellogg for the Kellogg & McDougall factory, Cosack & Company for its factory, and George Field and Edmund Hayes for their work on the Cantilever Bridge in Niagara Falls.

41. "Buffalo Expressions," *Buffalo Morning Express and Illustrated Buffalo Express*, November 19, 1886, 5.

42. "Some Distinguished Women of Buffalo," *American Woman's Illustrated World*, October 7, 1893, 197.

43. "Mostly about People," *Buffalo Times*, March 7, 1901, 2.

44. Ibid.

45. Fuchs Bros. declared bankruptcy in 1898, after the business was handed over to the next generation of sons, in 1898. "Fuchs Assignment," *Buffalo Morning Express and Illustrated Buffalo Express*, December 11, 1898, 14.

46. United States Census Report 1880, schedule 1, 124. He had two sisters and two brothers, Edwin and Charles.

47. "The Man About Town," *Buffalo Sunday Morning News*, December 9, 1888, 3.

48. "The Park," *Buffalo Morning Express and Illustrated Buffalo Express*, April 2, 1879, 4.

49. Buffalo City Directories for 1882–1884.

50. Adriana Barbasch, "AIA Accepts Its First Woman Architect," in *Architecture: A Place for Women*, ed. Ellen Perry Berkeley and Matilda McQuaid (Washington, DC: Smithsonian Institution Press, 1989), 17.

51. Edwards, *New York's Great Industries*, 143.

52. Burial Permits, Forest Lawn Cemetery. Tragically, but all too common at the time, they had two very small daughters who died suddenly in the late 1890s: four-month-old Helen died of bronchitis on Christmas Day of 1896, and the following year, two-year-old Louisa died of meningitis.

53. AIA Archives, Robert Bethune.

Chapter 3. Home Work

Epigraph

Page 53: Quoted in "Woman's Work: Women as Architects," *Buffalo Daily Courier*, July 13, 1884.

1. City of Buffalo Directories, 1882–1891. The name "Bethune & Bethune Architects" was never listed in the directory; however, in 1891 the firm's new name "Bethune, Bethune & Fuchs Architects" first appeared. By this time, the firm had taken on Will Fuchs as its third partner and moved its office to 51 W. Huron.

2. Bethune, "Women and Architecture," 21.

3. Nancy Woloch, *Women and the American Experience* (New York: McGraw-Hill, 2011), 283.

4. Frances B. Cogan, *All-American Girl: The Ideal of Real Womanhood in Mid-Nineteenth Century America* (Athens: University of Georgia Press, 1989), 245.

5. Woloch, *Women and the American Experience*, 283.

6. Virginia Penny, *The Employments of Women: A Cyclopaedia of Woman's Work* (Boston, MA: Walker, Wise, 1863), 36.

7. Ibid.

8. Buffalo City Directory, 1885.

9. Cogan, *All-American Girl*, 250.

10. Ibid., 237.

11. Ibid., 244.

12. Maria Malatesta, *Professional Men, Professional Women: The European Professions from the 19th Century until Today* (Thousand Oaks, CA: Sage, 2010), 134.

13. Janice P. Nimura, *The Blackwell Doctors* (New York: W. W. Norton, 2021), 75.

14. Ibid., 42.

15. Malatesta, *Professional Men, Professional Women*, 136.

16. Ibid., 140.

17. Mary Jane Mossman, *The First Women Lawyers: A Comparative Study of Gender, Law and the Legal Professions* (Oxford: Hart, 2006), 35.

18. Ibid., 24.

19. Woloch, *Women and the American Experience*, 283.

20. Lamia Doumato, "Louisa Tuthill's Unique Achievement," in *Architecture: A Place for Women*, ed. Ellen Perry Berkeley and Matilda McQuaid (Washington, DC: Smithsonian Institution Press, 1989), 7.

21. Gwendolyn Wright, *Moralism and the Modern Home* (Chicago: University of Chicago Press, 1980), 19.

22. Ibid., 22.

23. David P. Handlin, *The American Home: Architecture and Society, 1815–1915* (Boston: Little, Brown, 1979), 58.

24. Gwendolyn Wright, "Women in Architecture," in *The Architect*, ed. Spiro Kostoff (Oxford: New York University Press, 1977), 285.

25. Allaback, *The First American Women Architects*, 17.

26. Lisa Koenigsberg, "Mariana Van Rensselaer," in *Architecture: A Place for Women*, ed. Ellen Perry Berkeley and Matilda McQuaid (Washington, DC: Smithsonian Institution Press, 1989), 43.

27. Ibid.

28. Bethune, "Women and Architecture."

29. Wright, *Moralism and the Modern Home*, 19.

30. "Occupations of Women: What the Field of Architecture Offers to the Well Trained Practical Woman," *New York Tribune*, August 26, 1901, 7.

31. Martha N. McKay, "Women as Architects," in *The Western*, ed. H. H. Morgan (St. Louis: G. I. Jones, 1880), 22–39.

32. Ibid.

33. Ibid.

34. Association for the Advancement of Women, *Historical Account of the Association for the Advancement of Women, 1873–1893: Twenty-First Women's Congress, World's Columbian Exposition, Chicago, 1893* (Denham, MA: Transcript Stream Job Print., 1893), 25.

35. "Female Competition," *American Architect and Building News*, December 1890, 196.

36. Several projects were composed of multiple houses.

37. "Woman's Work: Women as Architects," *Buffalo Daily Courier*, July 3, 1884, 3.

38. "Woman Architects," *Buffalo Courier*, March 7, 1891, 6.

39. Ibid.

40. "She handles all the dwelling houses that come to the office of the firm of which she is a member." "A Clever Woman's Work," *Buffalo Enquirer*, February 9, 1892, 4.

41. "Woman's Work: Women as Architects," *Buffalo Daily Courier*, July 13, 1884, 3.

42. Allaback, *The First American Women Architects*, 161.

43. Joseph Dana Miller, "Women as Architects," *Frank Leslie's Popular Monthly* 50 (June 1900): 199.

44. Ibid.

45. Allaback, *The First American Women Architects*, 100.

46. "A Woman Who Builds Homes," *Ladies Home Journal*, October 1914.

47. Josephine Wright Chapman, "How to Make the Home Beautiful," *Success Magazine*, March 1905, 197.

48. Sarah Allaback, "Mary Nevan Gannon," Pioneering Women of American Architecture, Beverly Willis Architecture Foundation, https://pioneeringwomen.bwaf.org/mary-nevan-gannon, accessed August 15, 2021.

49. Ibid.

50. Allaback, *The First American Women Architects*, 83.

51. Severance, "Talks by Successful Women," 314–316.

52. Ibid.

53. Ibid.

54. Tuthill, *History of Architecture from Earliest Times*, ix.

55. Mark Girouard, *Sweetness and Light: The Queen Anne Movement, 1860–1900* (Oxford: Clarendon Press, 1977), 209.

56. John J. Stevenson, *House Architecture* (London: Macmillan, 1880), 340.

57. Ibid.

58. Girouard, *Sweetness and Light*, 62.

59. Annmarie Adams, *Architecture in the Family Way: Doctors, Houses, and Women, 1870–1900* (Montreal: McGill-Queen's University Press, 1996), 139.

60. Ibid., 150.

61. Ibid., 158.

62. Robert S. Peabody, "A Talk about 'Queen Anne,' " *American Architect and Building News*, April 28, 1877, 133.

63. Girouard, *Sweetness and Light*, 211.

64. "The Queen Anne Style," *American Architect and Building News*, February 21, 1880.

65. Vincent Scully, *Shingle Style and the Stick Style* (New Haven: Yale University Press, 1955), 22.

66. Leland Roth, *American Architecture: A History* (Boulder: Westview Press, 2001), 242.

67. Bethune, "Women and Architecture."

68. "Strong Society Organized to Beautify City," *Buffalo Evening News*, December 17, 1901, 4.

69. Catherine Faust, Austin M. Fox, Edward B. Green, Gerald C. Mead, Burchfield Penney Art Center, *E. B. Green: Buffalo's Architect* (Buffalo: Buffalo State College Foundation, 1997), 13.

70. Steve Cichon, "Black Rock's Pratt & Letchworth: Buffalo's Original Ironworks," *Buffalo News*, July 29, 2021.

71. Bruce McCausland, *1887–2012 History: First Presbyterian Church*, https://buffaloah.com/a/sym/1/mcc.html, accessed October 11, 2021.

72. Twentieth Century Club Membership Directory.

73. Catherine Faust, *The Architecture of E. B. Green: A Vanishing Legacy*, https://buffaloah.com/a/archs/ebg/bp/faust/index.html, accessed October 11, 2021.

74. Forest Lawn Cemetery Directory.

75. Ibid.

76. AIA Archives.

77. US Census report, 1880.

78. "Dwelling Houses," *Buffalo Morning Express and Illustrated Buffalo Express*, November 21, 1886, 11.

79. Susan Eck, "805 Delaware: The Kelloggs, Town Club, and Temple Beth Zion," Western New York History, https://www.wnyhistory.org/portfolios/whowhere/kellogg_805_delaware/kellogg_delaware.html, accessed October 11, 2021.

80. Zina Bethune Archive of Louise Bethune, University at Buffalo.

81. *Chautauqua Atlas*, 1881, courtesy of Dunkirk Historical Society.

82. Ibid.

83. Scully, *Shingle Style and Stick Style*, 63.

84. *Building a Healthy Community: Brooks Memorial Hospital . . . The First 100 Years*, https://brookshospital.org/wp-content/uploads/2020/11/brooksbook.pdf.

85. "Real Estate Transfers," *Buffalo Morning Express and Illustrated Buffalo Express*, July 24, 1889, 8.

86. "Some Distinguished Women of Buffalo," *American Woman's Illustrated World*, October 7, 1893, 197.

87. Buffalo City Directories, 1908–1911.

Chapter 4. Welcome to the Club

Epigraph

Page 85: American Institute of Architects Twenty-Second Annual Convention, Buffalo, New York, 1888, *AIA Convention Proceedings*. AIA Archives.

1. Woods, *From Craft to Profession*, 40.

2. Paul R. Baker, *Richard Morris Hunt* (Cambridge, MA: MIT Press, 1980), 109.

3. Woods, *From Craft to Profession*, 32.

4. Arthur C. Weatherhead, "The History of Collegiate Education in Architecture in the United States," PhD diss., Columbia University, 1941, 14–15.

5. Woods, *From Craft to Profession*, 37.

6. Ibid., 38.

7. Henry H. Saylor, *The A.I.A.'s First Hundred Years* (Washington, DC: American Institute of Architects, 1957), 15. The cities initially participating: New York City, 1867; Philadelphia and Chicago, 1869; Boston and Cincinnati, 1870; Baltimore, 1871; Albany, 1873; Rhode Island, 1875; San Francisco, 1881; St. Louis and Indianapolis, 1884; and Washington, DC, 1887.

8. *AIA Convention Proceedings*, 1882.

9. *WAA Convention Proceedings*, 1884. AIA Archives.

10. Woods, *From Craft to Profession*, 39.

11. The first three presidents of the AIA were: Richard Upjohn, 1857–1876; Thomas Ustick Walter, 1877–1887; and Richard Morris Hunt, 1888–1891. AIA Archives

12. *WAA Convention Proceedings*, 1884. AIA Archives.

13. *WAA Convention Proceedings*, 1884. AIA Archives.

14. Woods, *From Craft to Profession*, 41.

15. Ibid.

16. Dankmar Adler, president of the WAA in 1888, threatened to leave negotiations over this point. *Inland Architect and News Record* 12, no. 6 (November 1888).

17. Ibid.

18. Woods, *From Craft to Profession*, 41.

19. *AIA Convention Proceedings*, 1888, 49. AIA Archives.

20. Fifth Annual Convention of the Western Association of Architects. *Inland Architect and News Record* 12, no. 6 (November 1888).

21. Woods, *From Craft to Profession*, 39.

22. Fifth Annual Convention of the Western Association of Architects. *Inland Architect and News Record* 12, no. 6 (November 1888).

23. *Inland Architect and News Record and Builder* 6, no. 5 (November 1885): 68.

24. Woods, *From Craft to Profession*, 39.

25. Louise Bethune Letter to Henry Lord Gay, Secretary of the WAA, November 12, 1885. AIA Archives.

26. Louise Bethune Letter to John Root, December 7, 1885. AIA Archives.

27. *WAA Proceedings*, AIA Archives. November 18, 1885.

28. Ibid.

29. *Inland Architect and Builder* (November 1888): 69.

30. *Inland Architect and Record News* (November 1887): 81.

31. A. J. Bloor Secretary's Report to the AIA, December 1, 1886. AIA Archives.

32. Ibid. The discussion regarding this amendment was led by Louis Sullivan.

33. AIA Archives.

34. "Talk," *Woman's Exponent*, January 1, 1886, 8.

35. "Women as Architects," *Weekly Wisconsin*, January 2, 1886, 3.

36. Ibid.

37. "The Graduates," *Buffalo Courier*, November 10, 1889, 11.

38. AIA Meeting Minutes, March 1888. AIA Archives.

39. AIA Meeting Minutes, September 1888, AIA Archives.

40. AIA Archives. A. J. Bloor in a letter to Bethune regarding her AIA submission waived the third reference letter requirement.

41. The originals are in the Zina Bethune Collection on Louise Bethune, UB Special Collections.

42. AIA Archives. A. J. Bloor in a letter to Bethune regarding her AIA submission waived the third reference letter requirement.

43. 1888 Annual Report. AIA Archives.

44. AIA Meeting Minutes, March 1888. AIA Archives.

45. AIA Meeting Minutes, March 1888. AIA Archives. Letter from A. J. Bloor to Louise Bethune, April 6, 1888. AIA Archives. Of the other three new Associate members, one also had twelve years of experience and the other two had less than four years.

46. AIA Meeting Minutes, February 1888. AIA Archives. Bloor reviewed Bethune's initial application letter and his response with the board.

47. *Inland Architect and News Record* (August 1887): 1.

48. *AIA Convention Proceedings*, 1888. AIA Archives.

49. Ibid.

50. Ibid.

51. John W. Root, *Convention Proceedings of the American Institute of Architects, the Western Association of Architects, and the Consolidation of the American Institute and the Western Association* (Chicago: Inland Architect Press, 1890).

52. AIA Archives.

53. *AIA Convention Proceedings*, 1901. AIA Archives.

54. In her 1889 presentation to the Graduate Association in Buffalo, Louise noted that Smith was another member of the architectural association.

55. "W. S. Smith & Co.," *North Alabama Illustrated*, 1888, 105.

56. "WAA Convention Proceedings," *Inland Architect and News Record* (1887): 81.

57. Membership records for Ida Annah Ryan, AIA Archives. Blackall wrote a letter in opposition to Ryan's 1907 application for AIA admission on the grounds that women should have more experience and he stated that Lois Howe was only elected because the members mistook her name as Louis.

58. AIA Members List, 1916. AIA Archives.

59. AIA Archives.

60. AIA Archives. Ida Annah Ryan file.

61. Allaback, *The First American Women Architects*, 135.

62. Ibid., 177.

63. "Convention Proceedings of the Western Association of Architects." *Inland Architect* (December 1886): 79.

64. AIA Archives.

65. *History of the Buffalo Society of Architects*, 1908. UB Special Collections.

66. Root, *Convention Proceedings of the American Institute of Architects the Western Association of Architects and the Consolidation of the American Institute and the Western Association.*

67. Western New York State Association of Architects, *Architectural Era* 1–2, 201.

68. *Architectural Era* 3–4.

69. *AIA Convention Proceedings*, 1892, 66. AIA Archives.

70. Ibid.

71. Clifford Ricker, "Results of Licensing Law for Architects in Illinois," *Brickbuilder* 10, no. 2 (1902): 28.

72. Conversation with Robert Lopez, executive secretary to the New York State Board for Architecture and the State Board for Landscape Architecture, July 6, 2014.

73. *AIA Convention Proceedings*, 1897, 17. AIA Archives.

74. Sidney Smith, 1888. Western New York State Association of Architects, *Architectural Era* 1–2, 201.

75. https://foit-albert.com/about-us/.

76. AIA Archives. The upstate AIA members are:

Louise Blanchard Bethune (1856–1913), Buffalo, NYWAA 1885; AIA
  1888–1904; FAIA 1889
Florence England Bishop (1910–1987), Penfield, NYAIA 1945–
Patricia Day Earle, Lafayette, NYAIA 1967–1969
Beverly Foit-Albert, Buffalo, NYAIA 1966–1970
Helen Chittenden Gillespie (1907–1983), Syracuse, NYAIA 1943–
Barbara Carstairs Lewis (1912–2001), Fayetteville, NYAIA 1949–1970
Jane Hamblin Lewis, Albany, NYAIA 1967–1973
Laurel Anderson Mussman, New Hartford, NYAIA 1963–1978
Lucille Strauss, Katonah, NYAIA 1968–
Reba Thompson, Westchester, NYAIA 1951–
Olive Frances Tjaden (1904–1997), Garden City, NY; Ft. Lauderdale,
  FL. AIA 1938–1948
Maria Halina Twirbutt, Forest Hills, NYAIA 1966–
Olga Narovna Valvano (1922–1980), Victor, NYAIA 1952–1954
Marjorie Katherine Wright (1895–1949), Fayetteville, NYAIA 1944–

77. "Women in Architecture," *Buffalo Morning Express and Illustrated Buffalo Express*, March 7, 1891, 6.

Chapter 5. The Architecture of Education

1. "Woman's Work," *Buffalo Daily Courier*, July 13, 1884.
2. Lawrence A. Cremin, *American Education: The National Education, 1783–1876* (New York: Harper & Row, 1980), 1.
3. David B. Tyack, *The One Best System: A History of American Urban Education* (Cambridge, MA: Harvard University Press, 1974), 5.
4. Neil Gislason, *Building Innovation: History, Cases, and Perspectives on School Design* (Big Tankook Island, Nova Scotia: Backalong Books, 2011), 1.
5. Tyack, *The One Best System*, 22.
6. Dale Allen Gyure, *The Schoolroom: A Social History of Teaching and Learning* (Santa Barbara, CA: Greenwood, 2018) 10.
7. Henry Barnard, *School Architecture; or Contributions to the Improvement of School-Houses in the United States* (New York: A. S. Barnes, 1850), 6.
8. Ibid., 16.
9. Gislason, *Building Innovation*, 7.
10. Edward Robert Robson, *School Architecture: Being Practical Remarks on the Planning, Designing, Building and Furnishing of School-houses* (London: Murray, 1874), 27.
11. Robson, *School Architecture*, 80.
12. Gyure, *The Schoolroom*, 17.

13. John D. Philbrick, *City School Systems in the United States* (Washington, DC: Circulars of Information of the Bureau of Education, 1885).

14. Morton G. Weed, *School Days of Yesterday: The Story of the Buffalo Public Schools* (Buffalo: Buffalo Board of Education, 2001), 4–12.

15. Ibid.

16. James F. Crooker, *Department of Education: Annual Report, Superintendent of Education, City of Buffalo: 1890–91* (Buffalo: Haas & Klein Print., 1892), 71. Hereafter, *Superintendent's Report.*

17. "Candidates for Superintendent of Public Instruction," *Buffalo Courier*, March 12, 1883.

18. Crooker, *Superintendent's Report, 1882*, 21.

19. Crooker, *Superintendent's Report, 1882*, 19.

20. "The Schools of Buffalo," *Buffalo Courier*, June 13, 1883, 2.

21. "Lamps in Daytime," *Buffalo Sunday Morning News*, June 14, 1883, 1.

22. Ibid.

23. "Antiquated School Buildings," *Buffalo Courier*, May 31, 1882, 1.

24. *Proceedings of the Common Council of the City of Buffalo, from January 2, 1882, to December 29, 1882* (Buffalo: Courier Company Print., 1882), 795.

25. Crooker, *Superintendent's Report, 1882*, 21.

26. Crooker, *Superintendent's Report, 1890–91*, 25.

27. *Proceedings of the Common Council of the City of Buffalo, from January 1, 1883, to December 31, 1883* (Buffalo: Times Print., 1884), 403.

28. Ibid.

29. The *Buffalo Courier* as quoted in the *Superintendent's Report, 1883–84*, 33.

30. *Proceedings of the Common Council, 1882*, 1106.

31. Crooker, *Superintendent's Report, 1886–87*, 39.

32. Crooker, *Superintendent's Report, 1885–86*, 41.

33. Ibid., 42.

34. Ibid.

35. Crooker, *Superintendent's Report, 1889–90*, 95.

36. "Building Operations," *Buffalo Courier*, October 3, 1891, 6.

37. "False Statements: The Commercial's Way of Making a Sensation Exemplified: Distorting the Truth—A Libelous Article on Commissioner Sliker," *Buffalo Times*, September 4, 1886, 5.

38. AIA Correspondence. April 6, 1888. AIA Archives.

39. Henry P. Emerson, *Department of Public Instruction Annual Report: 1900–1901* (Buffalo: Wenbourne-Sumner Co. Print., 1902), 12.

40. "Many Honor Memory of James F. Crooker," *Buffalo Courier*, February 10, 1919, 3.

41. "Building Operations," *Buffalo Courier*, October 3, 1891, 6.

42. *100 Years of Education in the Public Schools of Lockport, New York* (Lockport: Board of Education, 1947), 19.

43. Ibid., 21.

44. Bethune, "Women and Architecture."

45. "Synopsis of Building News," *Inland Architect and Building News*, October 1889, 43.

46. "The Lock City: Laying the Corner-Stone of the Union School," *Buffalo Morning Express and Illustrated Buffalo Express*, July 13, 1890, 15.

47. *100 Years of Education*, 54.

Chapter 6. Innovation, Industry, and Entertaining the Public

1. Roth, *American Architecture*, 266.

2. "Illinois State Association," *Inland Architect and News Record* (March 1887): 23.

3. Roth, *American Architecture*, 268.

4. Ibid.

5. "Mostly About People," *Buffalo Times*, March 7, 1901, 2.

6. "14 Story Building," *Buffalo Commercial*, January 3, 1891, 11.

7. As reported by the Index of Building Permit Values. Charles Hoffmann, *The Depression of the Nineties: An Economic History* (Westport: Greenwood, 1970), 22.

8. "Annual Convention of the Ohio State Chapter, A.I.A.," *American Architect and Building News*, October 6, 1894.

9. *American Architect and Building News*, March 24, 1894, 139.

10. *American Architect and Building News*, May 8, 1897, 42.

11. *Queen of the Lakes . . . Buffalo: The Electric City of the Future: Souvenir of the Tenth Convention of the National Association of Builders. Sept. 14–19, 1896* (Buffalo: Courier, 1896), 57.

12. "New Buildings," *Buffalo Evening News*, November 10, 1896, 9.

13. *Superintendent's Report, 1900–1901*, 12.

14. "Mostly about People," *Buffalo Times*, March 7, 1901, 2.

15. "Women in Architecture," *Buffalo Morning Express and Illustrated Buffalo Express*, March 7, 1891, 6.

16. "Building Operations," *Buffalo Courier*, October 3, 1891, 6.

17. Nancy L. Todd, *New York's Historic Armories: An Illustrated History* (Albany: State University of New York Press, 2006), 2.

18. "Buffalo Expressions," *Buffalo Morning Express and Illustrated Buffalo Express*, November 19, 1886, 5.

19. Ibid.

20. "Buffalo Society of Architects," *Inland Architect and Builder* (December 1886).

21. "Seeing Buffalo of the Olden Time: A Historical Block," *Buffalo Times*, Tuesday, June 1, 1909, 4.

22. "Real Estate Movements," *Buffalo Times*, December 30, 1898, 1.

23. "To Have a Private Market," *Buffalo Courier*, July 10, 1903, 7.

24. "Exterior View of the New Market to Be Built at Black Rock," *Buffalo Evening News*, July 23, 1903, 1.

25. "City Will Have to Build Black Rock Market, Harp Says," *Buffalo Evening News*, November 10, 1903, 19.

26. Newspaper articles between 1903 and 1904 describe the project in development but the topic is not published after 1904.

27. "Fred Jehle," *Buffalo Times*, January 24, 1899, 4.

28. Ibid.

29. "Shea's New Theater," *Buffalo Commercial*, February 23, 1895, 11.

30. "Shea's New Theater," *Buffalo Evening News*, January 29, 1895, 7.

31. Ibid.

32. "Mr. Shea's Theater," *Buffalo Commercial*, May 14, 1895, 11.

33. "Building Permits," *Buffalo Courier*, July 2, 1895, 6.

34. "Buried to His Neck," *Buffalo Courier*, July 16, 1895, 6.

35. "Falling of a Wall," *Buffalo Commercial*, December 20, 1895, 13.

36. "Roof Fell In," *Buffalo Enquirer*, December 21, 1895. 1.

37. "Fuchs Building Collapse," *Buffalo Evening News*, December 24, 1895, 6.

38. "Architects Object," *Buffalo Commercial*, February 1, 1896, 10.

39. Francis R. Kowsky, Mark Goldman, Austin Fox, John D. Randall, Jack Quinan, Teresa Lasher, Reyner Banham, Charles Beveridge, and Henry-Russell Hitchcock, *Buffalo Architecture: A Guide* (Cambridge, MA: MIT Press, 1996), 82.

40. "Our Growing City," *Buffalo Courier*, September 19, 1891, 6.

41. "Building Operations," *Buffalo Courier*, October 3, 1891, 6.

42. "Woodlawn Beach," *Buffalo Express and Buffalo Morning Express*, April 16, 1893, 16.

43. "At Woodlawn," *Buffalo Enquirer*, August 10, 1894, 3.

44. "At Woodlawn," *Buffalo Enquirer*, August 10, 1894, 3.

45. *The Birth of Woodlawn*, courtesy of the Hamburg History Museum, 11.

46. "Basehits," *Buffalo Express and Buffalo Morning Express*, February 9, 1890, 14.

47. Joseph M. Overfield, *The 100 Seasons of Buffalo Baseball* (Kenmore, NY: Partners Press, 1985), 14.

48. "Good for East Buffalo," *Buffalo Morning Express and Illustrated Buffalo Express*, August 10, 1890, 8.

49. Ibid.

50. Elstner Publishing Company, *Industries of Buffalo: A Resume of the Mercantile and Manufacturing Progress of the Queen City of the Lakes in 1887* (Buffalo: Author, 1887).

51. "New Terminal Station," *Buffalo Times*, August 6, 1898, 5.

52. "Cereal Coffee Company Sold," *Buffalo Times*, January 4, 1900, 1.

Chapter 7. Riding into the Future

Epigraph

Page 151: Louise Bethune, Women's Wheel and Athletic Club Annual Dinner Program, April 29, 1894.

1. Nellie Bly, "Champion of Her Sex," *New York World*, February 2, 1896.
2. Ibid.
3. "A Runaway Accident," *Buffalo Commercial*, June 15, 1891, 9.
4. "Notes on Sports," *Buffalo Morning Express and Illustrated Buffalo Express*, February 9, 1890, 3.
5. "As a Cycling City, Buffalo Occupies a Position in the Front Rank," *Buffalo Courier*, November 18, 1894, 11.
6. Carl F. Burgwardt, "The Buffalo Bicycle Clubhouse: A Hidden Landmark," *Western New York Heritage Magazine*, Spring 2004, 51.
7. E. D. Sewall, "The Women's Bicycle and Its Predecessors," *Iron Age*, May 13, 1897, 8.
8. "Wheelwomen and Their Winter Sports," *American Wheelman*, 1892, 361.
9. "Fair Riders on Modern Wheels," *Outing* 17 (1890–1891): 305, https://hdl.handle.net/2027/nnc1.cu09397639.
10. "The Women's Wheel and Athletic Club 1892," Grosvenor Library, Buffalo and Erie County Central Library.
11. "Dr. Ida C. Bender Called by Death; Long an Educator," *Buffalo Courier*, June 12, 1916, 5.
12. "The Children's Home," *Dunkirk Evening Observer*, December 3, 1890, 2.
13. "The Women's Wheel and Athletic Club 1892," Grosvenor Library, Buffalo and Erie County Central Library.
14. "Ladies of the Wheel," *Buffalo Illustrated Express*, August 14, 1892, 7.
15. "The World Awheel," *Munsey's* 15 (1896): 157.
16. "Ladies of the Wheel," *Buffalo Illustrated Express*, August 14, 1892, 7. The three bicycles that the club members owned were the Swift, Dart, and Psycho. Bethune would have owned one of these brands.
17. "A Clever Woman's Work," *Buffalo Courier*, February 9, 1892, 4.
18. "Ladies of the Wheel," *Buffalo Illustrated Express*, August 14, 1892, 7.
19. Women's Wheel and Athletic Club meeting notes, Grosvenor Library, Buffalo and Erie County Central Library.
20. "What to Wear on a Wheel," *American Wheelman*, 1892.
21. Women's Wheel and Athletic Club meeting notes, Grosvenor Library, Buffalo and Erie County Central Library.
22. "Ladies of the Wheel," *Buffalo Illustrated Express*, August 14, 1892, 7.

23. Quoted in Lynn Sherr, *Failure Is Impossible: Susan B. Anthony in Her Own Words* (New York: Times Books, 1995), 196.

24. "Mrs. Stanton Likes Bloomers," *Rocky Mountain News*, August 11, 1895.

25. Letter to the Editor, *Sidepaths* magazine, 1898.

26. Frances E. Willard, *How I Learned to Ride the Bicycle: Reflections on an Influential 19th Century Woman*, ed. Carol O'Hare, with an introduction by Edith Mayo (Sunnyvale, CA: Fair Oaks, 1895; republished 1991).

27. "Miss Willard's Wheel Views," *Buffalo Morning Express and Illustrated Buffalo Express*, Sunday, February 23, 1896, 1.

28. "Woman's Club Banquet: Bright Buffalo Women Meet to Dine and Make Speeches," *Buffalo Evening News*, Thursday, April 26, 1894, 8.

29. Louise Bethune, Women's Wheel and Athletic Club Annual Dinner Program, 1895.

30. Louise Bethune, Women's Wheel and Athletic Club Annual Dinner Program, April 29, 1894.

31. "Cycles," *Buffalo Courier*, Monday, April 8, 1889, 3.

32. "Wheel Club Incorporated," *Buffalo Morning Express and Illustrated Buffalo Express*, Friday, March 24, 1893, 3.

33. "Ladies of the Wheel," *Buffalo Illustrated Express*, August 14, 1892.

34. "Bicycles in the Cemetery," *Buffalo Commercial*, June 13, 1892.

35. Women's Wheel and Athletic Club meeting notes, Grosvenor Library, Buffalo and Erie County Central Library. Possibly this is the petition that Anthony was referencing in her letter to *Sidepaths* magazine.

36. "Is Bicycling Immoral?," *Brooklyn Daily Eagle*, August 19, 1896, 1.

37. Association for the Advancement of Women, *Historical Account of the Association for the Advancement of Women, 1873–1893*, 25.

38. "Women as Architects," *Architect and Engineer of California*, June 1910.

39. "Some Distinguished Women of Buffalo," *American Woman's Illustrated World*, December 7, 1893, 197.

40. "Women's Work," *Buffalo Daily Courier*, July 13, 1884.

41. Bethune, "Women and Architecture."

42. Jean V. Matthews, *The Rise of the New Woman* (Chicago: Ivan R. Dee, 2003), 14.

43. Caroline Tichnor, "The Steel-Engraving Lady and the Gibson Girl," *Atlantic Monthly*, 1901, 107.

44. Ibid., 108.

45. Barbara Welter, "The Cult of True Womanhood, 1820–1860: Part 1," *American Quarterly* 18, no. 2 (Summer 1966): 152.

46. Julia Blackwelder, *Now Hiring: The Feminization of Work in the United States 1900–1995* (College Station: Texas A&M University Press, 1997), 39.

47. Patricia Marks, *Bicycles, Bangs, and Bloomers: The New Woman in the Popular Press* (Lexington: University Press of Kentucky, 1990), ix.

48. Matthews, *The Rise of the New Woman*, 13.

49. Marks, *Bicycles, Bangs, and Bloomers*, 150.

50. https://www.pbs.org/wgbh/americanexperience/features/triangle-fire-what-shirtwaist/, accessed June 23, 2019.

51. "Club Life for Women," *Harper's Bazaar*, October 25, 1890, 826.

52. Matthews, *The Rise of the New Woman*, 15.

53. Ibid., 23.

54. DAR History Website, https://www.dar.org/national-society/about-dar/dar-history.

55. Matthews, *The Rise of the New Woman*, 17.

56. Lillian W. Betts, "The New Woman," in *The American New Woman Revisited: A Reader, 1894–1930*, ed. Martha H. Patterson (New Brunswick, NJ: Rutgers University Press, 2008).

57. Woloch, *Women and the American Experience*.

58. "Married Women's Property Laws," American Women, Library of Congress, retrieved January 18, 2021.

59. "Woman's Club Banquet," *Buffalo Evening News*, April 26, 1894, 8.

60. "Education for Women," *Buffalo Evening News*, Monday, April 3, 1893, 7.

61. "The Women Objected," *Buffalo Enquirer*, Wednesday, April 12, 1893, 4.

62. "Agrees with Mrs. Lyon," *Buffalo Enquirer*, Thursday, April 13, 1893, 4.

63. "It Was Wound Up Last Night," *Buffalo Courier*, January 6, 1897, 6.

64. "Women's Organizations," in *A History of the City of Buffalo and Niagara Falls* (Buffalo: Times, 1896), 128.

65. "News for Wheelmen," *Buffalo Commercial*, March 7, 1895, 12.

66. "Century Riders," *Buffalo Morning Express and Illustrated Buffalo Express*, June 26, 1893, 8.

67. "News for Wheelmen," *Buffalo Commercial*, March 7, 1895, 12.

68. "A Rush for Bloomers," *Buffalo Commercial*, October 8, 1894, 10.

69. "The Woman's A.G.," *Buffalo Times*, January 5, 1897, 3.

Chapter 8. A Question of Equality

Epigraphs

Page 177: Louise Bethune, "Women and Architecture," *Inland Architect and News Record* 17 (March 1891).

Page 180: "Chicago," *American Architect and Building News*, November 26, 1892.

1. Mary Pepchinski, "The Woman's Building and the World Exhibitions: Exhibition Architecture and Conflicting Feminine Ideals at European and Amer-

ican World Exhibitions, 1873–1915," *Wolkenkucksheim* 5, no. 1 (2000), available at https://www.cloudcuckoo.net/openarchive/wolke/eng/Subjects/001/Pepchinski/ pepchinski.htm, accessed on January 22, 2022.

2. Ibid.

3. Jeanne Madeline Weimann, *The Fair Women* (Chicago: Academy Chicago, 1981), 1.

4. Elizabeth Duane Gillespie, *A Book of Remembrance* (Philadelphia: J. B. Lippincott, 1901), 297–351.

5. Pepchinski, "The Woman's Building and the World Exhibitions."

6. Gillespie, *A Book of Remembrance*, 316.

7. Mary F. Cordato, "Towards a New Century: Women and the Philadelphia Centennial Exhibition, 1876," *Pennsylvania Magazine of History and Biography* 107, no. 1 (January 1983): 113–135.

8. Elizabeth Cady Stanton, *Eighty Years and More* (New York: European, 1898), 313.

9. Cordato, "Towards a New Century."

10. Ibid. The newsletter was published from May 13 to November 11, 1876.

11. "Chicago," *American Architect and Building News*, November 26, 1892, 133.

12. Ibid.

13. Weimann, *The Fair Women*, 27.

14. Ibid.

15. Ibid.

16. Nancy F. Cott, *The Grounding of Modern Feminism* (New Haven, CT: Yale University Press, 1987), 17.

17. Weimann, *The Fair Women*, 40.

18. Ibid.

19. Ibid.

20. Ibid.

21. *Report of the President to the Board of Directors of the Columbian Exposition*, Chicago, 1892–1893, 28.

22. F. D. Millet, "The Designers of the Fair," *Harper's New Monthly Magazine*, November 1892, 876.

23. Robert Muccigrosso, *Celebrating the New World: Chicago's Columbian Exposition of 1893* (Chicago: Ivan R. Dee, 1993), 58.

24. The architects presented their schematic design documents on March, 6, 1891. *Report of the President to the Board of Directors of the Columbian Exposition*, Chicago, 1892–1893, 26.

25. Weimann, *The Fair Women*, 144.

26. Ibid.

27. "Columbian Exposition Women's Building," *Inland Architect and News Record* (February 1891): 1.

28. Weimann, *The Fair Women*, 144.

29. "Columbian Exposition Women's Building," *Inland Architect and News Record* (February 1891): 1.

30. Ibid., 1.

31. Weimann, *The Fair Women*, 146.

32. Ibid.

33. "Columbian Exposition Women's Building," *Inland Architect and News Record* (February 1891): 1.

34. Ibid.

35. "Progress in Work on World's Fair," *Inland Architect and Building News* (March 1891): 18.

36. Weimann, *The Fair Women*, 150.

37. Allaback, *The First American Women Architects*, 104.

38. Weimann, *The Fair Women*, 153.

39. Ibid.

40. Ibid.

41. Wanda Corn, *Women Building History: Public Art at the 1893 Columbian Exposition* (Berkeley, CA: University of California Press, 2011), 89.

42. Dianne Sachko Macleod, *Enchanted Lives, Enchanted Objects: American Women Collectors and the Making of Culture, 1800–1940* (Berkeley: University of California Press, 2008), 107.

43. Ibid.

44. Sophia Hayden, "1894 Report to the Lady Board of Managers," in *Addresses and Reports of Mrs. Potter Palmer: President of the Board of Lady Managers, World's Columbian Commission*, ed. Bertha Honore Palmer (Chicago: Rand, McNally, 1894).

45. Weimann, *The Fair Women*, 177.

46. "Chicago," *American Architect and Building News*, November 26, 1892, 134.

47. Minerva Parker Nichols, "A Woman on the Woman's Building," *American Architect and Building News*, December 10, 1892, 170.

48. *American Architect and Building News*, December 10, 1892, 158.

49. "Woman Architects," *Buffalo Courier*, March 7, 1891, 6.

50. Ibid.

51. Judith Paine, "Pioneer Women Architects," in *Women in American Architecture: A Historic and Contemporary Perspective*, ed. Susana Torre (New York: Watson-Guptill, 1977), 55.

52. Bethune, "Women and Architecture."

53. Ibid.

54. Woods, *From Craft to Profession*, 43.

55. Allaback, *The First American Women Architects*, 94.

56. Allaback, *The First American Women Architects*, 159.

57. "Women in Buffalo's Professional and Business Life," *Buffalo Sunday Morning News*, November 9, 1913, 19.

Chapter 9. The Triumphant Hotel Lafayette—and Beyond

Epigraphs

Page 199: "Women in Buffalo's Professional and Business Life," *Buffalo Sunday Morning News*, November 9, 1913, 19.
Page 204: "Buffalo's Fine New Hotel," *Buffalo Sunday Morning News*, October 19, 1902, 14.

1. Brooklyn Museum, *The American Renaissance* (New York: Pantheon Press, 1979), 29.
2. Ibid., 11.
3. "Buffalo Hotel Opened," *New York Times*, June 2, 1904, 6.
4. "Old French Church," *Buffalo Morning Express and Illustrated Buffalo Express*, May 13, 1900, 25.
5. "A New Hotel," *Buffalo Commercial*, March 3, 1899, 9.
6. *American Contractor*, October 21, 1899, 11: "Hotels. Buffalo, NY—Archts. Bethune, Bethune & Fuchs, 45 W. Chippewa st., have plans for a hotel for Jos. A. Oaks, Spaulding & Boldt, of the Broezel house, and Chas. A. Pooley. Twelve stories, brick and steel and contain 300 rooms."
7. "Hotel Lafayette," *Buffalo Commercial*, April 2, 1900, 10.
8. Ibid.
9. "Improvements," *Buffalo Commercial*, November 23, 1900, 8.
10. "Monument Square Hotel," *Buffalo Review*, August 8, 1901, 6.
11. "Hotel Project Has New Life," *Buffalo Evening News*, June 7, 1901 11.
12. "To End in Foreclosure," *Buffalo Commercial*, March 10, 1902, 12.
13. "Rochester Man May Put Up a Hotel Here," *Buffalo Courier*, July, 26, 1902, 7.
14. "Will Build a Hotel," *Buffalo Commercial*, August 2, 1902, 10.
15. "Woman Architect, First in the Country, Dies in Buffalo," *Buffalo Courier*, 1913, 7.
16. In correspondence with friends, Louise wrote that both she and Robert traveled to New York to meet with prominent hotel operator George Sweeney regarding the Lafayette. Letter to Clara H. Manning, September 23, 1903, Buffalo Genealogical Society, Grosvenor Library, Buffalo and Erie County Library.
17. Louise Bethune, "It Is to Laugh," Zina Bethune Archive on Louise Bethune, University at Buffalo.
18. The History of Buffalo, New York website. Original Richmond Hotel / New Richmond Hotel / Iroquois Hotel, http://www.buffaloah.com/h/iroqH/.
19. Donald Albrecht and Jeannine Falino, Susan Gail Johnson, Phyllis Magidson, and Thomas Mellins, *Gilded New York: Design, Fashion, and Society* (New York: Museum of the City of New York; Monacelli Press, 2013), 152.

20. Ibid., 143.

21. Lafayette Hotel Buffalo, Buffalo History Museum.

22. "New Hotel Is Buffalo's Finest," *Hotel Courier*, June 2, 1904, 6.

23. Ibid.

24. "New Hotel Opened," *Buffalo Morning Express and Illustrated Buffalo Express*, June 1904, 7.

25. "New Hotel Is Buffalo's Finest," *Hotel Courier*, June 2, 1904, 6.

26. "New Hotel Opened," *Buffalo Morning Express and Illustrated Buffalo Express*, June 1904, 7.

27. Lafayette Hotel Buffalo, Buffalo History Museum.

28. Ibid.

29. Bethune, "It Is to Laugh."

30. "Built the Lafayette," *Illustrated Buffalo Express*, June 16, 1912, 11.

31. Ibid.

32. Jacqueline Albarella, *The Restoration of the Hotel Lafayette* (Buffalo: Albarella Media, 2014), 36.

33. "Built the Lafayette," *Illustrated Buffalo Express*, June 16, 1912, 11.

34. Reyner Banham, *A Concrete Atlantis: U.S. Industrial Building and European Modern Architecture, 1900–1925* (Cambridge: MIT Press, 1986), 45.

35. "The Magnificent Success of a Firm," *Buffalo Free Press*, February 4, 1902, 2.

36. "An Old Firm in a New Store; Denton, Cottier & Daniels to Move from Main Street," *Buffalo Courier*, February 9, 1908, 20.

37. Ibid.

38. Ibid.

39. Ibid.

40. Ibid.

41. "The Bricka & Enos Store—And What It Stands For," *Buffalo Courier*, October 15, 1911, 31.

42. Letter to Mr. Williams H. Manning, West Somerville, Massachusetts, May 23, 1910, Bethune Genealogy Paper, Grosvenor Special Collections, Buffalo and Erie County Central Library.

43. Brooklyn Museum, *The American Renaissance*, 41.

44. These documents are housed at the Grosvenor Special Collections, Buffalo and Erie County Central Library. Some originals are part of the Zina Bethune Archive on Louise Bethune, University at Buffalo.

45. The Bethune and Blanchard genealogical records are located at the Grosvenor Special Collections, Buffalo and Erie County Central Library.

46. Letter to Mr. Alexander Mackenzie, Toronto, Ontario, July 14, 1910, Bethune Genealogy Papers, Grosvenor Special Collections, Buffalo and Erie County Central Library.

47. Letter to Mr. Alexander Mackenzie, Toronto, Ontario, August 3, 1910, Bethune Genealogy Papers, Grosvenor Special Collections, Buffalo and Erie County Central Library.

48. Bethune, "It Is to Laugh."

49. Ibid.

50. Ibid.

51. Letter to Miss Abbot, Buffalo, New York, April 1, 1912, Bethune Genealogy Papers, Grosvenor Special Collections, Buffalo and Erie County Central Library.

52. Letter to Mr. Carlos P. Darling, Buffalo, New York, July 19, 1912, Bethune Genealogy Papers, Grosvenor Special Collections, Buffalo and Erie County Central Library.

53. Letter to Mr. Isaac D. Blodgett, Buffalo, New York, March 2, 1912, Bethune Genealogy Papers, Grosvenor Special Collections, Buffalo and Erie County Central Library.

54. Letter to Miss Woodcock, Buffalo, New York, May 8, 1911, Bethune Genealogy Papers, Grosvenor Special Collections, Buffalo and Erie County Central Library.

55. Letter to Hon. Mr. Charles E. Williams, Bridgeport, Colorado, April 16, 1912, Bethune Genealogy Papers, Grosvenor Special Collections, Buffalo and Erie County Central Library.

56. Letter to Hon. Ezra S. Stearns, Buffalo, New York, January 24, 1913, Bethune Genealogy Papers, Grosvenor Special Collections, Buffalo and Erie County Central Library.

57. Ibid.

58. Clara Erskine Clement, *Women in the Fine Arts, from the Seventh Century B.C. to the Twentieth Century A.D.*, 1904, https://www.gutenberg.org/files/12045/12045-h/12045-h.htm, accessed May 25, 2022.

59. "Feminism and Architecture," *Western Architect*, April 1914, 34.

60. Jennie Louise Bethune Last Will and Testament, January 4, 1908, Erie County Records.

61. Forest Lawn Cemetery Records.

62. To address this situation, the American Institute of Architects New York State and Buffalo/WNY corrected the omission by placing a foot marker at the gravesite on December 18, 2013, in honor of the centennial of Louise's death.

Conclusion: The Forgotten Woman Architect—Rediscovered

1. Steve Cichon, "Torn-Down Tuesday: Elmwood Music Hall," *Buffalo News*, March 20, 2017.

2. Interview of Zina Bethune by the author, March 2006.

3. AIA Archives.

4. Ida Annah Ryan file, AIA Archives.

5. Sara Holmes Boutelle, *Julia Morgan, Architect* (New York: Abbeville Press, 1988), 7.

6. Meredith Gaglio, "Mary Elizabeth Jane Colter," Pioneering Women of American Architecture, https://pioneeringwomen.bwaf.org/mary-elizabeth-jane-colter/.

7. Jan Cigliano Hartman, *The Women Who Changed Architecture* (Princeton, NJ: Princeton Architectural Press, 2022), 50.

8. Despina Stratigakos, *Where Are the Women Architects?* (Princeton, NJ: Princeton University Press, 2016), 15.

9. Ada Louise Huxtable, "The Last Profession to Be 'Liberated by Women,'" *New York Times*, April 13, 1977, 93.

10. Gabrielle Esperdy, "The Incredible True Adventures of the Architectress in America," *Places Journal*, September 2012, https://placesjournal.org/article/the-incredible-true-adventures-of-the-architectress-in-america/?cn-reloaded=1, accessed April 20, 2020.

11. Ibid.

12. Stratigakos, *Where Are the Women Architects?*, 19.

13. Bethune, "Women and Architecture."

Bibliography

Archives

AIA Archive, Washington, DC
AIA Buffalo/WNY Chapter
Bethune Genealogy Archive, Buffalo and Erie County Library, Grosvenor Collection
Blanchard Genealogy Archive, Buffalo and Erie County Library, Grosvenor Collection
Buffalo and Erie County Library
Buffalo City Records
Buffalo Genealogical Society, Buffalo and Erie County Library, Grosvenor Collection
Buffalo History Museum
Buffalo Women's Wheel and Athletic Club, Buffalo and Erie County Library, Grosvenor Collection
DAR Buffalo Chapter, Buffalo and Erie County Library, Grosvenor Collection
Dunkirk Historical Society
Forest Lawn Cemetery, Buffalo, NY
Hamburg Historical Society
Lockport Public Library
New York State Library
Kerry S. Grant Pan-American Exposition Collection, University at Buffalo Special Collections
Ryerson and Burnham Archives, Chicago Institute of Art
Twentieth Century Club, Buffalo, NY
Zina Bethune Archive on Louise Bethune, University at Buffalo Special Collections

Books and Book Chapters

Adams, Annmarie. *Architecture in the Family Way: Doctors, Houses, and Women, 1870–1900*. Montreal: McGill-Queen's University Press, 1996.

Adams, Edward Dean. *Niagara Power: History of the Niagara Falls Power Company, 1886–1918; Evolution of Its Central Power Station and Alternating Current System.* Niagara Falls: Privately printed for the Niagara Falls Power, 1927.

Albarella, Jacqueline. *The Restoration of the Hotel Lafayette.* Buffalo: Albarella Media, 2014.

Allaback, Sarah. *The First American Women Architects.* Urbana: University of Illinois Press, 2008.

Albrecht, Donald, Jeannine Falino, Susan Gail Johnson, Phyllis Magidson, and Thomas Mellins. *Gilded New York: Design, Fashion, and Society.* New York: Museum of the City of New York; Monacelli Press, 2013.

Association for the Advancement of Women. *Historical Account of the Association for the Advancement of Women, 1873–1893: Twenty-First Women's Congress, World's Columbian Exposition, Chicago, 1893.* Denham, MA: Transcript Stream Job Print., 1893.

Bailey, George M. *Illustrated Buffalo: Queen City of the Lakes.* New York: Acme Publishing and Engraving, 1890.

Baker, Paul R. *Richard Morris Hunt.* Cambridge, MA: MIT Press, 1980.

Banham, Reyner. *A Concrete Atlantis: U.S. Industrial Building and European Modern Architecture, 1900–1925.* Cambridge, MA: MIT Press, 1986.

Barnard, Henry. *School Architecture; or Contributions to the Improvement of School-Houses in the United States.* New York: A. S. Barnes, 1850.

Berkeley, Ellen Perry, and Matilda McQuaid, eds. *Architecture: A Place for Women.* Washington, DC: Smithsonian Institution Press, 1989.

Bernstein, Peter L. *Wedding of the Waters.* New York: W. W. Norton, 2006.

Betts, Lillian W. "The New Woman." In *The American New Woman Revisited: A Reader, 1894–1930,* edited by Martha H. Patterson. New Brunswick, NJ: Rutgers University Press, 2008.

Blackwelder, Julia. *Now Hiring: The Feminization of Work in the United States 1900–1995.* College Station: Texas A&M University Press, 1997.

Blank, Carla, and Tania Martin. *Storming the Old Boys' Citadel: Two Pioneer Women Architects of Nineteenth Century North America.* Montreal: Baraka Books, 2014.

Bloomfield, Ron. "Leverette A. Pratt and Walter Koeppe in the Drafting Room, May 8, 1895." In *Legendary Locals of Bay City, Michigan.* Charleston: Arcadia, 2012.

Blumenson, John J. G. *Identifying American Architecture: A Pictorial Guide to Styles and Terms, 1600–1945.* Walnut Creek, CA: AltaMira Press, 1995.

Boisseau, Tracey Jean, and Abigail M. Markwyn. *Gendering the Fair: Histories of Women and Gender at World's Fairs.* Urbana: University of Illinois Press, 2010.

Boutelle, Sara Holmes. *Julia Morgan, Architect.* New York: Abbeville Press, 1988.

Boyle, Bernard Michael. "Architectural Practice in America, 1865–1965: Ideal and Reality." In *The Architect,* edited by Spiro Kostof. Oxford: New York University Press, 1977.

Brooklyn Museum. *The American Renaissance.* New York: Pantheon Press, 1979.

Buffalo Central School: 1874–'75, 1875.

Building a Healthy Community: Brooks Memorial Hospital . . . The First 100 Years. Institutional Advancement Series, 1998. https://brookshospital.org/wp-content/uploads/2020/11/brooksbook.pdf.

Burke, B. Doreen. *In Pursuit of Beauty: Americans and the Aesthetic Movement.* New York: Metropolitan Museum of Art; Rizzoli, 1986.

Burnham, Daniel H. *The Final Official Report of the Director of Works of the World's Columbian Exposition.* Chicago: World's Columbian Exposition, 1893; reprint, Joan E. Draper, ed., New York: Garland, 1897.

Briggs, Martin S. *The Architect in History.* New York: Da Capo Press, 1974.

Briggs, Warren R. *Modern American Schools: Being a Treatise upon, and Designs for the Construction of School Buildings.* New York: Wiley & Sons, 1899.

Brooklyn Museum. *The American Renaissance.* New York: Pantheon Press, 1979.

City of Buffalo. *Our Police and Our City.* Buffalo: Author, 1893.

Clark, Robert Judson. *The Shaping of Art and Architecture in Nineteenth-Century America.* New York: Metropolitan Museum of Art, 1972.

Clement, Clara Erskine. *Women in the Fine Arts, from the Seventh Century B.C. to the Twentieth Century A.D., 1904.* Release date April 15, 2004. https://www.gutenberg.org/files/12045/12045-h/12045-h.htm. Accessed May 25, 2022.

Cogan, Frances B. *All-American Girl: The Ideal of Real Womanhood in Mid-nineteenth-Century America.* Athens: University of Georgia Press, 1989.

Corn, Wanda. *Women Building History Public Art at the 1893 Columbian Exposition.* Berkeley: University of California Press, 2011.

Cott, Nancy F. *The Grounding of Modern Feminism.* New Haven, CT: Yale University Press, 1987.

———. *History of Women in the United States, Part 1, Theory and Method in Women's History: Historical Articles on Women's Lives and Activities.* Berlin: K. G. Saur, 2012.

———. *No Small Courage: A History of Women in the United States.* Oxford: Oxford University Press, 2000.

Cremin, Lawrence A. *American Education: The Metropolitan Experience, 1876–1980.* New York: Harper & Row, 1988.

Cremin, Lawrence A. *American Education: The National Experience, 1783–1876.* New York: Harper & Row, 1980.

Crooker, James F. *Department of Education Annual Report: Superintendent of Education, City of Buffalo: 1882.* Buffalo: Henry Nauert Print., 1883.

———. *Department of Education: Report, Superintendent of Education, City of Buffalo: 1883–1884.* Buffalo: Times Print., 1884.

———. *Department of Education: Report, Superintendent of Education, City of Buffalo: 1884–1885.* Buffalo: Haas & Klein Print., 1886.

———. *Department of Education: Report, Superintendent of Education, City of Buffalo:1885–1886.* Buffalo: Times Print., 1887.

———. *Department of Education: Report, Superintendent of Education, City of Buffalo: 1886–1887*. Buffalo: Laughlin, 1888.

———. *Department of Education: Report, Superintendent of Education, City of Buffalo: 1887–88*. Buffalo: Haas & Klein Print., 1889.

———. *Department of Education: Report, Superintendent of Education, City of Buffalo: 1888–1889*. Buffalo: Times Print., 1890.

———. *Department of Education: Annual Report, Superintendent of Education, City of Buffalo: 1889–1890*. Buffalo: Haas & Klein Print., 1891.

———. *Department of Education: Annual Report, Superintendent of Education, City of Buffalo:1890–1891*. Buffalo: Haas & Klein Print., 1892.

Cuff, Dana. *Architecture: The Story of Practice*. Cambridge: MIT Press, 1991.

Deamer, Peggy. *The Architect as Worker: Immaterial Labor, the Creative Class, and the Politics of Design*. London: Bloomsbury Academic Press, 2015.

Doumato, Lamia. "Louisa Tuthill's Unique Achievement." In *Architecture: A Place for Women*, edited by Ellen Perry Berkeley and Matilda McQuaid, 5–13. Washington: Smithsonian Institution Press, 1989.

Edwards, Lydia. *How to Read a Dress: A Guide to Changing Fashion from the 16th to the 20th Century*. London: Bloomsbury Press, 2017.

Edwards, Richard. *New York's Great Industries: Buffalo and Vicinity*. New York: Historical, 1884.

Egbert, Donald Drew. *The Beaux-Arts Tradition in French Architecture*. Edited by David Van Zanten. Princeton, NJ: Princeton University Press, 1980.

Elias, Stephen N. *Alexander T. Stewart: The Forgotten Merchant Prince*. Westport, CT: Praeger, 1992.

Elstner Publishing Company. *The Industries of Buffalo: A Resume of the Mercantile and Manufacturing Progress of the Queen City of the Lakes*. Buffalo: Author, 1887.

Emerson, Henry P. *Department of Public Instruction Annual Report: 1893–1894*. Buffalo: Wenbourne-Sumner, 1895.

———. *Department of Public Instruction Annual Report: 1894–1895*. Buffalo: Wenbourne-Sumner, 1896.

———. *Department of Public Instruction Annual Report: 1896–1897*. Buffalo: Wenbourne-Sumner, 1897.

———. *Department of Public Instruction Annual Report: 1899–1900*. Buffalo: Wenbourne-Sumner, 1901.

———*Department of Public Instruction Annual Report: 1900–1901*. Buffalo: Wenbourne-Sumner, 1902.

Faust, Catherine, Austin M. Fox, Edward B. Green, Gerald C. Mead, Burchfield Penney Art Center. *E. B. Green: Buffalo's Architect*. Buffalo: Buffalo State College Foundation, 1997.

Fergusson, James. *History of Modern Styles of Architecture*. Edited by Robert Kerr. New York: Dodd, Mead, 1891.

Gillespie, Elizabeth Duane. *A Book of Remembrance*. Philadelphia: J. B. Lippincott, 1901.

Gillis, John R. *The Human Shore: Seacoasts in History*. Chicago: University of Chicago Press, 2012.

Girouard, Mark. *Sweetness and Light: The Queen Anne Movement, 1860–1900*. Oxford: Clarendon Press, 1977.

Gislason, Neil. *Building Innovation: History, Cases, and Perspectives on School Design*. Big Tankook Island, Nova Scotia: Backalong Books, 2011.

Goldstein, Harriet Irene, and Vetta Goldstein. *Art in Everyday Life [by] Harriet Goldstein [and] Vetta Goldstein*. 4th ed. New York: Macmillan, 1954.

Gyure, Dale Allen. *The Schoolroom: A Social History of Teaching and Learning*. Santa Barbara, CA: Greenwood, 2018.

Haber, Francine, Kenneth R. Fuller, and David N. Wetzel. *Robert S. Roeschlaub: Architect of the Emerging West, 1843–1923*. Denver: Colorado Historical Society, 1988.

Hallenbeck, Sarah. *Claiming the Bicycle: Women, Rhetoric, and Technology in Nineteenth-Century America*. Carbondale: Southern Illinois University Press, 2016.

Handlin, David P. *The American Home: Architecture and Society, 1815–1915*. Boston: Little, Brown, 1979.

Hannaford, Phebe. *Daughters of America: Or Women of the Century*. Boston: B. B. Russell, 1883.

Hart, John F. *Industries of Buffalo: A Resume of the Mercantile and Manufacturing Progress of the Queen City of the Lakes*. Buffalo: Elstner Publishing Company, 1887.

Hartman, Jan Cigliano. *The Women Who Changed Architecture*. Princeton, NJ: Princeton Architectural Press, 2022.

Hayden, Sophia. "1894 Report to the Lady Board of Managers." In *Addresses and Reports of Mrs. Potter Palmer: President of the Board of Lady Managers, World's Columbian Commission*, edited by Bertha Honore Palmer. Chicago: Rand, McNally, 1894.

Hays, Johanna. *Louise Blanchard Bethune: America's First Female Professional Architect*. Jefferson, NC: McFarland, 2014.

Herlihy, David V. *Bicycle: The History*. New Haven, CT: Yale University Press, 2004.

Hoffmann, Charles. *The Depression of the Nineties: An Economic History*. Westport, CT: Greenwood, 1970.

Holliday, Kathryn. *Leopold Eidlitz: Architecture and Idealism in the Gilded Age*. New York: W. W. Norton, 2008.

Horowitz, Helen Lefkowitz. *Rereading Sex: Battles over Sexual Knowledge and Suppression in Nineteenth-Century America*. New York: Vintage Books, 2003.

Isenberg, Nancy. *Sex and Citizenship in Antebellum America*. Chapel Hill: University of North Carolina Press, 1998.

Jones, Howard Mumford. *Ideas in America*. Cambridge: Harvard University Press, 1945.

Jordan, R. Furneaux. *A Concise History of Western Architecture*. London: Thames and Hudson, 1969.

Jordy, William H., and William H. Pierson. *American Buildings and Their Architects.* Garden City, NY: Anchor Press, 1976.

Joselit, Jenna Weissman. *A Perfect Fit: Clothes, Character, and the Promise of America.* New York: Metropolitan Books, 2001.

Kegler, Richard. *The Aries Press of Eden.* Rochester, NY: RIT Press, 2016.

Kilde, Jeanne Halgren. *When Church Became Theatre: The Transformation of Evangelical Architecture and Worship in Nineteenth-Century America.* Oxford: Oxford University Press, 2002.

Klein, Maury. *The Power Makers: Steam, Electricity, and the Men Who Invented Modern America.* New York: Bloomsbury Press, 2008.

Kostoff, Spiro, ed. *The Architect: Chapters in the History of the Profession.* Oxford: New York University Press, 1977.

Kostoff, Spiro. *A History of Architecture: Settings and Rituals.* Revisions by Greg Castillo. Oxford: Oxford University Press, 1995.

Kowsky, Francis R. *The Best Planned City in the World: Olmsted, Vaux, and the Buffalo Park System.* Amherst: University of Massachusetts Press, 2013.

Kowsky, Francis R., Mark Goldman, Austin Fox, John D. Randall, Jack Quinan, Teresa Lasher, Rayner Banham, Charles Beveridge, and Henry-Russell Hitchcock. *Buffalo Architecture: A Guide.* Seventh printing. Cambridge: MIT Press, 1996.

Lears, T. J. Jackson. *No Place of Grace: Antimodernism and the Transformation of American Culture, 1880–1920.* Chicago: University of Chicago Press, 1994.

Macleod, Dianne Sachko. *Enchanted Lives, Enchanted Objects: American Women Collectors and the Making of Culture, 1800–1940.* Berkeley: University of California Press, 2008.

Macy, Sue. *Wheels of Change: How Women Rode the Bicycle to Freedom (with a Few Flat Tires Along the Way).* Washington, DC: National Geographic, 2011.

Malatesta, Maria. *Professional Men, Professional Women: The European Professions from the 19th Century until Today.* Thousand Oaks, CA: Sage, 2010.

Mankiller, Wilma, Gwendolyn Mink, Marysa Navarro, Barbara Smith, and Gloria Steinem, eds. *The Reader's Companion to U.S. Women's History.* Boston: Houghton Mifflin, 1998.

Marks, Patricia. *Bicycles, Bangs, and Bloomers: The New Woman in the Popular Press.* Lexington: University Press of Kentucky, 1990.

Martin, Justin. *Genius of Place: The Life of Frederick Law Olmsted.* Cambridge, MA: Da Capo Press, 2011.

Mason, George Champlin. *Architects and Their Environment, 1850–1907: Together with Notes and Reminiscences of the Fathers of the Profession, Their Clients and Assistants.* Ardmore, WA: Rubblestone, 1907.

Matthews, Jean V. *The Rise of the New Woman: The Women's Movement in America, 1875–1930.* Chicago: Ivan R. Dee, 2003.

McAlester, Virginia. *A Field Guide to American Houses: The Definitive Guide to Identifying and Understanding America's Domestic Architecture.* New York: Alfred A. Knopf, 2013.

McCausland, Bruce. *1887–2012 History: First Presbyterian Church*. https://buffaloah. com/a/sym/1/mcc.html.

McKay, Martha N. "Women as Architects." In *The Western*, edited by H. H. Morgan, 22–38. St. Louis, MO: G. I. Jones, 1880.

Men of Buffalo; A Collection of Portraits of Men Who Deserve to Rank as Typical Representatives of the Best Citizenship, Foremost Activities and Highest Aspirations of the City of Buffalo. Chicago: Marquis, 1902.

Middleton, Robin. *Architecture of the Nineteenth Century*. Milan: Electa Architecture; distributed by Phaidon Press.

Mingus, Nancy Blumenstalk. *Buffalo: Good Neighbors, Great Architecture*. Charleston, SC: Arcadia, 2003.

Moore, Charles. "Leverett A. Pratt." In *History of Michigan Volume II*. Chicago: Lewis, 1915.

Mossman, Mary Jane. *The First Women Lawyers: A Comparative Study of Gender, Law and the Legal Professions*. Portland, OR: Hart, 2006.

Muccigrosso, Robert. *Celebrating the New World: Chicago's Columbian Exposition of 1893*. Chicago: Ivan R. Dee, 1993.

National Cyclopedia of American Biography. New York: James T. White, 1904.

Nimura, Janice P. *The Blackwell Doctors*. New York: W. W. Norton, 2021.

Overfield, Joseph, M. *The 100 Seasons of Buffalo Baseball*. Kenmore, NY: Partners Press, 1985.

Paine, Judith. "Pioneer Women Architects." In *Women in Architecture: A Historic and Contemporary Perspective*, edited by Susana Torre, 54–69. New York: Watson-Guptill, 1977.

Penny, Virginia. *The Employments of Women: A Cyclopaedia of Woman's Work*. Boston, MA: Walker, Wise, 1863.

Philbrick, John D. *City School Systems in the United States*. Circulars of Information No. 1. Washington, DC: Bureau of Education, 1885.

Pierce, R. V. *The People's Common Sense Medical Advisor in Plain English; or Medicine Simplified*. Seventy-second edition. Buffalo: World's Dispensary Print., 1909.

Poppeliers, John C., Allen Chambers, and Nancy B. Schwartz. *What Style Is It?* Washington, DC: Preservation Press of the National Trust for Historic Preservation, 1977.

Randall, John D. *Buffalo and Western New York, Architecture and Human Values*. Buffalo: Artcraft-Burow, 1976.

Ravitch, Diane. *The Great School Wars: New York City, 1805–1973*. New York: Basic Books, 1974.

Reynolds, David. S. *Beneath the American Renaissance: The Subversive Imagination in the Age of Emerson and Melville*. New York: Alfred A. Knopf, 1988.

Robson, Edward Robert. *School Architecture: Being Practical Remarks on the Planning, Designing, Building and Furnishing of School-houses*. London: Murray, 1874.

Root, John W. *Convention Proceedings of the American Institute of Architects, the Western Association of Architects, and the Consolidation of the American Institute and the Western Association.* Chicago: Inland Architect Press, 1890.

Ross, Ishbel. *Silhouette in Diamonds: The Life of Mrs. Potter Palmer.* New York: Arno Press, 1975.

Roth, Leland M. *American Architecture: A History.* Boulder: Westview Press, 2001.

Ryan, Mary P. *Cradle of the Middle Class: The Family in Oneida County, New York, 1790–1865.* Cambridge: Cambridge University Press, 1981.

Rykwert, Joseph. "The Ecole des Beaux-Arts and the Classical Tradition." In *The Beaux-Arts and Nineteenth-Century French Architecture,* edited by R. D. Middleton, 8. Cambridge, MA: MIT Press, 1982.

Saint, Andrew. *Architect and Engineer: A Study in Sibling Rivalry.* New Haven, CT: Yale University Press, 2007.

———. *The Image of the Architect.* New Haven, CT: Yale University Press, 1983.

Saylor, Henry H. *The A.I.A.'s First Hundred Years.* Washington, DC: American Institute of Architects, 1957.

Scully, Vincent. *American Architecture and Urbanism.* New York: Henry Holt, 1988.

———. *Shingle Style and the Stick Style.* New Haven, CT: Yale University Press, 1955.

Segrave, Kerry. *Women and Bicycles in America, 1868–1900.* Jefferson, NC: McFarland, 2020.

Sherr, Lynn. *Failure Is Impossible: Susan B. Anthony in Her Own Words.* New York: Times Books, 1995.

Smith, Henry P. *History of the City of Buffalo and Erie County: With Biographical Sketches of Some of Its Prominent Men and Pioneers.* Syracuse, NY: D. Mason, 1884.

Sokolina, Anna. *The Routledge Companion to Women in Architecture.* New York: Routledge, 2021.

Stanton, Elizabeth Cady. *Eighty Years and More.* New York: European, 1898.

Stanton, Elizabeth Cady, Susan B. Anthony, and Matilda Joslyn Gage. *History of Woman Suffrage.* Vol. 1. New York: Fowler & Wells, 1881.

Stein, Susan R. *The Architecture of Richard Morris Hunt.* Chicago: University of Chicago Press, 1986.

Stern, Madeleine, B. *We the Women: Career Firsts of the 19th-Century America.* New York: Schulte, 1962.

Stevenson, John J. *House Architecture.* London: Macmillan, 1880.

Stratigakos, Despina. *Where Are the Women Architects?* Princeton, NJ: Princeton University Press, 2016.

Thomas, Tracy A. *Elizabeth Cady Stanton and the Feminist Foundations of Family Law.* New York: New York University Press, 2016.

Todd, Nancy L. *New York's Historic Armories: An Illustrated History.* Albany: State University of New York Press, 2006.

Torre, Susana, ed. *Women in American Architecture: A Historic and Contemporary Perspective.* New York: Watson-Guptill, 1977.

Tuthill, Louisa C. *History of Architecture from Earliest Times; Its Present Condition in Europe and the United States.* Philadelphia: Lindsay and Blakiston, 1848.

Tyack, David B. *The One Best System: A History of American Urban Education.* Cambridge, MA: Harvard University Press, 1974.

Weed, G. Morton. *School Days of Yesterday: The Story of the Buffalo Public Schools.* Buffalo: Buffalo Board of Education, 2001.

Weimann, Jeanne Madeline. *The Fair Women.* Chicago: Academy Chicago, 1981.

Wellman, Judith. *The Road to Seneca Falls: Elizabeth Cady Stanton and the First Woman's Rights Convention.* Chicago: University of Chicago Press, 2004.

Whiffen, Marcus, and Frederick Koeper. *American Architecture, Vol. 1, 1607–1860.* Cambridge, MA: MIT Press, 1984.

White, Gerald T. *The United States and the Problem of Recovery after 1893.* Tuscaloosa: University of Alabama Press, 1982.

Willard, Frances E. *How I Learned to Ride the Bicycle: Reflections of an Influential 19th Century Woman.* Edited by Carol O'Hare, with an introduction by Edith Mayo. Sunnyvale, CA: Fair Oaks Press, 1895; republished 1991.

Willard, Frances E., and Mary A. Livermore, eds. *A Woman of the Century: Fourteen Hundred-Seventy Biographical Sketches Accompanied by Portraits of Leading American Women in All Walks of Life.* New York: Charles Wells Moulton, 1893.

Wilson, Elizabeth. *Adorned in Dreams: Fashion and Modernity.* London: I. B. Tauris, 2014.

Wilson, Richard Guy. "The Great Civilization." In *The American Renaissance, 1876–1917,* 11–13. New York: Pantheon Books, 1979.

Withey, Henry F., and Elsie Rathburn Withey. *Biographical Dictionary of American Architects (Deceased).* Los Angeles: New Age, 1956; facsimile edition, Hennessey & Ingalls, 1970.

White, Lawrence. *Sketches and Designs by Stanford White.* New York: Architectural Book, 1920.

Woloch, Nancy. *Women and the American Experience.* New York: McGraw-Hill, 2011.

Wood, J. Henry. *Schools of Buffalo: A Souvenir History and Description of the Public Schools of Buffalo.* Buffalo: I. C. Wood, 1899.

Woods, Mary N. *From Craft to Profession: The Practice of Architecture in Nineteenth-Century America.* Berkeley: University of California Press, 1999.

Wright, Gwendolyn. *Moralism and the Model Home.* Chicago: University of Chicago Press, 1980.

OTHER BOOKS

100 Years of Education in the Public Schools of Lockport, New York. Lockport: Lockport Board of Education, 1947.

The Birth of Woodlawn. Courtesy of the Hamburg History Museum.

Daughters of the American Revolution. *Daughters of the American Revolution Lineage Book.* 1904.

A History of the City of Buffalo and Niagara Falls. Buffalo: Times Print., 1896.
Proceedings of the Common Council of the City of Buffalo, from January 2, 1882 to December 29, 1882. Buffalo: Courier Print., 1882.
Proceedings of the Common Council of the City of Buffalo, from January 1, 1883 to December 31, 1883. Buffalo: Times Print., 1884.
Proceedings of the Common Council of the City of Buffalo, from January 1, 1884 to December 31, 1884. Buffalo: Courier Print., 1885.
Proceedings of the Common Council of the City of Buffalo, from January 1, 1885 to December 31, 1885. Buffalo: Courier Print., 1886.
Proceedings of the Common Council of the City of Buffalo, from January 1, 1886 to December 31, 1886. Buffalo: Courier Print., 1887.
Proceedings of the Common Council of the City of Buffalo, from January 1, 1887 to December 31, 1887. Buffalo: Courier Print., 1887.
Proceedings of the Common Council of the City of Buffalo, from January 1, 1889 to December 31, 1889. Buffalo: Haas & Klein Print., 1889.
Proceedings of the Common Council of the City of Buffalo, from January 1, 1890 to December 31, 1890. Buffalo: Haas & Klein Print., 1890.
Queen of the Lakes . . . Buffalo: The Electric City of the Future: Souvenir of the Tenth Convention of the National Association of Builders, Sept. 14–19, 1896. Buffalo: Courier, 1896.
Report of the President to the Board of Directors of the Columbian Exposition. Chicago, 1892–1893.

Dissertations and Papers

Gardner, Deborah S. "The Architecture of Commercialism: John Kellum and the Development of New York, 1840–1875." PhD diss., Columbia University, 1979.
Hanlon, Sheila. "The Lady Cyclist: A Gender Analysis of Women's Cycling Culture in 1890s London." PhD diss., York University, 2009.
Harrington, Leroy. "Forestville, Its Environs, Past and Present." Prepared and read at a meeting of the Chautauqua County Historical Society, June 4, 1949.
Weatherhead, Arthur C. "The History of Collegiate Education in Architecture in the United States." PhD diss., Columbia University, 1941.
White, Erica Michelle. "Representations of the True Woman and the New Woman in *Harper's Bazaar.*" Graduate Theses and Dissertations, Iowa State University 2009.

Articles

"14 Story Building." *Buffalo Commercial,* January 3, 1891.
Akcigit, Ufuk, John Grigsby, and Tom Nicholas. "The Rise of American Ingenuity: Innovation and Inventors of the Golden Age." Harvard Business School Working Paper, No. 17–063, January 2017.

American Architect and Building News, December 10, 1892.
American Architect and Building News, March 24, 1894.
American Architect and Building News, May 8, 1897.
"Annual Convention of the Ohio State Chapter, A.I.A." *American Architect and Building News*, October 6, 1894.
"Antiquated School Buildings." *Buffalo Courier*, May 31, 1882.
"Architects Object." *Buffalo Commercial*, February 1, 1896.
"As a Cycling City, Buffalo Occupies a Position in the Front Rank." *Buffalo Courier*, November 18, 1894.
"At Woodlawn." *Buffalo Enquirer*, August 10, 1894.
Barbasch, Adriana. "The Buffalo/Western New York Chapter of the American Institute of Architects: Celebrates 100 Years of Architecture, 1886–1986." Buffalo: AIA, 1986.
Barbasch, Adriana. "A Tribute to the First Professional Woman Architect Admitted to the American Institute of Architecture: 1856–1913." Buffalo: AIA, 2001.
"Basehits." *Buffalo Express and Buffalo Morning Express*, February 9, 1890.
Berkeley, Ellen Perry. "Women in Architecture." *Architectural Forum* (September 1972): 46–53.
Bethune, Louise. "It Is to Laugh." Zina Bethune Archive on Louise Bethune, University at Buffalo.
———. "Women and Architecture." *Inland Architect and News Record* (March 1891): 21.
Betts, Lillian W. "The New Woman." *Outlook*, October 12, 1895, 587.
"Bicycles in the Cemetery." *Buffalo Commercial*, June 13, 1892.
Bly, Nellie. "Champion of Her Sex." *New York World*, February 2, 1896.
"The Bricka & Enos Store—And What It Stands For." *Buffalo Courier*, October 15, 1911.
Brown, Denise Scott. "Learning the Wrong Lessons from the Beaux-Arts." *Architectural Design Profiles* 17 (1979): 30–33.
"Buffalo Expressions." *Buffalo Morning Express and Illustrated Buffalo Express*, November 19, 1886.
"Buffalo Hotel Opened." *New York Times*, June 2, 1904.
"Buffalo Society of Architects." *Inland Architect and Builder* (December 1886): 95.
"Buffalo's Fine New Hotel." *Buffalo Sunday Morning News*, October 19, 1902.
"Building Operations." *Buffalo Courier*, October 3, 1891.
"Building Permits." *Buffalo Courier*, July 2, 1895.
"Built the Lafayette." *Illustrated Buffalo Express*, June 16, 1912.
Burgwardt, Carl F. "The Buffalo Bicycle Clubhouse: A Hidden Landmark." *Western New York Heritage Magazine*, Spring 2004.
"Buried to His Neck." *Buffalo Courier*, July 16, 1895.
"Candidates for Superintendent of Public Instruction." *Buffalo Courier*, March 12, 1883.

"The Cary Hotel." *Buffalo Morning Express and Illustrated Buffalo Express*, January 30, 1882.

"Century Riders." *Buffalo Morning Express and Illustrated Buffalo Express*, June 26, 1893.

"Cereal Coffee Company Sold." *Buffalo Times*, January 4, 1900.

Chapman, Josephine Wright. "How to Make the Home Beautiful." *Success Magazine*, March 1905.

"Chicago." *American Architect and Building News*, November 26, 1892.

"The Children's Home." *Dunkirk Evening Observer*, December 3, 1890.

Cichon, Steve. "Black Rock's Pratt & Letchworth: Buffalo's Original Ironworks." *Buffalo News*, July 29, 2021.

———. "Torn-Down Tuesday: Elmwood Music Hall." *Buffalo News*, March 20, 2017.

"City Will Have to Build Black Rock Market, Harp Says." *Buffalo Evening News*, November 10, 1903.

"A Clever Woman's Work." *Buffalo Enquirer*, February 9, 1892.

"Club Life for Women." *Harper's Bazaar*, October 25, 1890.

"Columbian Exposition Women's Building." *Inland Architect and News Record* (February 1891): 1.

Cordato, Mary F. "Towards a New Century: Women and the Philadelphia Centennial Exhibition, 1876." *Pennsylvania Magazine of History and Biography* 107, no. 1 (January 1983): 113–135.

"Cycles." *Buffalo Courier*, Monday, April 8, 1889.

"Dr. Charles W. Bethune." *Buffalo Courier Express*, October 3, 1952.

"Dr. Ida C. Bender Called by Death; Long an Educator." *Buffalo Courier*, June 12, 1916.

"Dwelling Houses." *Buffalo Morning Express and Illustrated Buffalo Express*, November 21, 1886.

Eck, Susan. "805 Delaware: The Kelloggs, Town Club, and Temple Beth Zion." Western New York History. https://www.wnyhistory.org/portfolios/whowhere/kellogg_805_delaware/kellogg_delaware.html.

Esperdy, Gabrielle. "The Incredible True Adventures of the Architectress in America." *Places Journal*, September 2012. https://placesjournal.org/article/the-incredible-true-adventures-of-the-architectress-in-america/?cn-reloaded=1.

"Exterior View of the New Market to Be Built at Black Rock." *Buffalo Evening News*, July 23, 1903.

"Falling of a Wall." *Buffalo Commercial*, December 20, 1895.

"False Statements." *Buffalo Times*, September 4, 1886.

"Fair Riders on Modern Wheels." *Outing* 17 (1890–1891): 305–307.

Fanton, Mary Annable. "Some Industrial Art Schools for Women." *Godey's Magazine*, June 1896, 632–633.

"Female Competition." *American Architect and Building News*, December 1890.

"Feminism and Architecture." *Western Architect*, April 1914.

Fifth Annual Convention of the Western Association of Architects. *Inland Architect* 12, no. 6 (1888): 62.

"Fred Jehle." *Buffalo Times*, January 24, 1899.

"Fuchs Building Collapse." *Buffalo Evening News*, December 24, 1895.

"Good for East Buffalo." *Buffalo Morning Express and Illustrated Buffalo Express*, August 10, 1890.

"The Graduates." *Buffalo Courier*, November 10, 1889.

"Hotel Lafayette." *Buffalo Commercial*, April 2, 1900.

"Hotel Project Has New Life." *Buffalo Evening News*, June 7, 1901.

Hitchcock, Henry-Russell. "French Influence on 19th Century Architecture in the USA." *Architectural Design Profiles* 17 (1979): 80–83.

Huxtable, Ada Louise. "The Last Profession to Be 'Liberated' by Women." *New York Times*, March 13, 1977.

"Illinois State Association." *Inland Architect and News Record* (March 1887): 28.

"Improvements." *Buffalo Commercial*, November 23, 1900.

"In Memory of the Dead." *Buffalo Enquirer*, August 22, 1891.

"Is Bicycling Immoral?" *Brooklyn Daily Eagle*, August 19, 1896.

"It Was a Triumph." *Buffalo Evening News*, February 7, 1890.

"It Was Wound Up Last Night." *Buffalo Courier*, January 6, 1897.

"A Jewel Palace." *New York Times*, November 12, 1870.

"Ladies of the Wheel." *Buffalo Illustrated Express*, August 14, 1892.

"Lamps in Daytime." *Buffalo Sunday Morning News*, June 14, 1883.

Letter to the Editor. *Sidepaths*, 1898.

"Local Observations." *Buffalo Courier*, December 11, 1881.

"The Lock City: Laying the Corner-Stone of the Union School." *Buffalo Morning Express and Illustrated Buffalo Express*, July 13, 1890.

"Louis XIV Rex." *Buffalo Evening News*, February 14, 1888.

"The Magnificent Success of a Firm." *Buffalo Free Press*, February 4, 1902.

"The Man About Town." *Buffalo Sunday Morning News*, December 9, 1888.

Mann, Horace. "Woman." *New-York Daily Tribune*, December 9, 1852, 3.

"Many Honor Memory of James F. Crooker." *Buffalo Courier*, February 10, 1919.

"Married Women's Property Laws." *American Women*. Library of Congress.

Miller, Joseph Dana. "Women as Architects." *Frank Leslie's Popular Monthly* 50 (June 1900): 199–204.

Millet, F. D. "The Designers of the Fair." *Harper's New Monthly Magazine*, November 1892.

"Miss Willard's Wheel Views." *Buffalo Morning Express and Illustrated Buffalo Express*, Sunday, February 23, 1896.

"Monument Square Hotel." *Buffalo Review*, August 8, 1901.

"Mostly about People." *Buffalo Times*, March 7, 1901.

"Mr. Shea's Theater." *Buffalo Commercial*, May 14, 1895.

"Mrs. Stanton Likes Bloomers." *Rocky Mountain News*, August 11, 1895.

"New Buildings." *Buffalo Evening News*, November 10, 1896.
"A New Hotel." *Buffalo Commercial*, March 3, 1899.
"New Hotel Is Buffalo's Finest." *Hotel Courier*, June 2, 1904.
"New Hotel Opened." *Buffalo Morning Express and Illustrated Buffalo Express*, June 1904.
"New Terminal Station." *Buffalo Times*, August 6, 1898.
"News for Wheelmen." *Buffalo Commercial*, March 7, 1895.
Nichols, Minerva Parker. "A Woman on the Woman's Building." *American Architect and Building News*, December 10, 1892.
"Notes on Sports." *Buffalo Morning Express and Illustrated Buffalo Express*, February 9, 1890.
"Occupations of Women: What the Field of Architecture Offers to the Well Trained Practical Woman." *New York Tribune*, August 26, 1901.
"Odd Oscar: How the Apostle of Aestheticism Lectured." *Hamilton Spectator*, May 31, 1882.
"An Old Firm in a New Store; Denton, Cottier & Daniels to Move from Main Street." *Buffalo Courier*, February 9, 1908.
"Old French Church." *Buffalo Morning Express and Illustrated Buffalo Express*, May 13, 1900.
"Our Growing City." *Buffalo Courier*, September 19, 1891.
"The Park." *Buffalo Morning Express and Illustrated Buffalo Express*, April 2, 1879.
Peabody, Robert S. "A Talk about 'Queen Anne.'" *American Architect and Building News*, April 28, 1877.
"People and Events." *Omaha Daily Bee*, February 9, 1914.
Pepchinski, Mary. "The Woman's Building and the World Exhibitions: Exhibition Architecture and Conflicting Feminine Ideals at European and American World Exhibitions, 1873–1915." *Wolkenkucksheim* 5, no. 1 (2000), available at https://www.cloudcuckoo.net/openarchive/wolke/eng/Subjects/001/Pepchinski/pepchinski.htm. Accessed on January 22, 2022.
Pettengill, George E. "How A.I.A. Acquired Its First Woman Member, Mrs. Louise Bethune." *AIA Journal* (March 1975).
"The Press Club Ball." *Buffalo Evening News*, April 10, 1893.
"Progress in Work on World's Fair." *Inland Architect and Building News*, March 1891.
"The Public Schools." *The Buffalo Commercial*, September 6, 1886.
"The Queen Anne Style." *American Architect and Building News*, February 21, 1880.
"Real Estate Movements." *Buffalo Times*, December 30, 1898.
"Real Estate Transfers." *Buffalo Commercial*, November 9, 1881.
"Real Estate Transfers." *Buffalo Morning Express and Illustrated Buffalo Express*, July 24, 1889.
"Republican Protest." *Buffalo Morning Express and Illustrated Buffalo Express*, October 10, 1882.

Ricker, Clifford, "Results of Licensing Law for Architects in Illinois." *Brickbuilder* 10, no. 2 (1902): 23–24.

"Rochester Man May Put Up a Hotel Here." *Buffalo Courier*, July, 26, 1902.

"Roof Fell In." *Buffalo Enquirer*, December 21, 1895.

"A Runaway Accident." *Buffalo Commercial*, June 15 1891.

"A Rush for Bloomers." *Buffalo Commercial*, October 8, 1894.

"School Principal Dead." *Buffalo Times*, August 18, 1891.

"The Schools of Buffalo." *Buffalo Courier*, June 13, 1883.

"Seeing Buffalo of the Olden Time: A Historical Block." *Buffalo Times*, June 1, 1909.

Severence, Alice. "Talks by Successful Women IX—Miss Gannon and Miss Hands on Architecture." *Godey's Magazine* 83 (September 1896): 314–316.

Sewall, E. D. "The Women's Bicycle and Its Predecessors." *Iron Age*, May 13, 1897.

"Shea's New Theater." *Buffalo Evening News*, January 29, 1895.

"Shea's New Theater." *Buffalo Commercial*, February 23, 1895.

"Some Distinguished Women of Buffalo." *American Woman's Illustrated World*, October 7, 1893.

Stern, Madeleine B. "America's First Woman Architect?" *Journal of the Society of Architectural Historians* 18 (May 1959): 66.

"Strong Society Organized to Beautify City." *Buffalo Evening News*, December 17, 1901.

"Synopsis of Building News." *Inland Architect and Building News* (October 1889): 43.

"Talk." *Woman's Exponent*, January 1, 1886.

Tichnor, Caroline. "The Steel-Engraving Lady and the Gibson Girl." *Atlantic Monthly*, 1901.

"To Have a Private Market." *Buffalo Courier*, July 10, 1903.

"To End in Foreclosure." *Buffalo Commercial*, March 10, 1902.

"Two Popular Architects." *American Architect and Building News*, March 1, 1879.

Van Ness, Cynthia. "Population Growth and Decline over the Years." http://www.buffaloah.com/h/bflopop.html.

Wachadlo, Martin, and Christopher Brown. "Richard A. Waite: A Forgotten Master." *Western New York Heritage*, Winter 2004.

Welter, Barbara. "The Cult of True Womanhood, 1820–1860: Part 1." *American Quarterly* 18, no. 2 (Summer 1966): 151–174.

Western New York State Association of Architects. *The Architectural Era*, 1–2.

"What to Wear on a Wheel." *American Wheelman*, 1892, 101.

"Wheel Club Incorporated." *Buffalo Morning Express and Illustrated Buffalo Express*, Friday, March 24, 1893.

"Wheelwomen and Their Winter Sports." *American Wheelman*, 1892.

"Will Build a Hotel." *Buffalo Commercial*, August 2, 1902.

"Woman Architect, First in the Country, Dies in Buffalo." *Buffalo Courier*, 1913.

"Woman Architects." *Buffalo Courier*, March 7, 1891.

"The Woman's A.G." *Buffalo Times*, January 5, 1897.
"Woman's Club Banquet," *Buffalo Evening News*, April 26, 1894.
"Woman's Work: Women as Architects." *Buffalo Daily Courier*, July 13, 1884.
"A Woman Who Builds Homes." *Ladies Home Journal*, October 1914.
"Women as Architects." *Weekly Wisconsin*, January 2, 1886.
"Women as Architects." *Architect and Engineer of California*, June 1910.
"Women in Architecture." *Buffalo Morning Express and Illustrated Buffalo Express,* March 7, 1891.
"Women in Art." *American Builder and Journal of Art*, September 1, 1872.
"Women in Buffalo's Professional and Business Life." *Buffalo Sunday Morning News*, November 9, 1913.
"Woodlawn Beach." *Buffalo Express and Buffalo Morning Express*, April 16, 1893.
"The World Awheel." *Munsey's* 15 (1896): 157–159.
"W. S. Smith & Co." *North Alabama Illustrated*, 1888.

Other Sources

Bethune, Louise. *Women's Wheel and Athletic Club Annual Dinner Program*, April 29, 1894.
———. *Women's Wheel and Athletic Club Annual Dinner Program*, 1895.
"The Women's Wheel and Athletic Club 1892." Grosvenor Library, Buffalo and Erie County Central Library.
Women's Wheel and Athletic Club meeting notes. Grosvenor Library, Buffalo and Erie County Central Library.

Websites

https://buffaloah.com
https://nyheritage.org/collections/buffalo-city-directories
https://www.minervaparkernichols.com
https://pioneeringwomen.bwaf.org
https://www.cayugacounty.us/918/Military-Tract-of-Central-New-York
http://history.rays-place.com/ny/onon-manlius-ny.htm
https://www.newspapers.com
https://www.ancestry.com
https://www.pbs.org/wgbh/americanexperience/features/triangle-fire-what-shirtwaist/
https://www.dar.org/national-society/about-dar/dar-history

Index

97, 99, 183; attitude toward women members, 96, 104; merger with American Institute of Architects, 98–100, 105, 200, 221; position on design competitions, 89, 100, 102

Wetmore, Dr. Mary, 96

Wetmore, Samuel, 253

Wheeling, 4, 150–160, 173–174

White Brothers Livery Stable, 242, 245

Whitman, Walt, 69

Wilde, Oscar, 30, 69

Willard, Frances E., 158, 184

Williams, Ebenezer, 10, 220, 261n3

Williams, Elizabeth Fenner, 11

Williams, Jonathon Whitney, 10

Woman's Building. *See* World's Columbian Exposition

Women as Architects, 1–3, 5, 22–26, 33, 48–49, 53, 55, 58, 59–65, 67–68, 70–72, 78, 86, 96, 100–104, 132–133, 137, 150, 160–161, 176, 179, 181–185, 188–195, 223, 227, 231–236

Women's Clothing, 4, 64, 152, 166, 170

Women in the Professions, 54, 55–58, 60, 102, 132, 155, 165, 191, 232

Women Wheelers, 150–160, 172

Women's Clubs, 64, 71, 165, 167–169, 192

Women's Education and Industrial Union, 54, 62, 191, 241

Women's Equality, 3, 4, 14, 15, 49, 57, 71, 101, 150, 152, 157, 170, 172, 175–180, 188, 192, 193, 195, 235

Women's Suffrage, 4, 11, 14, 15, 48, 57, 67, 152, 158, 159, 170–172, 177–179, 193, 231

Women's Wheel and Athletic Club, 4, 6, 42–43, 150–159, 166–173, 220, 253

Woods, Mary, 46, 87

World's Columbian Exposition, 22, 131; Board of Lady Managers, 182, 185, 188, 189, 192; chief of construction, 178, 181, 185, 188, 192; selection of architects, 88, 185; Woman's Building, 176–179, 185–186, 193–194, 234

Wright, Frank Lloyd, 46, 71, 213